"A tour de force. Not only the best available introduction to Marx's thought and to post-Marx Marxist theories, but also of interest to specialists. The organization is excellent, and the writing is always clear and jargon-free. It covers all the main topics that a book on Marx should address. It is remarkably fair and balanced, sympathetic to Marx's ideas, but also appropriately critical of them."

Allen Buchanan, Duke University, USA

"A philosophical introduction to Marx which manages to be genuinely accessible without avoiding controversy or consigning its subject to history. Edwards and Leiter bring Marx into a productive conversation with current work in the social sciences in order to develop and defend distinctive accounts of his views on history, ideology, and capitalism. A very welcome addition to the literature."

David Leopold, University of Oxford, UK

T0372876

Marx

The writings of Karl Marx (1818–1883) have left an indelible mark not only on the understanding of economics and political thought but on the lives of millions of people who lived in regimes that claimed (wrongly) his influence. Trained as a philosopher and steeped in the thought of Hegel, Marx turned away from Hegelian philosophy after 1845 towards a philosophy that incorporated economics and history. It is this Marx that endures and to which this outstanding introduction is devoted.

Jaime Edwards and Brian Leiter begin with an overview of Marx's life and intellectual development, including his early years as a journalist in Germany before his exile in London. They then introduce and assess the fundamental elements of Marx's thought:

* Marx's theory of history and historical change (historical materialism)
* class conflict, the state, and the Communist revolution
* Marx's theory of economics, especially the labour theory of value, and his prediction of the collapse of capitalism
* the nature and role of ideology in Marx's thought
* Marx's theory of human nature and the good life, including his arguments concerning alienation
* Marx's legacy and influence, including Western Marxism, the Frankfurt School, and "feminist Marxism".

Including annotated further reading suggestions at the end of each chapter and a glossary of technical terms, this is an indispensable introduction to Marx's philosophical thought. It will also be extremely useful to those in related disciplines such as politics, sociology, history, and political economy.

Jaime Edwards is a Lecturer in Law at the University of Chicago, USA, where he teaches political philosophy.

Brian Leiter is the Karl N. Llewellyn Professor of Jurisprudence and Director of the Center for Law, Philosophy, and Human Values at the University of Chicago, USA, where he teaches and writes about moral, political, and legal philosophy in both the Anglophone and Continental European traditions.

The Routledge Philosophers

Edited by Brian Leiter

University of Chicago, USA

Routledge Philosophers is a major series of introductions to the great Western philosophers. Each book places a major philosopher or thinker in historical context, explains and assesses their key arguments, and considers their legacy. Additional features include a chronology of major dates and events, chapter summaries, annotated suggestions for further reading and a glossary of technical terms.

An ideal starting point for those new to philosophy, they are also essential reading for those interested in the subject at any level.

Also available:

Darwin
Tim Lewens

Rawls
Samuel Freeman

Spinoza
Michael Della Rocca

Russell
Gregory Landini

Wittgenstein
William Child

Heidegger
John Richardson

Adorno
Brian O'Connor

Husserl, second edition
David Woodruff Smith

Aristotle, second edition
Christopher Shields

Kant, second edition
Paul Guyer

Hume
Don Garrett

Dewey
Steven Fesmire

Freud, second edition
Jonathan Lear

Habermas
Kenneth Baynes

Peirce
Albert Atkin

Plato
Constance Meinwald

Plotinus
Eyjólfur Emilsson

Einstein
Thomas Ryckman

Merleau-Ponty, second edition
Taylor Carman

Leibniz, second edition
Nicholas Jolley

Bergson
Mark Sinclair

Arendt
Dana Villa

Cassirer
Samantha Matherne

Adam Smith
Samuel Fleischacker

Descartes
David Cunning

Marx
Jaime Edwards and Brian Leiter

For more information about this series, please visit: https://www.routledge.com/The-Routledge-Philosophers/book-series/ROUTPHIL

Jaime Edwards and
Brian Leiter

Marx

Routledge
Taylor & Francis Group

LONDON AND NEW YORK

First published 2025
by Routledge
4 Park Square, Milton Park, Abingdon, Oxon OX14 4RN

and by Routledge
605 Third Avenue, New York, NY 10158

Routledge is an imprint of the Taylor & Francis Group, an informa business

© 2025 Jaime Edwards and Brian Leiter

British Library Cataloguing-in-Publication Data
A catalogue record for this book is available from the British Library

Library of Congress Cataloging-in-Publication Data
Names: Edwards, Jaime (Professor of philosophy), author. | Leiter, Brian, author.
Title: Marx / Jaime Edwards and Brian Leiter.
Description: Abingdon, Oxon ; New York, NY : Routledge, 2025. | Series: The Routledge philosophers | Includes bibliographical references and index.
Identifiers: LCCN 2024018235 (print) | LCCN 2024018236 (ebook) | ISBN 9781138938502 (hardback) | ISBN 9781138938519 (paperback) | ISBN 9781315658902 (ebook)
Subjects: LCSH: Marx, Karl, 1818-1883. | Philosophy, Marxist.
Classification: LCC B3305.M74 E39 2025 (print) | LCC B3305.M74 (ebook) | DDC 335.4092--dc23/eng/20240603
LC record available at https://lccn.loc.gov/2024018235
LC ebook record available at https://lccn.loc.gov/2024018236

ISBN: 978-1-138-93850-2 (hbk)
ISBN: 978-1-138-93851-9 (pbk)
ISBN: 978-1-315-65890-2 (ebk)

DOI: 10.4324/9781315658902

Typeset in Joanna
by SPi Technologies India Pvt Ltd (Straive)

For my teachers and my students
—JE

For Celia
artist, chef, rebel
—BL

Contents

Preface and Acknowledgments

In keeping with the goals of the *Routledge Philosophers* series, we have tried to write a book that is *genuinely* introductory, that is, one that does not presuppose any knowledge of Marxian jargon, or even too much knowledge of philosophy (although we venture into some complex philosophical terrain at points, but we try to provide all the building blocks for these points for the reader). At the same time, we hope there is material of interest here for more advanced students and scholars. Marx is the object of a huge secondary literature; and, while we confine disputes with others mostly to the footnotes, we also stake out definite positions, and offer evidence and arguments for them, on a range of issues: on the centrality of causal explanation (via class struggle) to historical materialism; on the problems with the labor theory of value and how much of Marx's critique of capitalism survives rejecting that theory; on the role of "ideologists" in Marx's account of ideology; on Marx's (justified) lack of interest in questions of moral and political philosophy (including the question of the "injustice" of capitalism); and on the priority of the mature Marx over the "early" Marx prior to 1845. Throughout, we also try to integrate contemporary work in cognitive science, political science, and neoclassical economics with our exposition and assessment of Marxian ideas, from his theory of ideology to his views on class and ruling class domination, to the likelihood of the displacement of labor by technology. Although we defend definite views on many interpretive questions, we hope there is material here that will be helpful to teachers and students, including those who end up disagreeing with us.

Edwards did initial drafts of Chapters 1, 3, 5, and 7, while Leiter did initial drafts of Chapters 2, 4, and 6. We then traded chapters, discussed them, and edited and revised each other's initial drafts, sometimes substantially.

Professor Brian O'Connor at University College Dublin kindly hosted a workshop with Leiter on drafts of Chapters 2, 4, and 6 in June 2022. We are grateful for helpful comments and questions from not only Professor O'Connor but also Antoine Athanassiadis, Eileen Brennan, Maeve Cook, Killian Favier, Samuel Ferns, and Clémence Saintemarie. Material from Chapter 4 also benefitted from presentation by Leiter at a conference at the University of Amsterdam on global capital as the Leviathan of the 21st century organized by Enzo Rossi. Thanks especially to Ugur Aytac, Albena Azmanova, Stephanie Classman, and James Muldoon for helpful suggestions as well as literature references. Earlier versions of Chapters 4 and 6 were also greatly improved by presentation (again, by Leiter) at the Colloquium on Legal, Social and Political Philosophy at New York University; particular thanks are due to Samuel Scheffler and Jeremy Waldron. A very early draft of Chapter 4 was saved from many errors thanks to the economist Roberto Veneziani, who is absolved from our remaining mistakes. Discussions with Daniel Burnfin, as well as his detailed commentary, were also invaluable for our understanding of Marx's economics, although Dr. Burnfin should not be supposed to agree with the final product. A later version of Chapter 4 benefitted from skeptical reactions at a faculty workshop at the University of Chicago Law School, with particular thanks to Adam Chilton, William Hubbard, Aziz Huq, Eric Posner, Adriana Robertson, Julie Roin, and David Weisbach.

Very early drafts of Chapters 3 and 5 were presented by Edwards at Allen Wood's Marx course at Stanford University in 2019. Comments from Professor Wood and S.M. Love were especially useful. A draft of Chapter 3 was presented by Edwards at the Philosophy, Politics, and Economics conference in 2020, and particular thanks are due to the feedback of Graham Hubbs. An earlier version of some of the material in Chapter 5 appeared in Transformation and the History of Philosophy (Routledge, 2023) and received very helpful feedback from the editors, G. Anthony Bruno and Justin Vlasits. A later version was presented by Edwards at Marquette University in 2021, and particular thanks are due to Yoon Choi, Javiera Perez Gomez, and Kimberly Ann Harris. This version was subsequently presented at the University of Wisconsin, Milwaukee, receiving especially helpful feedback from Stan Husi and the uniformly excellent graduate students in attendance.

Leiter taught with Michael Forster a seminar on Marx and 20th-century Marxism in early 2023, in which Edwards also participated. Forster's detailed comments on Chapters 2, 4, 5, and 6 were very helpful, and we also benefitted from comments by students in the seminar, especially Kate Petroff. Edwards worked through a draft of the entire manuscript with his students Abbigail Bender and Brooklyn Filtzkowski, and their suggestions helped improve the accessibility and clarity of the manuscript. Leiter presented related work on the Marxian concept of ideology at both the University of Arizona and Stanford University, and feedback at both places helped, indirectly, improve Chapter 5 of this volume.

Peter Povilonis provided excellent research assistance on several chapters, as well as good advice on a number of translation issues. Dr. Hana Nasser did an initial draft of the glossary, and provided valuable research assistance on references in the penultimate version of the manuscript. The Alumni Faculty Fund of the University of Chicago Law School provided financial support for this research assistance.

In January 2024, Chicago's Center for Law, Philosophy, and Human Values hosted a conference on the penultimate draft of the manuscript; extended commentaries were presented by Allen Buchanan, David Leopold, Jake McNulty, Paul Raekstad, and Allen Wood. In addition, we were fortunate to get useful suggestions and criticisms from the audience at this conference, and we should acknowledge, especially, Pascal Brixel, Daniel Brudney, Daniel Burnfin, Chiara Cordelli, Lawrence "Dusty" Dallman, Anton Ford, Ben Laurence, Hana Nasser, Martha Nussbaum, Kate Petroff, Sara Wexler, and Vanessa Wills. We are especially grateful to Professors Brixel and Leopold for sharing detailed written comments with us. All these scholars saved us from errors and helped improve the final manuscript. No doubt we erred in not taking more of their advice!

Finally, Edwards would like to express his immense gratitude to Katherine Gibson, Nethanel Lipshitz, Agnes Malinowska, and Francey Russell for their intellectual companionship and years of insightful conversations about the themes explored in this book. Leiter would like to express his gratitude to the late Maurice Leiter for introducing him to Marx long ago; to Edwards and Dusty Dallman, whose dissertations on Marx taught him so much; and to Sheila, Sam, William, and Celia for everything else!

March 2024

1

Life, Work, and Intellectual Development

1. An Overview of Marx's Key Ideas

Karl Marx (1818–1883) is arguably history's most influential, if often misunderstood, philosopher—although his contributions went well beyond philosophy as it had been previously understood, to include questions in economics, history, and social theory. Over the course of his life, he enjoyed only periods of modest recognition due primarily to his work as a political activist, newspaper editor, and essayist. However, in the decades after his death, his ideas came to prominence throughout Europe with the rise of revolutionary political movements inspired by his writings, particularly by *Capital*, his most sustained work on the political economy of capitalism published towards the end of his life. The 1917 Russian Revolution established the first nominally Marxist regime; and, as the century progressed, roughly a third of the world's population came to live under governments that self-identified as such, even when they obviously had nothing to do with Marx's own ideas. Unsurprisingly, it was outside of these regimes that his actual ideas received their most sustained critical engagement and subsequently achieved their most lasting influence. While generations of social and political activists continue to look to Marx for inspiration, anyone with a serious education in the social sciences or the humanities will encounter his ideas throughout their studies, either explicitly or implicitly, presented at times as truisms while at others as matters of profound controversy.

DOI: 10.4324/9781315658902-1

So, what are these ideas? Here we highlight five key areas of his thought, each of which will receive sustained treatment in subsequent chapters of this volume.

A. Historical Materialism

A theory of the transformation of societies animated Marx's thinking throughout his decades-long career. His core idea—historical materialism—is distinctive both for the way that it tries to explain conscious human activity in terms of the material (or economic) conditions in which it arises (hence the theory's materialism) and for the way that it explains shifts from one epoch to the next in virtue of transformations of these conditions, in particular, the growth of technology (hence its historical dimension).

Marx begins his analysis with "real" people laboring to satisfy their basic needs and creating new needs in the process. Each historical period has a specific mode of production constituted by the available raw materials, current technologies, and the prevailing division of labor that determines who will produce what and under which conditions. Each mode of production gives rise to a corresponding legal and political structure, as well as to the society's economic, political, moral, and religious thought more generally—all of which is primarily explained in virtue of its role in supporting and sustaining the mode of production itself. In this way, Marx traces our ideas back to our practical activity—a fact that often escapes first-personal conscious thought itself, which can "flatter" itself that it is free from such workaday concerns. Things do change, and often in revolutionary ways. The impetus for these transformations, according to Marx, occurs when the economic structure and its corresponding legal and political institutions become impediments rather than complements to the ever-developing productive forces. At such moments, those best positioned to maximize these productive forces seize power, revolutionizing the economic structures as well as the corresponding legal and political structures, and with this the character of the society's thinking more generally.

B. Class Conflict

Marx's historical materialism is animated by his account of classes and their conflicts:

The history of all hitherto existing society is the history of class struggles ... oppressor and oppressed, stood in constant opposition to one another, carried on an uninterrupted, now hidden, now open fight, a fight that each time ended, either in a revolutionary re-constitution of society at large, or in the common ruin of the contending classes.

(MECW 6: 482)

Prevailing economic systems sort individuals into different groups whose members are similarly situated with respect to realizing their material interests. For example, the central players in Marx's Europe are those who own the factories, those who own vast tracts of land, those who own small farms, and those who do the actual work in the factories or on the land. However, this is never a society characterized by "social cooperation among equals for mutual advantage" (Rawls 2009: 14) as traditional political philosophy supposes. Rather, groups acting in pursuit of their own interests inevitably find themselves in conflict with one another. Those best positioned to exploit the existing productive forces attain ruling-class status, monopolizing political power either through governing directly or through controlling the political figures who rule nominally, and then leveraging this power to ensure and enhance their own economic position. The others either toil away unware of the class dynamics shaping their lives, or they develop a "class consciousness"—understanding their place in the class struggle, fighting for gains where possible, and challenging the ruling class itself for control if and when they are fortunate enough to find themselves in the right position vis-à-vis the prevailing economic structure at the right time historically.

C. Capitalism

Marx is most widely known for his analysis and critique of capitalism—the economic system in which he expects the history of class conflict to crescendo before finally ushering in the age of communism. Capitalism, according to Marx, is characterized by capitalists (paradigmatically for Marx factory owners) employing wage laborers to produce commodities for exchange on the market for a profit. These profits stem from "exploitation"—paying the laborer a wage that is less than the value they contribute in production. Marx was one of the first thinkers to recognize and celebrate the incredible power of capitalism to expand human productivity. However, he also argues that the system is fundamentally unstable. The capitalist is incentivized to exploit workers as much as possible, either by extending their working hours or by supplementing and/or replacing their labor through automatization. This ensures that a worker will be poor and either overworked or unemployed. Additionally, this ultimately undermines the capitalist system itself. Adopting but modifying the labor theory of value prevalent among economists of his era—according to which the value of a commodity was the result of the labor socially necessary to produce it—Marx concludes that, as the value-producing labor is increasingly displaced by technology, the rate of profit will ultimately fall across the system.

Though the labor theory of value has generally been rejected, and with it some of the specific features of Marx's analysis, he remains the forebearer of a more general criticism—namely that capitalism generates a population that will be increasingly unable to support the system by buying the goods it produces, and that grows increasingly frustrated at it as their immiseration deepens. At the moment when both the productive capacities of the system and the immiseration of the population are sufficiently extensive, Marx expects the newly class-conscious industrial workers to recognize and seize the historical moment by carrying out a communist revolution, abolishing private ownership of the means of production and the system of exploitation it enables.

D. Ideology

Marx's account of ideology grows out of his historical materialism, but its interest and importance do not depend ultimately on the truth of historical materialism. In his earlier writings, he employs the term "ideology" (and its cognates) narrowly as one of abuse directed at a particular kind of philosophical opponent, one who believes ideas rather than material conditions are the motor of history. However, while Marx retains the pejorative connotation, he soon expands his usage to critique moral, political, economic, and religious thought more generally and for reasons extending beyond their simply being idealist in nature. Although Marx never provides a precise definition of ideology, the main line of thought emerging from his various remarks is that an ideology is a cluster of inferentially related *beliefs* (and also *causally related attitudes*[1]) that have three characteristics: (1) at least some of the ideology's central beliefs are false; (2) the ideology is the product of ideologists (economic, religious, and philosophical "theorists") who systematically make claims underdetermined (or even contradicted) by evidence (typically due to shared biases that undermine their theorizing); and (3) the ideology supports the interests (in a sense to be explained) of the ruling class, and harms the interest of the vast majority, most often by misrepresenting how the existing state of affairs affects their interests. This puts the concept of "interests" at the center of the critique of ideology, a point to which we return in detail in Chapter 5. Thus, an ideological critique aims to unmask false beliefs that harm the interests of those who hold them, while also explaining their genesis in a way that simultaneously explains their prevalence and intractability.

E. Human Nature and the Good Life

In the early 1840s, Marx articulated—although mostly in work he never published—something like a normative theory about what a good human life requires and the ways in which life under modern capitalism falls short. This early normative theory involves several claims and commitments:

1. Human beings have an *essential* nature, which determines the conditions under which they could flourish (i.e., lead good lives).
2. It involves an *objectivist* theory of the good—i.e., what is good for a person does not depend on a person's desires, actual or idealized.
3. Human beings are essentially creatures who need to engage in free productive activity, i.e., to produce things (to labor)—not simply to survive but to express themselves as productive beings (including producing things for aesthetic reasons).
4. Human beings are also essentially creatures who need *reconciliation* (*Versöhnung*) with the world in which they live, including

with their fellow human beings, on whose productive labor they depend. A person is in a condition of alienation/estrangement (Entfremdung) to the extent that their essential nature is thwarted from expression or realization in various ways (an objective fact about their circumstances, which they might or might not experience psychologically), and capitalism produces in a state of alienation par excellence, reducing the worker to an automaton endlessly producing widgets on a factory line (or delivering Amazon packages to doorsteps).

In his mature work, Marx retains a conception, often implicit, of the human good and human flourishing, and his objections to capitalism are informed by these conceptions, especially by the ideal of "freedom from necessity"—that is, freeing people from having to work as a necessity for survival rather than as an expression of their nature[2] However, he thinks a successful critique of capitalism does not depend on moral theorizing. The masses who are being immiserated in times of potential abundance will not need a moral theory to explain why they are badly off, but rather a clear-eyed understanding of what is happening and what could be done to change it. In such circumstances, at best moral theorizing will be ineffectual, and at worst it will be marshaled by the ideological classes to distract or discourage meaningful change.

The task of this volume will be to present the ideas sketched briefly above as perspicuously as possible, to offer our own assessment of their relative strengths and weaknesses, and ultimately to provide an orientation to readers so that they can better explore Marx's ideas on their own. Such exploration is especially daunting in his case. First, Marx was prolific. The definitive edition of his writings, the Marx-Engels-Gesamtausgabe (MEGA 2), will consist of roughly 100 large volumes when complete. Second, while some of this work was published in his lifetime, most of it was not, and the unpublished works range from haphazardly jotted down notes to nearly completed works that he simply set aside for one reason or another. Third, Marx wrote extensively in a variety of mediums—philosophical essays, volumes exploring economic history and ideas, journal and newspaper articles, political tracts and speeches, and extensive correspondence with friends and colleagues. Finally, the core of his writing was largely focused on the events and figures of his time, even as his insights often transcend them. This writing ranges from some of the greatest political analysis ever recorded to petty score-settling with minor figures that can stretch on for hundreds of pages. In either case, Marx presumes that his audience will be well-acquainted with the targets of his critique, though most present-day readers are not.

For all of these reasons, it can prove difficult for someone coming to Marx for the first time to know where to begin and what to make of the work one encounters. Therefore, it will behoove us to begin by situating Marx's writings in his life and times. This will provide the requisite context for approaching his ideas. As a bonus, in contrast to many philosophical biographies, we'll find that Marx's life was an interesting one—a semi-tragic figure engaged on multiple fronts with the tumultuous events of his age.

2. Marx's Early Life

Karl Marx was born in 1818 in the German Rhineland city of Trier, a region that had been relatively content under the liberalizing influence of recent Napoleonic rule, but which was now controlled by the Prussians who were typically viewed as an oppressive occupying force. His father Heinrich was born into a rabbinical family, though he received a secular education and, because of Prussia's recently instituted anti-Jewish laws, converted to Christianity in order to continue a successful law career. Though understandably cautious, Heinrich was a man inspired by the Enlightenment and was involved locally in agitating for political reform. It is clear that he and Karl admired one another and shared a deep affection until the father's death just after Karl turned twenty. The same cannot be said for Karl's relationship with his mother, Henriette. An émigré from the Netherlands also of rabbinical descent, her and Karl's relationship over the course of her long life seems to have consisted primarily of a financially desperate son petitioning a disapproving mother from afar in vain for an advance on his relatively sizable inheritance. Most significant for Karl was his relationship with the von Westphalen family in Trier. The father, Ludwig, was a well-educated man who took young Karl as a mentee, inspiring in him a passion for Greek, French, and English literature and thought. His daughter, Jenny, would marry Karl after a six-year engagement, and the two would remain together until her death nearly forty years later, having lived together in four countries, mostly under difficult conditions as exiles, but quite clearly devoted to one another.

Marx was afforded an excellent education, though he tended to be as undisciplined as he was precocious, and much of his erudition came from intellectual pursuits outside of the classroom. He was tutored by his father until he entered the local *Gymnasium* (high school), which was run by the liberal humanist Hugo Wyttenbach, someone admired by Marx but despised by the local Prussian government, which went so far as ordering the police to raid the school to recover the seditious liberal literature they rightly suspected was being distributed to students. Marx received a classical education, studying math, history, literature, and languages. Upon graduating, he enrolled at the University of Bonn desiring to study philosophy and literature, though compelled by his father to study law. However, in Bonn Marx soon turned his attention away from his studies altogether and towards writing poetry, debating ideas with fellow student radicals after hours, and general troublemaking (drinking, dueling, and so on). His father, sensing that Karl's future was in jeopardy, had him transferred to the more academically serious climate of the University of Berlin. The calculation was partly successful: Karl was more academically focused, but his attention quickly turned from law to philosophy—an enthusiasm that would soon jeopardize his future more than either he or his father could have imagined.

3. Intellectual Influences on the Young Marx: Hegel, Feuerbach, Bauer

The Berlin Marx encountered was one still intellectually dominated by Georg Wilhelm Friedrich Hegel (1770–1831), the famed philosopher who had chaired the Berlin department from 1818 until his death five years before Marx's arrival. Hegel was regarded as the great philosophical system builder who had promoted a historicized version of idealism: idealistic in that it placed *Geist* (spirit or mind) at the center of philosophy, an agent of sorts whose central project was self-actualization, which it accomplished through acting on the whole of the world and then coming to comprehend itself through an interpretation of this action; historicized in that this process was understood as a progressive one that *Geist* accomplished slowly across the whole of history.[3]

Both *Geist* itself and the world it manifests through its activity are made intelligible through philosophy, whose task is to articulate this process. However, what this means precisely was already a matter of controversy in Hegel's time and has remained so ever since. His writings are notoriously obscure—partly owing to the difficulty and scope of his subject matter, partly to the philosophical style that had gripped many philosophers of the Romantic era, and partly to the fact that he was a prominent figure working somewhat cautiously under the watchful eye of the state censors whom he did not want to offend. Most controversial was how to understand the nature of *Geist* itself. Hegel encouraged the idea that he was providing a philosophically defensible account of the Christian God, though some suspected that he was secretly a pantheist or even an atheist interested only in providing an account of the development of human rationality as such. We will see that Marx will come to reject Hegel's idealism, and he will certainly reject the religious idiom in which it is often cast; but there are three general features of Hegel's philosophy that influence Marx's thought, albeit to varying degrees, throughout his life.

A. Holism

A characteristic move in Hegel's works—whether articulating the categories of thought in his *Logic*, the shapes of human consciousness in his *Phenomenology of Spirit*, or the relationship of individuals to their society in his *Elements of the Philosophy of Right*—is to begin with something seemingly simple and show how it must finally be understood as part of a larger complex. For example, the *Philosophy of Right* begins by picturing an individual bearer of rights, reminiscent of the sort of person a social contract theorist like Locke would have us imagine. The picture is initially minimalist—the subject bears only Abstract Right (*Recht*), which lacks reference to any particular interests and simply has as its imperative "Be a person and respect others as persons" (Hegel 1991: ¶ 36). However, the account so far is too minimal: we do not yet have a recognizably determinate human being before us, and so this is too thin a basis from which to theorize social life more generally. So, Hegel begins to explore what actually makes a human life determinate, arguing that this involves externalizing our wills by taking possession of objects and transforming them, but that this activity itself already presupposes that we are involved in relationships of reciprocity with others, a "common will" even, whereby each individual holds their possessions through the common assent of the others, and that this in turn structures notions of rights violations and retribution, which in turn informs notions of morality, which finally leads us to Hegel's account of ethical life more generally. In the end, we are meant to see that there is very little sense in thinking about our initial individual abstracted from the holistic forms of social life that precede the individual and through which their life is made determinate.

Details aside, Marx remains drawn to the idea that, although particular things may appear to be simple, they are typically part of a larger complex, and the condition of adequately understanding any particular thing requires understanding its position in this whole. (For example, we will later see Marx in a Hegelian fashion begin his sweeping analysis of capitalism from an account of a simple commodity.)

B. Teleology and Dialectic

A second standard move in Hegel's work is to present an initially plausible way of seeing things, show how this vision leads to contradictions, and then offer a new account that overcomes the contradictions while preserving something of the original picture. Hegel's various accounts are teleological in that they present a progression towards an end (adequate understanding), and they are dialectical in that this end can only ever be reached through confronting and reconciling contradictions that necessarily arise along the way. For example, in the *Logic*, Hegel sets out to articulate the most fundamental metaphysical category. He begins with "Being," which soon proves inadequate insofar as it is only intelligible with respect to a second, seemingly distinct, category, "Nothing," both of which are eventually reconciled into a third category, "Becoming." The initial categories are both negated (as fundamental) and preserved (as moments within the more fundamental category)—a process nicely captured by Hegel's beloved German verb *aufheben*, which can mean both "to destroy" and "to raise." Similarly, in the *Phenomenology*, Hegel traces out increasingly adequate philosophical standpoints in this dialectic fashion, from "sense certainty" (something like sense-data theory) through to "Absolute Knowing."

Hegel's account of world history is one in which successive societies are characterized by various principles implicitly aimed at freedom and rationality, which they act out before becoming conscious of these principles and their inadequacies; and these societies are subsequently replaced by others better able to reconcile these contradictions into new social forms. A parallel pattern shapes Hegel's account of the domains of "absolute spirit"—art, religion, and the history of philosophy—each of which displays a dialectical shape internally as well as with respect to one another.

C. Progressivism

Hegel's teleological and dialectical presentations end well. In every domain the successive accounts are improvements over the previous ones, increasing the adequacy of *Geist*'s understanding of itself and the world that it manifests until, in the end, we recognize "the History of the world is none other than the progress of the consciousness of Freedom" (Hegel 2004: 19). This aim is not one generally recognized in advance by the various historical actors generally acting on motives and reasons of a personal sort, but "Reason" itself proves "cunning" by using them to move history forward toward this goal. Even philosophers, those best positioned to grasp and articulate the particular principles animating their own times, are only able to finally do so as their epoch draws to a close and another begins.[4] This process continues until we reach Hegel himself, who seems to have finally been in a position to complete philosophy's ultimate aim of tracing *Geist*'s journey through to the end:

> [I have] tried to exhibit their ... necessary procession out of one another, so that each philosophy necessarily presupposes the one preceding it. Our standpoint is the cognition of spirit, the knowledge of the idea as spirit, as absolute spirit ... To

recognize that absolute spirit can be for it is this finite spirit's principle and vocation.

(Hegel 2009: 212)

As controversial as his suggestion that he had completed philosophy was his suggestion that the Prussian state he belonged to was sufficiently rational for him to have done so. "The state," Hegel writes, "is the divine idea as it exists on earth" (2004: 39), and "the march of God in the world" (1991: 279). To many of his contemporaries, Hegel seemed to be claiming that God's march had reached its final destination at the Prussian constitutional monarchy of his own day, and, however contestably, they read the *Philosophy of Right's* famous dictum—"What is rational is actual; and what is actual is rational" (Hegel 1991: 20)—as an ode to its arrival.

After Hegel's death in 1831, the philosophical following he had cultivated fractured along theological and political lines into several competing schools. "Right" (or "Old") Hegelians leaned into the conservative defense of the Prussian state as the embodiment of reason and fulfillment of history while defending traditional Christianity with Hegelian tools. "Center" Hegelians largely focused on developing themes in his Logic and Aesthetics, while reinterpreting religious dogma through a Hegelian lens. "Left" (or "Young") Hegelians were inspired by Hegel's vision of history as the progressive advance of reason and freedom, though they scorned the idea that this great advance could truly have reached its goal in the stultifying Prussian state in which they lived; and they targeted religion in particular as an obstacle to freedom to be critiqued away rather than accommodated or rationally rehabilitated.

The watershed moment in this movement was David Strauss's 1835 publication of *The Life of Jesus*. Strauss argued that the New Testament was too filled with contradictions to be considered an actual historical record. Rather, the New Testament was a written record of the early church's increasingly mythologized account of the life of Jesus which had developed through an oral tradition over time. In other words, the Bible was myth. Strauss's publication scandalized the conservative academic community, though it initiated a decade of religious critique from Left Hegelian quarters, most notably Ludwig Feuerbach and Bruno Bauer, both of whom would soon have a direct influence on Marx before themselves becoming the targets of his critiques.

Ludwig Feuerbach (1804–1872), arguably the most influential of the Young Hegelians, developed Hegelian themes in the broadly materialist direction that would characterize significant parts of German philosophy for the remainder of the 19th century.[5] He studied philosophy in Berlin, attending Hegel's lectures from 1825 to 1827. After his own academic career was soon cut short because of his attacks on the conservative religious establishment that dominated the academy, Feuerbach retreated from public life to write. In 1841 he published his best-known work, *The Essence of Christianity*, arguing that God does not exist and that human liberation depends on recognizing this fact.

Echoing a thought that goes at least as far back as Xenophanes's *Fragments* of 6th-century BC Greece, Feuerbach begins by claiming that what we call God is merely the projection of human qualities onto an imagined supernatural being.[6] Christianity, however, is a particular sort of projection, one in which finite humans take their greatest qualities and project them onto a being who is imagined to possess them infinitely. Humans have the capacity for knowledge, power, and generosity; God is seen as omniscient, omnipotent, and omnibenevolent. In projecting what is best in themselves, people come to feel alienated from these very same qualities; and, dominated by an image of perfection before which they inevitably fall short, they denigrate themselves and the human community more generally. Therefore, Feuerbach concludes, we need to break the spell: we should renounce religion as the illusory projection that it is and finally recognize that those powers we have worshiped are in fact our own, developing them in ways that will enable us to finally realize a non-alienated community here in this world.

Bruno Bauer (1809–1882) occupied a similarly prominent role in Young Hegelian circles marshalling Hegelian ideas against the prevailing conservative political and religious establishment. Bauer arrived as a student in Berlin in 1828, just as Feuerbach was leaving. He too studied with Hegel, writing an essay on aesthetics that was awarded the Prussian royal prize in philosophy on Hegel's recommendation. After completing his studies, Bauer attained a lectureship position and remained in Berlin teaching theology through the

1830s. His early work from this period focused primarily on interpreting the Old and New Testaments as exemplifications of various Hegelian themes.

As the decade progressed, Bauer's writing began to emphasize what he saw as the negative consequences of religion, namely, a dogmatism that valued an other-worldly abstraction over this-worldly community. Then, as Strauss had done, Bauer turned his attention to a textual analysis aimed at establishing the true origins of the Gospels. Like Strauss, Bauer argued that the Gospels could not be read as a historical record; unlike Strauss, he explicitly argued against the existence of a historical Jesus, and he claimed that three of the Gospels were mere attempts to rewrite Mark's original. In short, Bauer's ideas in this period developed from highlighting the rational (i.e., Hegelian) ideas religious texts and practices embodied (even if inchoately) to dismissing these as dogmatic illusions.

Marx arrived in Berlin in 1836, began attending the lectures of the Hegelian legal theorist Eduard Gans, and eventually found his way into the "Doctors Club," a circle of prominent Young Hegelians led by Bauer who met regularly to discuss philosophy and politics. Bauer became a mentor to Marx, enlisting his help with editing Hegel's *Lectures on the Philosophy of Religion* and advising on his doctoral thesis in philosophy, *The Difference Between the Democritean and Epicurean Philosophy of Nature*. Marx admired Epicurus's materialism, which the latter uses to criticize religion as an invention by the priesthood to maintain power by leveraging the fear of death. He believes that understanding reality as a combination of atoms and void negates the concept of an afterlife, lessening the dread of death and reconciling us with our physical existence.[7]

Although its central topic is the competing accounts of atomic theory in ancient Greek philosophy, a topic Marx would not pursue, the dissertation approaches this topic largely through the lens of German idealist preoccupations (freedom, the unity of thought and being, etc.) with several of Marx's characteristic qualities already on display: attempting to work out what is right and wrong in the philosophy of the "giant thinker" Hegel; castigating the conservative tendencies of contemporary followers of Hegel; and enthusiastic antagonizing of the dominant conservative religious and political establishment ("Philosophy makes no secret of it. The confession of Prometheus: 'In simple words, I hate the pack of Gods'").

Marx completed his thesis in 1841, submitting it to the more liberal University of Jena, and left to join Bauer, who had been transferred to the University of Bonn two years prior because of his own outspokenness. However, Bauer's academic position was again cut short when Friedrich Wilhelm IV, the new King of Prussia, personally ordered his dismissal, making it very clear that Marx could not expect an academic appointment himself.

4. Marx in the 1840s: Journalism, Politics, Persecution

Marx, now twenty-four years old, turned to journalism. The *Rheinische Zeitung* was a fledgling Cologne newspaper under the editorial influence of the socialist-leaning philosopher and Zionist Moses Hess. Marx began there as a journalist, contributing a series of articles critical of the Rhineland Diet's (the regional parliament's) lack of transparency and its restrictions on press freedom, and later articles critical of the Diet's treatment of the region's poor. Marx's writing was popular with the readership and he was promoted through the editorial ranks, eventually taking over as the paper's editor. It is in this period that we see the beginning of Marx's break from Bauer and other Young Hegelians. Marx, busy investigating real-world politics with which he finds Bauer increasingly out of step, published an article critical of the group of thinkers (the "free") that Bauer had assembled in Berlin. It is also in this period that Marx begins to become more radical.

The initial tenor of most of his journalism from this period was that of a reform-minded liberal, optimistic that the system could transition from a monarchy to a constitutional democracy without violence, and largely dubious of the socialist ideas circulating at that time. Under Marx's leadership, the struggling paper had established itself into one of Germany's most widely circulated. However, the Protestant Prussian government that had initially supported the *Rheinische Zeitung*, in the hopes that it would provide a non-Catholic counterweight to Cologne's more established and often critical Catholic newspaper, soon realized that their hopes were misplaced and began to suppress the paper, which shifted Marx's writing in an increasingly radical direction and eventually led to his resignation in protest in 1843.

Marx, now married to Jenny after their long engagement, moved to Paris in the fall of 1843 to establish the *Deutsch–Französische Jahrbücher*. Although France was ruled by the center-right July Monarchy (1830–1848), Paris itself was the creative center of cultural and intellectual life in Europe. French socialist thought was flourishing. Henri de Saint-Simon's (1760–1825) often charismatic followers were promoting his hopes of a society renewed through science and brotherly love; Charles Fourier's (1772–1837) followers were beginning their attempts to realize his vision that human harmony would be achieved through communes built to his specifications; and Pierre-Joseph Proudhon (1809–1865), the first philosopher to declare himself an anarchist, had recently published his widely read *What is Property?*, which famously concluded that "property is theft!"

Paris had also developed a population of notable radical German expatriates, including the poet Heinrich Heine (1797–1856) and fellow members of the "Young Germany" movement.[8] It was also in Paris that Marx would soon meet Friedrich Engels (1820–1895), a wealthy German industrialist's son who would become his life-long collaborator, financial patron, literary executor, and intellectual champion. Marx, together with co-editor and fellow expatriate Arnold Ruge (1802–1880), intended the *Deutsch–Französische Jahrbücher* to be a forum that would foster exchange between the generally disconnected French and German radical intellectuals of this period.

Marx contributed two articles to the journal's premiere (and only) edition. The first, "Contribution to a Critique of Hegel's Philosophy of Right, Introduction," accepts Feuerbach's claim that humans have created God in their own image, an image before which they now bow, not recognizing its powers as theirs and unable to employ these for their own benefit. Marx criticizes Feuerbach, however, for failing to recognize the material conditions that give rise to the religious impulse in the first place, and consequently for misidentifying the remedy for alienation. Feuerbach seems to think that alienation will dissipate once people come to see religion for the myth that it is. However, Marx writes, "religion is the opiate of the people," though it certainly fills their heads with illusions—simply telling them to quit their addiction will not alleviate the suffering that compels them to medicate. Truly overcoming alienation requires changing the material conditions that give rise to it, and Marx here first identifies this as a job for the proletariat, the relatively new class of industrial workers who will remain the protagonists of his writings throughout his life.

The second article, "On the Jewish Question," is a response to Bauer's recent essay on the same subject. The "Jewish Question" referred to the societal and political debates about the status and treatment of Jews in Europe, particularly in German-speaking regions, during the late 18th and 19th centuries. Following Feuerbach, Bauer saw religion as an alienated form of consciousness, and so argued that Jews and Christians alike could only achieve personal emancipation by renouncing their religious identity and political emancipation by renouncing any public role for religion in the state. Marx argues that even if religious constraints were removed from the political sphere, individuals would still face economic and social alienation in the larger society. The secular state not only fails to ensure emancipation, but its guiding preoccupations can be an obstacle to it. For instance, Marx argues that the liberal rights of "politically emancipated" states enshrine an ideal of isolated individuals in competition with and under threat from one another, whereas true "human emancipation" requires us acting in concert with others for everyone's mutual benefit.

The *Deutsch-Französische Jahrbücher* was soon beset by troubles. Its hoped-for radical French contributors never materialized, the first edition was quickly suppressed back in Germany, and Ruge and Marx soon fell out over intellectual differences. Nevertheless, Marx remained productive while in Paris. He began contributing to the radical German-language newspaper *Vorwärts!* (*Forward*), and increasingly devoted himself to studying the British economic writings of Adam Smith (1723–1790), David Ricardo (1772–1823), and James Mill (1773–1836), whose works he first encountered during this period. He also worked on what has become known as *The Economic and Philosophical Manuscripts of 1844* (or *Paris Manuscripts*). These notebooks sketched out an amalgam of Hegelian themes of production and alienation with Smith's account of the division of labor that enabled capitalist productive expansion. Most notably, it is here that Marx argues that the worker under capitalism is subjected to four types of alienation: first, workers are alienated from the product of their labor, since it is made for another who takes it away as soon as it is finished; second, they are alienated from the activity of work itself, which is experienced as an unfortunate burden they must bear; third, workers are alienated from their species-being (*Gattungswesen*), the distinctively human power which is both expressed and recognized through their world-transforming productive activity—an activity and accomplishment that is obscured from the vantage point of those working on a factory line; and fourth, workers are alienated from other humans, who are seen as a means to an end rather than as fellow members of a community transforming the world for everyone's benefit.

At the beginning of 1845, at Prussia's request, Marx was expelled from France. With a return to Germany off-limits, Marx unhappily relocated to Brussels, where he would remain for most of the next three years. Brussels was a much smaller and less culturally active city than Paris, and one where Marx did not speak the language; but it was a place that offered respite to him on condition that he did not publish anything political. Brussels at this time was attracting many other radicals in similar situations, including many of his friends and associates from Paris, and Marx was soon joined by Engels as well, with whom he lived for a time.

In Brussels, Marx began working out his account of historical materialism, and in so doing completed his intellectual break with both the Young Hegelians and French socialists. In his *Theses on Feuerbach* (1845), Marx critiques both existing materialism, for ignoring the active role humans play in shaping their world, and idealism, specifically Hegel's form, for limiting human activity to thought or contemplation. Marx acknowledges the partial insights of both philosophical theories: the physical reality of the world emphasized by materialism, and the active nature of the human subject recognized by idealism. However, he proposes a new perspective, suggesting that humans transform the world not just through thought but through actual physical labor and material activity. The 11th thesis, engraved on Marx's tomb, concludes "the philosophers have only interpreted the world, the point is to change it" (MECW 5: 5).

Over the next year, Marx and Engels collaborated to develop this thought in the *German Ideology*. This work establishes the "premises of the materialist method"—human beings are creatures who must produce in order to satisfy their basic needs, and in so doing expand their powers and develop new material and social needs, which gives rise to distinct ways of organizing their productive activities, which itself explains the structure of any particular society more generally as well as its prevailing ideas. Marx would later publish an important precis of this view in his 1859 Preface to *A Contribution to the Critique of Political Economy*; yet the *German Ideology*, unpublished in his life, would remain the most detailed account of historical materialism that he would ever provide.

In February of 1848, Marx would violate the prohibition from publishing anything political in truly spectacular fashion by co-authoring with Engels one of history's most well-known and incendiary political works, *The Communist Manifesto*. During his time in Brussels, Marx cultivated a network of political activists. Early on he had established a small group of fellow exiles called the "Communist Corresponding Committee," with satellite groups in London and Paris. During this time, Marx was also in contact with the "League of the Just"—a secret society of radicals with messianic tendencies that he had known from his time in Paris. Now based in London after a failed coup in France, this group proposed, and Marx accepted, merging the two organizations to form one above-ground political organization, namely the "Communist League." Marx and Engels were tasked with drawing up the League's program, and the result was the *Manifesto*. In magisterial rhetoric, this work animates the general outlines of historical development that Marx had been theorizing in *The German Ideology* and elsewhere, with a pronounced emphasis on the role that class conflict plays in this process. We are told that we are presently on the eve of a revolution: in a short time capitalism has developed human productive capacities to a degree previously unimaginable, yet this has come at the expense of the proletariat (the vast majority), who are now in a position to transform society in a way that finally transcends class altogether. The *Manifesto* ends with a call to arms: "The proletarians have nothing to lose but their chains. They have a world to win. Working Men of All Countries, Unite!" (MECW 6: 519).

As fate would have it, 1848 would in fact witness the most wide-spread revolutionary wave in Europe's history. In February, the July Monarchy was overthrown in France and the Second Republic (1848–1852) assumed power.[9] Within a short time, uprisings were threatening to topple most of the other European powers as well. Marx was expelled from Belgium, but, due to the upheavals, he was able to return first to Paris and then to Cologne. In June, financed by a recent inheritance, Marx began publishing the *Neue Rheinische Zeitung*, a daily newspaper that he edited and to which he was the primary contributor. Marx advocated for revolution; though, to the consternation of many fellow revolutionaries (but in keeping with his own historical materialist principles), he argued for a two-step process. First, revolutionaries needed to support the bourgeoisie overthrowing of the feudal remnants that still dominated Germany's politics; then they could topple the bourgeoisie themselves.[10] However, neither of these steps was to occur. Most of the uprisings of 1848 soon faltered with conservative powers gradually reasserting themselves. Marx was frequently harassed and even put on trial, and finally, in May of 1849, he was expelled from Germany altogether. Marx returned briefly to Paris, but now in the midst of its own conservative reaction, he was soon expelled from France as well and sought asylum in England.

5. Marx in Exile in London

Marx left for London when he was thirty-one years old, and would spend the remaining three decades of his life there as an exile, devoted to his writing and intermittent political organizing, though generally under desperate financial conditions and beset by chronic ill-health. Marx was one of a large diaspora of 1848 exiles; but the community would provide little support, embittered as it was by the failed revolution, cut off from its home countries, and increasingly fractured through infighting and mistrust. Marx and Jenny already had three children when they arrived in London, and they would have four more together in their time there; but, partly owing to their extreme poverty, only three of the seven would survive to adulthood.

During their initial years in London, the family subsisted largely on what help Engels was able to provide through his father. Throughout most of the 1850s, Marx was able to earn a modest living writing articles as a European correspondent for the progressive New York *Daily Tribune*, though this work dried up towards the end of the decade, at which point the family was again largely dependent on Engels. Their finances finally stabilized when the family received two sizable inheritances in the mid-1860s. However, though finally financially secure, the terrible health that had afflicted Marx throughout much of his adulthood now made his life increasingly unbearable: liver and gall problems, chronic headaches, neuralgia, rheumatic pains, and boils, among other ailments.

Despite the generally terrible circumstances, Marx worked tirelessly throughout these years in London as a political organizer, a political commentator, and most famously as an economic theorist. Let us say a bit about each of these roles that defined the rest of his life.

A. *Political Organizer*

During his first few years in London, Marx continued to take an active role in the Communist League, organizing members throughout Europe as well as publishing the party's journal, the *Neue Rheinische Zeitung Revue*. During this same period, Marx was active in the German Workers' Educational Society (GWES), a public-facing educational and charitable organization that served to attract artisans to the Communist League. However, by 1851 the League had disintegrated, and Marx had resigned from the GWES—both events the result of a split between one faction that wanted to agitate for revolution straight away and Marx's faction that continued to press for his two-step program (the working class should partner with the bourgeoisie to stamp out the remnants of feudal power before stamping out the bourgeoisie themselves).

Marx stepped away from political organizing until the formation in 1864 of the International Workingmen's Association (IWA), or "the First International" as it would come to be known. The IWA aimed to unite the numerous left-wing organizations throughout Europe to advocate for the working classes, and at its height is estimated to have had a membership in the millions. Marx drafted the IWA's constitution and delivered its inaugural address, and over much of the next decade he would assume an increasingly dominant role until, in 1872, long-standing differences finally split the organization into two competing factions—one led by Marx and the other led by the famed Russian anarchist Mikhail Bakunin. The dissolution of the IWA marked the end of Marx's most direct political activity, though he would continue to serve at a distance as a mentor to political organizers elsewhere, particularly to the emerging socialist parties in Germany.

B. Political Commentator

Marx wrote several important essays responding to contemporary political events that complement his theory of history while helping to clarify his views on class conflict and the nature of the state. Shortly after his arrival in London, he published The Class Struggles in France, which analyzed the still-unfolding political turmoil taking place. A popular uprising had toppled the July Monarchy in February of 1848 and a seemingly progressive provisional government had been installed. However, in June a workers' uprising was put down and the government lurched in a conservative direction. In Marx's analysis, these events do not demonstrate a failure of the radical left (as many had thought at the time) since it was never really their struggle to begin with. The real conflict was between the petty bourgeoisie (small business owners), who had enlisted the radicals for a time with sentimental talk of brotherhood, against the bourgeoisie proper (the industrialists and financiers).

Marx developed these themes in his small masterpiece The Eighteenth Brumaire of Louis Napoleon, written after Louis's assumption of dictatorial powers, which tasks itself with answering "how the class struggle in France created circumstances and relationships that made it possible for a grotesque mediocrity to play a hero's part." Marx's answer was that France's class divisions had resulted in a stalemate in which the various elements of the bourgeoisie were divided amongst themselves, the workers remained too small a minority in a nation that was still industrially underdeveloped, and the great masses of peasants were unable to recognize themselves as a class. Louis, who in his vacuousness could appear as all things to all people, was able to take advantage of this division. Marx bookended his time in London with 1871's "The Civil War in France," a tribute to the ultimately doomed radical government that ruled Paris for two months that year, and 1875's "Critique of the Gotha Programme," Marx's entreaty that German socialists not compromise their radical principles for moderate concessions from the government and his most programmatic suggestions for how a transition to communism could take place.

C. Economic Theorist

Above all, Marx remains known as a trenchant critic of capitalism, detailing its inherent destructiveness and instability. Marx obtained a ticket to the British Museum's reading room soon after his arrival in 1850 and devoted large parts of the next two decades there to developing his account over thousands of pages. During 1857–1858, he worked on the *Grundrisse*, a large, complex, and unfinished work that touches on some themes from his earlier economic writings (especially alienation) but mostly begins developing those that would characterize his mature work (detailing the inner workings of the capitalist exchange economy and of its supposedly self-undermining nature). The following year he published *A Contribution to the Critique of Political Economy*, less known for its economic content than for the Preface's precis of historical materialism. Soon after, Marx produced an enormous collection of writings now known as the *1861–2 Manuscripts* that he considered a continuation of the *Critique* (which remained unpublished in his life, though a substantial portion of these was published after his death as *Theories of Surplus Value*).

Finally, in 1867, after two decades of research and drafting, Marx published the first volume of *Capital*. Here he argues that the essence of capitalism is the production of commodities to exchange on the market for a profit; that this profit is the result of exploiting workers who themselves own nothing but their labor power, and so are forced on pain of starvation to exchange it for a wage; that the demand for profit that ultimately determines whether businesses succeed or fail compels capitalists to drive workers harder or replace them through automatization, and that this produces misery in the population and instability in the system itself. The work was a modest success, and Marx oversaw a second German-language edition as well as the French-language edition, reworking some of the text each time. *Capital* itself was intended only as the first volume in a larger project, though one Marx would never complete. Engels, in a heroic effort with controversial results, would later assemble roughly ten years' worth of Marx's writings into *Capital* volume II (1885) and III (1894).

Marx died in March of 1883, fifteen months after Jenny. He was buried in London's Highgate Cemetery, in a section designated for atheists, on an overcast day with roughly a dozen mourners in attendance. Engels spoke:

> Just as Darwin discovered the law of development or organic nature, so Marx discovered the law of development of human history: the simple fact, hitherto concealed by an overgrowth of ideology, that mankind must first of all eat, drink, have shelter and clothing, before it can pursue politics, science, art, religion, etc.; that therefore the production of the immediate material means, and consequently the degree of economic development attained by a given people or during a given epoch, form the foundation upon which the state institutions, the legal conceptions, art, and even the ideas on religion, of the people concerned have been evolved, and in the light of which they must, therefore, be explained, instead of vice versa … But that is not all. Marx also discovered the special law of motion governing the present-day capitalist mode of production, and the bourgeois society that this mode of production has created … Marx was before all else a revolutionist. His real mission in life was to contribute, in one way or another, to the overthrow of capitalist society and of the state institutions which it had brought into being, to contribute to the liberation of the modern proletariat, which he was the first to make conscious of its own position and its needs, conscious of the conditions of its emancipation. Fighting was his element. And he fought with a passion, a tenacity and a success such as few could rival.

Within twenty years of Marx's death, socialist parties inspired by his work gained in prominence throughout Europe; within another twenty, revolutions were being fought and won in his name. The century that followed would see pitched intellectual and political battles fought among those who admired his ideas, as well as between these admirers and those who opposed Marx's ideas altogether. It is to a detailed examination of the ideas themselves that we now turn.

Notes

1 Beliefs can be true or false, and can stand in logical relations with other beliefs, while attitudes (which are neither true nor false) can stand in causal relations with beliefs and other attitudes. So, for example, the belief that Kings have a divine right to rule may cause attitudes of approbation and respect in some, and attitudes of dismay and anger in others. The belief itself is false (Kings do not have a divine right to rule), and, while the attitudes may be caused by the belief that it is false, the attitudes themselves are neither true nor false.

2 See esp. the discussion in Chapter 3, Section 4C.

3 "The history of spirit is its own deed; for spirit is only what it does, and its deed is to make itself – in this case, as spirit – the object of its own consciousness, and to comprehend itself in its interpretation of itself to itself" (Hegel 1991: 372).

4 "Philosophy … always comes too late … As the thought of the world, it appears only at a time when actuality has gone through its formative process and attained its completed state … When philosophy paints its grey in grey, a shape of life has grown old, and it cannot be rejuvenated, but only recognized, by the grey in grey of philosophy; the owl of Minerva begins its flight only with the onset of dusk" (Hegel 1991: Preface).

5 The other dominant movement in German philosophy after the decline of Hegel's influence in the 1840s was a "back to Kant" movement in the hands of various Neo-Kantian philosophers.

6 "Mortals deem that the gods are begotten as they are Ethiopians say that their gods are snubnosed and black, Thracians that they are blue-eyed and red-haired … if horses or oxen or lions had hands or could draw with their hands and accomplish such works as men, horses would draw the figures of the gods as similar to horses, and oxen as similar to oxen, and they would make the bodies of the sort which each of them had" (Xenophanes 1992: 14–16).

7 We are grateful to Martha Nussbaum for helping us to better appreciate the force of Epicurus's argument and its significance for Marx.

8 The "Young Germany" movement emerged in 19th-century Germany as a literary and cultural movement. It aimed to challenge the conservative social and political climate of the time. The movement consisted of writers and intellectuals who advocated for liberal and progressive ideas, criticizing established institutions such as the monarchy and the church. Influenced by the ideals of the French Revolution and the Enlightenment, they called for political reform, freedom of

speech, and social justice. Writers like Heinrich Heine, Ludwig Börne, and Karl Gutzkow produced literature addressing social inequality and religious intolerance. For an assessment of the role of the "Young Germany" movement in the development of German national culture, see Hohendahl (2016).

9 After Napoleon Bonaparte's fall in 1814, the conservative Bourbon Monarchy was restored in France under Louis XVIII (reigned 1814–1824) and his brother Charles X (1824–1830). However, Charles's absolutist policies provoked the July Revolution in 1830. This led to the establishment of the July Monarchy under Charles's cousin, Louis-Philippe d'Orléans (1830–1848), who ruled in a more liberal manner. However, widespread discontent led to the February Revolution in 1848, toppling Louis-Philippe and leading to the creation of the Second Republic. Louis Napoleon, nephew of Napoleon Bonaparte, was elected as the first President of the Second Republic in December 1848 (and in 1851 would overthrow the Republic and declare himself Emperor). See Mansel (2003).

10 In 1848, Germany was not a unified nation but a collection of individual states under the German Confederation. Despite the emergence of modern ideas and institutions, remnants of the feudal system persisted. These remnants included the manorial system and serfdom, particularly in eastern regions like Prussia. Additionally, the nobility retained considerable local autonomy and privileges, including judicial and administrative powers in some cases. Various German states had legislative assemblies composed of different "estates," representing the nobility and sometimes the clergy, a holdover from feudal society. Guild systems in cities, while not strictly feudal, also contributed to social and economic stratification. These feudal remnants were a target of the revolutions of 1848, which sought to modernize and democratize German society and governance.

Further Reading

Brudney (1998) has several chapters on the Young Hegelians and Marx's engagement with them, and is especially good on Bauer.

Leopold (2007) is a study of Marx's early works that also provides a helpful overview of their intellectual context.

Liedman (2018) offers an intellectual biography of Marx with helpful historical background to many of Marx's key texts.

Seigel (1978) is an illuminating and subtle psychoanalytic biography.

Sperber (2014) is an exhaustively researched and highly readable biography of Marx that illuminates the intellectual currents to which he was responding.

2

Marx's Theory of History

Historical Materialism and the Hegelian Background

1. Historical Materialism: Forces of Production (Productive Power), Relations of Production, Ideological Superstructure

Marx's most important and influential theoretical contribution is an account of how history unfolds; more precisely, how and why societies and, most importantly, their forms of economic organization change over the course of history. How did feudalism give way to early forms of capitalism? Why should capitalism give way to communism? A theory of historical evolution and change is, for Marx, a theory of how the economic activity of human beings evolves and changes, and how those changes affect everything else in human society.

Economic activity, for Marx, encompasses all the productive activity human beings engage in to meet their basic physical needs (for example, for food and shelter) as well as their other wants and desires (for example, *certain kinds* of food and shelter).[1] Basic needs, for Marx, are brute—a function of what human beings are like and what the world is like: humans need nutrition; they are vulnerable to heat and to cold; they are vulnerable to disease, to physical harm by others, and so on. How human beings meet their basic needs is the fundamental economic fact from which his theory, usually called *historical materialism*, begins.

Marx observes that, throughout human history, the *productive power* of human beings—that is, the power of human beings to produce what

DOI: 10.4324/9781315658902-2

they need—has varied widely. In Marxian lingo, productive power is usually called "the forces of production" (or "means of production" or the economic "base"), but we will use "productive power" and "forces of production" interchangeably. One relative constant in the forces of production in human history has been the physical strength of human beings, their ability to wield a hoe, pick fruit, lift a rock, chop wood. Humans also have a variety of cognitive capacities that enhance their productive power—for example, the ability to plan, to calculate, to do physics, chemistry, and mathematics.

The productive power of human beings *qua* human beings does not change significantly: our bodies and our brains have not gotten significantly bigger over the last several millennia (although the *knowledge* acquired with our brains has expanded exponentially); however humans today are, on average, somewhat taller and stronger than in the past. What has changed dramatically is another aspect of productive power: namely, the *instruments*, *tools*, or *technology* available to human beings, as well as the ways in which humans organize their production (e.g., contrast the individual producer with the assembly line[2]). We shall refer to all of these simply as "technology."

The forces of production grow throughout history because of advances in technology: more and more can be produced with the existing natural resources and with even less human labor power thanks to technological advances. The invention of arrows and spears for hunting was an advance in technology; the invention of guns and gunpowder another. The invention of hoes and plows was an advance in farming technology; the invention of the tractor another. The invention of the spinning wheel was an advance in technology for producing fabrics; the development of the power loom another. The invention of the computer, one of the most significant developments of productive power of the last half-century, has marked a further dramatic increase in what human labor can produce.

Marx's basic idea is that historical change is explained by changes in technology, which affect how human beings meet their basic needs as well as their wants and desires. A human life is very different when the first question in the morning is not "Will I be able to kill animals today to feed my family?" but instead, "When will the grocery delivery arrive?" These differences in the material circumstances of life are also crucial to understanding dramatic differences

in ideas, culture, and values, according to Marx.[3] As he writes in
The German Ideology: "What [individuals] are … coincides with their
production, both with *what* they produce and with *how* they produce.
Hence what individuals are depends on the material conditions of
their production" (MECW 5: 31–32).

In his 1859 Preface to *A Contribution to the Critique of Political Economy*
(hereafter, "the 1859 Preface"), Marx puts it this way:

> In the social production of their existence, men inevitably enter
> into definite relations, which are independent of their will,
> namely relations of production appropriate to a given stage in
> the development of their material forces of production [i.e.,
> technology]. The totality of these relations of production con-
> stitutes the economic structure of society, the real foundation,
> on which arises a legal and political superstructure and to which
> correspond definite forms of social consciousness. The mode of
> production of material life conditions the general process of
> social, political and intellectual life. It is not the consciousness
> of men that determines their existence, but their social existence
> that determines their consciousness.
>
> (MECW 29: 263)

Marx is here concerned with two additional features of human
societies, which he calls "relations of production" and a society's
"superstructure" (crudely, what we just called "ideas, culture and
values"—that is, ideology [but see Chapter 5 for a narrowing of
this gloss]). "Relations of production" refer to the distribution of
property rights in productive forces (or, more generally, control over
productive forces in the case of societies without established systems
of property rights). As technology and productive power increase,
not all humans have equal control of the new technologies or equal
access to their benefits. Human societies are stratified into "classes,"
which we can characterize provisionally as groups of people defined
by the kind of control they have over technology and productive
power (we complicate this account considerably in Chapter 3).
Feudal lords, for example, control not just the land but also the tools
that serfs use in tilling the land and harvesting its fruits. Serfs (generally) control only their own ability to work: if they work for the

feudal lord, if they use his land and his tools to produce food, they are permitted to keep a bit for themselves, while the rest goes to the lord. A serf who refuses to work is finished: there is no other option for meeting his basic needs since serfs did not generally have the option of working for others (they were generally "tied to the land"). Chattel slaves do not even have control over their own labor power: they must work or face punishment, including death. "Wage slaves," by contrast, sell their labor power in return for a wage, and can, under certain circumstances, sell their labor for better wages, thus having an advantage over serfs and chattel slaves, at least as long as there are buyers for their labor power.

Almost all humans everywhere and at all times have "labor power," an ability to work with the physical and cognitive capacities they have; although, as the example of serfs makes clear, sometimes even having labor power is not enough to meet basic needs (and even "wage slaves" [those who must sell their labor power to survive] face the same problem if there are no other buyers for their labor). One constant, however, is that human societies differ dramatically in terms of which humans have control over technology and resources such as land. Feudal lords own the tools and the land but not the labor power of serfs.[4] Southern plantation owners before the American Civil War owned the tools, the land, *and the labor power* of their slaves. Capitalists may own the land, the factory on that land, and the technology that factory employs, but not anyone's labor power; but capitalists can purchase the labor of workers needed to produce things with the factory and technology the capitalist owns. Under capitalism, the contemporary worker owns her labor power, which she can sell in the marketplace, but usually not the technology which is owned by the capitalist.[5]

These class differences—that is, differences between groups of people in terms of what productive power they own (or control) and can sell to others, and what productive power they do not own (or control)—are crucial to understanding historical processes precisely because classes have conflicting interests that arise from what productive power they do and do not own. Capitalists, for example, have an interest in paying the lowest wages possible; wage slaves have the opposite interest.

Capitalism is of special interest for Marx, and is the subject of the extended economic analysis we discuss in Chapter 4. Consider a worker in an Amazon warehouse: he sells his labor power for an hourly wage, but he does not own the warehouse, the merchandise, or the technology platforms by which consumers order goods through Amazon. This worker could refuse to sell his labor to Amazon, which might not be a life-and-death decision, depending on whether there are other buyers for the labor power he has to offer. In this capitalist society, we would say that capitalists own the technology ("means of production") while the worker owns only his own labor power. The wage laborer can refuse to work at any wage offered, and may die as a result, but he will not be killed for refusing. The chattel slave, however, lacks even that limited privilege: he does not own his own labor power, let alone the land, tools, or technology he is ordered to use. (The serf is somewhere in between: there is no market in which he can sell his labor power; but, at the same time, the feudal lord typically cannot sell the serf to someone else,[6] although he can sell the land on which the serf works.) Capitalist relations of production that involve "wage slavery" are thus importantly different from those involved in "chattel slavery": in the former, but not the latter, the individual owns his labor power; and, while both kinds of slaves may end up dead (the former if no one wants to buy his labor power, or if he refuses to sell his labor power to those buying), the relations of production are different.

The other feature of human societies that historical materialism aims to explain is its "ideological superstructure." For Marx, the ideological superstructure refers to the dominant or influential religious, philosophical, moral, and economic ideas in that society.[7] We shall devote a later chapter to Marx's notion of "ideology" (Chapter 5); but here it will suffice to note that Marx's claim is that the dominant religious, philosophical, moral, and economic ideas in any society are those favorable to (in the interests of) the class that controls the most important forces of production (what Marx calls "the ruling class"). For example, in slave societies, the idea emerges that slaves are inferior human beings who are, indeed, better off being enslaved: we see this in antiquity with Aristotle's defense of Greek slavery, and in the American South with racist stereotypes of

African peoples that were proffered as justification for their being enslaved.[8] We see this also in the history of Europe with its ideology of the "divine right of Kings," where religion rationalized the dominance of absolute rulers based on heredity, and in contemporary capitalist societies where the mass media associate capitalism with "freedom" and opposition to capitalism is vilified as leading to tyranny and ruin. (We return to the issue of "freedom" in Chapters 3 and 6.)

These are the basic underpinnings of Marx's theory of history. We start by situating Marx's theory against its Hegelian background, before turning to a more formal statement of Marx's theory of history, some of the interpretive and philosophical puzzles it raises, and, finally, the question whether it is true.

2. Hegel's Theory of History and Historical Materialism

As we discussed in Chapter 1, Marx went through a period of devotion to the philosophy of Hegel before breaking with him. Marx's historical materialism is presented by Marx himself as a rejection of Hegel's views, and in some crucial respects it certainly is. But Marx hewed closer to Hegel's general view of history than was probably wise for an atheist philosopher like Marx with no adequate grounds for confidence in history following a predictable course of development—something more congenial to a view of the world, like Hegel's, in which, on some interpretations, God is supposed to play a role.[9]

Five claims are distinctive of the Hegelian philosophy of history, as reflected in his *Phenomenology of Spirit* and his later *Reason in History* essay. The first claim—the one Marx most clearly rejects—is also the one most distinctive of Hegel's idealism, which we can formulate as follows:

- History—more precisely, "world history" as Hegel calls it—is the history of "spirit striving to attain knowledge of its own nature" (*Reason in History*, III.1). Each historical epoch, in turn, has a distinctive form of consciousness, that is, a distinctive way in which Spirit (*Geist*) understands itself at that time.

Even here, Marx really rejects only the idea that history is the history of "spirit striving to attain knowledge of its own nature." It is true, for Marx, that each historical epoch has "a distinctive form of consciousness" (roughly, an ideology), but that ideology is explained by what is truly driving history—namely, developments in technology.

The other four distinctive claims in Hegel's philosophy of history are ones that Marx essentially retains, but again without their idealist interpretation. According to Hegel, the process of Spirit coming to know itself through history exhibits a structure that is *dialectical, teleological, progressive,* and *cunning:*

1. It is a *dialectical* process insofar as each later form of consciousness arises from (a) the contradictions of the earlier form, which lead to (b) the sublation (i.e., a negation that refashions or transfigures some element) of that earlier form.[10]
2. It is *teleological* (i.e., end-directed) insofar as the whole process has as its inevitable endpoint in Spirit's self-knowledge (i.e., "the progress of the consciousness of Freedom" [Hegel 2004: 19]).
3. It is *progressive* insofar as later forms represent *improvements* over earlier forms.[11]
4. It is *cunning* (the "cunning of Reason" as Hegel calls it) insofar as the actual structure of the process is unknown to historical actors, who act for motives and reasons unrelated to the *dialectical* and *teleological* structure of the process—at least until Hegel makes it explicit.

Although Marx rejects the idea that "Spirit"—how human beings understand themselves at any particular historical moment (e.g., our forms of consciousness, including ideologies)—is the motor of historical change, he accepts materialist versions of claims 1 through 4, above.

First, history for Marx is the history of the growth of the productive forces and the attendant class struggles. Each historical epoch is characterized by a distinctive level of development of the productive forces, which, in turn, explains everything else about that historical epoch, including what Hegel calls its "spirit"—i.e., the form of consciousness characteristic of that epoch (what Marx would call, with some qualifications, the "ideology"). Here is one formulation of the idea from *The German Ideology*:

> History is nothing but the succession of the separate generations, each of which exploits the materials, the capital funds, the productive forces handed down to it by all preceding generations, and thus, on the one hand, continues the traditional activity in completely changed circumstances and, on the other, modifies the old circumstances with a completely changed activity.
>
> (MECW 5: 50)[12]

Thus, for Marx, history is a *dialectical* process,[13] but only insofar as each later stage of development of the productive forces arises from: (a) the contradiction of the earlier form (i.e., the situation where the existing relations of production are a "fetter" on the further development of the productive forces); and (b) the sublation of that earlier form (i.e., it negates the earlier relations of production, while taking over the earlier development of the productive forces). We shall discuss this idea further below.

Second, for Marx, history is *teleological* insofar as the whole process has as its endpoint communist relations of production—that is, a situation where the main forces of production are collectively owned and used for collective benefit (the endpoint is not, as Hegel would have it, Spirit's self-understanding, although it would be a situation of "freedom from necessity") (see, e.g., MECW 29: 133; MECW 30: 750; MECW 35: 749). (In Chapter 4, we return to the question whether this is plausible.) This explains in turn why, third, history is *progressive*, since later historical epochs represent improvements in the development of the productive forces. And, fourth, history is *cunning* insofar as the actual structure of the process is unknown to historical actors, who act for motives and reasons that manifest no awareness of the *dialectical* and *teleological* structure of the process.

As we discuss in more detail below: nascent bourgeoisie struggle with the remnants of the feudal order not because they want to develop the productive forces and pave the way for capitalism and then communism, but because they want to make money by producing more things people want by doing so more efficiently than their predecessors. Historical materialism exposes the import of their individual acts and motives, but the actors themselves are unaware of the broader process of which they are part. A crucial exception occurs in the transition from capitalism to communism, according to Marx: it is the task of a communist political party to make explicit to members of the working class (those who sell their labor power to capitalists) the dialectical and teleological structure of historical change (cf. *German Ideology*, in MECW 5: 35–36, for example.) We also return to this topic in Chapter 4.

Marx's break with the idealism of Hegel's account of historical change also explains why he repudiates the approach to critique associated with Hegel and the Young Hegelians, especially those known as the "Left" Young Hegelians, such as Bruno Bauer. Crucially, for Marx—and *contra* the Young Hegelians—"the products of consciousness" are *not* "the real chains [*Fesseln*] of men" (MECW 5: 30). Criticizing philosophical ideas, and showing them to be "contradictory," was not important for Marx: it did not matter that the conservative and reactionary professors had contradictory ideas or theories.[14] The only thing that matters are the "contradictions" in the material circumstances of existence:

> [A]ll forms and products of consciousness cannot be dissolved by mental criticism … but only by the practical overthrow of the actual social relations which gave rise to this idealistic humbug; that not criticism but revolution is the driving force of history, also of religion, of philosophy and all other types of theory.
> (MECW 5: 54)

The Young Hegelians want "merely … to produce a correct consciousness about an *existing* fact; whereas for the real communist it is a question of overthrowing the existing state of things" (MECW 5: 58). But, according to historical materialism, "overthrowing the existing state of things" is only possible when the existing ideologies and relations of production prevent the growth of productive power.

Because mere criticism of ideas is inefficacious according to historical materialism, it follows, unsurprisingly, that propounding good and uplifting ideas about freedom and equality and justice will also be inefficacious, unless the material conditions are present for their realization: "if these material elements of a complete revolution are not present ... then it is absolutely immaterial for practical development whether the *idea* of this revolution has been expressed a hundred times already, as the history of communism proves" (MECW 5: 54). Propounding communism in the year 1500 would be a practically irrelevant exercise: the level of development of productive forces was so inadequate that communist relations of production were impossible. It would be akin to saying today that, since Martian Gods can dispense bounty from the skies, it does not make sense for most people to be wage slaves. That is true, but irrelevant: Martian Gods do not exist, and bounty does not fall from the skies. Theories of historical change can only make a difference to practice *under certain economic conditions*, an idea central to historical materialism:

> Where speculation ends ... there real, positive science begins: the representation of the practical activity, of the practical process of the development of men. Empty talk about consciousness ceases, and real knowledge has to take its place. When reality is depicted, philosophy as an independent [or self-sufficient] branch of knowledge loses its medium of existence.[15]
>
> (MECW 5: 37)

Marx opposes "empty talk" and philosophy disconnected from the real facts. In this, as in other respects, he is prescient.

3. Functional Explanation in Historical Materialism

Marx's 1859 Preface, which we quoted earlier, is the *locus classicus* of what we will henceforth refer to as the "Orthodox Functionalist" version of historical materialism.[16] According to Orthodox Functionalism, the level of development of the forces of production *explains functionally* the other features of society. A functional explanation explains the existence of something by appeal to the function it performs: for example, cheetahs run fast because that trait fulfills the function of contributing to their survival and reproductive success (i.e., their speed enables them to catch their prey and avoid other predators).

Historical materialism claims that the relations of production and the ideological superstructure in a society are explained by the level of development of the forces of production (i.e., technology and the modes of cooperation in production). More precisely, historical materialism claims that societies have the relations of production and the ideological superstructure that are most conducive to the development and growth of productive power: the function they perform is to support the development and growth of productive power. When they fail to perform that function—when the relations of production and ideological superstructure impede or "fetter" the further development of productive power—societies change. Here is how Marx's 1859 Preface puts it:

> At a certain stage of development, the material productive forces of society [i.e., the forces of production] come into conflict with the existing relations of production, or—this merely expresses the same thing in legal terms—with the property relations within the framework of which they have operated hitherto. From forms of development of the productive forces these relations turn into their fetters. Then begins an era of social revolution. The changes in the economic foundation lead sooner or later to the transformation of the whole immense superstructure. In studying such transformations it is always necessary to distinguish between the material transformation of the economic conditions of production ... and the legal, political, religious, artistic [künstlerischen] or philosophical—in short, ideological forms in which men become conscious of this conflict and fight it out. Just as one does not judge an individual by what he thinks about himself, so one cannot judge such a period of transformation by its consciousness, but, on the contrary, this consciousness must be explained rather from the contradictions of material life, from the conflict existing between the social forces of production and the relations of production.
>
> (MECW 29: 263)[17]

A "contradiction" for Marx exists when the growth of productive power is stymied ("fettered") by the existing relations of production and the existing ideology.[18] More precisely, a "contradiction" exists when the dominant ideology serves to legitimate and sustain relations of production that, in fact, are a hindrance to (or "fetter") the further development of the productive forces.

Here is a stylized and fictional example that runs roughshod over historical details (we say more about those in the endnotes)[19] but still illustrates the core idea. The invention of the power loom to weave fabrics represented a massive increase in the ability to produce fabrics. A factory with power looms and a handful of workers could produce far more than even hundreds of individual weavers could. But where would the workers to run the power looms come from? Serfs trapped on feudal estates would have been useless: they were bound to the land and the feudal lord. Journeymen—weavers, cobblers, bakers, leatherworkers, etc.—owned their tools and would sell their products to others; but they were both paid by and regulated by guild-masters and the various trade guilds. However, neither guilds nor the journeymen could produce on the scale of the new factories that the power loom made possible. What was needed were workers, freed from the control of the feudal lords and guild-masters, who had the legal right to sell their labor power to those who owned the new technologies. Thus, the owners of factories and power looms—the "bourgeoisie" as Marx calls the class that owns the main technologies under capitalism—had economic interests diametrically opposed to those defenders of the older feudal order (and its pre-capitalist descendant)—not just the feudal lords, but the various guilds, with their restrictions on the work of craftsmen and individual journeymen.[20] The feudal and pre-capitalist order gave way *because* the nascent capitalist class could make better use of the available productive power.[21] Here is how Marx puts it in volume I of *Capital*, describing the transition from the pre-capitalist world to the capitalist one:

> This [pre-capitalist] mode of production presupposes parcelling of the soil, and scattering of the other means of production. As it excludes the concentration of these means of production, so also it excludes co-operation, division of labour within each separate process of production, the control over, and the productive application of the forces of Nature by society ... It is compatible only with a system of production, and a society, moving within narrow and more or less primitive bounds ... At a certain stage

of development it brings forth the material agencies for its own dissolution. From that moment new forces and new passions spring up in the bosom of society; but the old social organisation fetters them and keeps them down. It must be annihilated; it is annihilated. Its annihilation, the transformation of the individualised and scattered means of production into socially concentrates ones, of pigmy property of the many into the huge property of the few, from the means of subsistence, and from the means of labour, this fearful and painful expropriation of the mass of the people forms the prelude to the history of capital.

(MECW 35: 749)

It is a crucial feature of Marx's account that it appears inevitable, indeed necessary, that capitalism itself give way to communism (much as feudalism had to give way to capitalism, as the prior passage suggests): capitalism too contains the seeds of its own destruction. On the one hand, capitalism harnesses and develops the productive potential of humanity like no other economic system in the history of the world: "The bourgeoisie, during its rule of scarce one hundred years [roughly 1750–1850], has created more massive and more colossal productive forces than have all preceding generations together" (MECW 6: 489). But at a certain point, capitalist relations of production also become a "fetter" and yield "contradictions," which then usher in the transformation to communism, in which productive power is collectively owned and used for the benefit of all. As Marx famously puts it in volume I of *Capital*:

The monopoly of capital becomes a fetter upon the mode of production which has sprung up and flourishing along with, and under it. Centralisation of the means of production and socialisation of labour at least reach a point where they become incompatible with their capitalist integument. This integument is burst asunder. The knell of capitalist private property sounds. The expropriators are expropriated.

(MECW 35: 750)

Marx gives different accounts of why communism is inevitable, some of which depend on aspects of his economic theory that may not be sound, while others stand independent of the more dubious

portions of his economic theory.[22] We will devote Chapter 4 to a
more detailed account of Marx's economics and his account of why
capitalism should (or, more plausibly, is likely to) self-destruct. What
is important to emphasize here is that just as, according to historical
materialism, capitalism necessarily displaced feudalism, so too will
communism necessarily displace capitalism: history, for Marx (as for
Hegel before him), is heading in a particular tradition (it is end- or
goal-directed), and the theory of historical materialism allows us to
see what that direction is, or so he claims.

4. Functional Explanation and Class Struggle

The idea that the history of social and economic change is explained
by the functional role of relations of productions and ideology in
facilitating or hindering the growth of productive power—Orthodox
Functionalism as we have been calling it—presents some puzzles.

Philosophically, functional explanations are peculiar because
the thing to be explained (the *explanandum*) is prior in time to the
explanans (the thing that explains it): for example, that cheetahs run
fast (the explanandum) is, in evolutionary theory, explained by
the fact that it allows them to survive and then reproduce successfully. Surviving and reproducing, however, occur *after* cheetahs are
able to run fast. Ordinary causal explanations involve an explanandum that comes temporally *after* the explanans: for example, the
window broke *because* the brick was thrown through it (the brick
caused the window to break). How can something that comes after
"explain" something that came before, as functional explanation
would have it?

Philosophers of science have argued that a successful functional
explanation must really be a shorthand gloss on ordinary causal
explanation, one that respects the temporal priority of explanans
over explanandum.[23] "Cheetahs run fast because doing so fulfills the
function of promoting reproductive success" is really shorthand for
a more complicated set of causal relations that are central to evolution by natural selection. Early proto-cheetahs—ancestors of the
current ones, as it were—had differing genes, which produced different phenotypic (i.e., physically observable) traits. Some of these
proto-cheetahs had, by chance, genes conducive to running fast

(the phenotype), while some did not. In the ancestral environment, being able to run fast turned out to be a big advantage, in terms of avoiding predators and catching food. As a result, the fast-running proto-cheetahs (unlike their slower-running brethren) lived longer and had more offspring that they could feed; and most of those offspring, in turn, had the genes conducive to developing the phenotypic trait of being able to run fast. Note that this much more complicated causal explanation—genes conducive to running fast enable their bearers to have more offspring, most of whom have the same gene—is a causal explanation that preserves the temporal priority of explanans to explanandum. Having a gene conducive to the phenotypic trait of running fast is prior to surviving and reproducing. But—and this is the crucial bit—*the reason that gene becomes predominant in a population of cheetahs is the function it performs: contributing (causally) to survival and reproduction.*

Something similar, as we will see shortly, is true of Marx's explanation of historical change: there is a causal mechanism underlying the functional explanations, what Marx usually calls "class struggle." Marx's texts, themselves, make this clear. Indeed, it is striking that the Orthodox Functionalism of the 1859 Preface is not articulated with the same theoretical clarity elsewhere: there are some hints of it in *The German Ideology* of 1845–1846, but it appears to be replaced by the "history is the history of class struggle" slogan of *The Communist Manifesto*, written in 1848. Marx's own practice of explaining historical events (e.g., *The Eighteenth Brumaire of Louis Bonaparte*) is also far closer to the "class struggle" version of historical explanation than to the Orthodox Functionalism of the 1859 Preface.

In the *German Ideology*, Marx (with Engels) does say some things that sound like Orthodox Functionalism, such as the following:

> Thus the chief form of property during the feudal epoch consisted on the one hand of landed property with serf labour chained to it, and on the other of the labour of the individual with small capital commanding the labour of the journeymen. The organisation of both was *determined* [emphasis added] by the restricted conditions of production—the small-scale and primitive cultivation of land, and the craft type of industry.
>
> (MECW 5: 34–35)

[A]ll collisions in history have their origin, according to our view, in the contradiction [*Widerspruch*] between the productive forces and the form of intercourse [the relations of production].
(MECW 5: 74)

A rather different passage, however, with its emphasis on class struggle, also comes from the *German Ideology*:

[A]ll struggles within the State, the struggle between democracy, aristocracy, and monarchy, the struggle for the franchise, etc., etc., are merely the illusory forms ... in which the real struggles of the different classes are fought out among one another.
(MECW 5: 46–47)

This emphasis on class struggle as explaining historical change takes center stage just two years later in *The Communist Manifesto* and in Marx's own subsequent historical writing.[24] (It is also the strand of historical materialism most influential in work by later historians.[25]) Part I of the *Manifesto* famously begins as follows:

The history of all hitherto existing society is the history of class struggles.

Freeman and slave, patrician and plebian, lord and serf, guild-master and journeyman, in a word, oppressor and oppressed, stood in constant opposition to one another, carried on an uninterrupted, now hidden, now open fight, a fight that each time ended, either in a revolutionary reconstitution of society at large, or in the common ruin of the contending classes.
(MECW 6: 482)

So what is the relationship between Orthodox Functionalism and the invocation of class struggle as explaining historical change? In fact, as we will show, they are complementary, not competing, explanations. More precisely, the 1859 Preface is the functionalist shorthand or gloss on the more elaborate causal theory of historical change that appeals to class struggle.

Cheetahs run fast because doing so results in their survival and successful reproduction: that is the functionalist gloss on the evolution of fast-running cheetahs. But the real, underlying causal mechanism, as we have seen, appeals to the fact that early proto-cheetahs with genes that disposed them to running fast fared much better in terms of surviving and reproducing, with the effect that those genes became predominant in the population of cheetahs over evolutionary time. So too with historical materialism: the relations of production and ideological superstructure of a society are explained by their fulfilling the function of developing the forces of production in that society; and historical change occurs when the existing relations of production and ideologies cease to fulfill that function. But there is an underlying causal mechanism here—namely, class struggle, which we will refer to as the "Causal Theory" of historical materialism. Thus, while Orthodox Functionalism says:

> Relations of production X are explained by the contribution they make to the use and development of forces of production Y,

the Causal Theory says:

> Because they make effective use of forces of production Y, members of Class A flourish and dominate; but when technological developments make more advanced forces of production Y* possible, and Class A fails to make use of Y*, then Class A's competitors in Class B, who can make effective use of Y*, struggle with Class A and ultimately triumph.

The nascent bourgeois class of capitalist society sees the productive potential of the new industrial technologies (e.g., the power loom), but realizes that, to exploit that productive power, it must have the legal right to purchase the labor power of other people—people who, under existing relations of productions, may be serfs, peasants, or journeymen beholden to trade guilds. Thus the bourgeois class must "struggle" to change the existing relations of production so it can take advantage of the new technology and its productive power.

5. The "Materialism" in Historical Materialism

This is a good point at which to ask: In what regard is Marx's theory of historical change a *materialist* theory? There is a sense of "materialism" in the history of philosophy that is *irrelevant* to understanding historical materialism: namely, "materialism" as an ontological or metaphysical thesis according to which the only things that actually exist in the world are material or physical. What counts as "material" or "physical"? Philosophers have meant different things by these concepts at different times and in different traditions. Examples include: only that which one can touch or see (the contrast would be with abstract objects like "the number 4"); everything that is not mental (what you are experiencing as you read this is not physical); or only those things that the physical sciences posit as existing.

None of the preceding metaphysical interpretations of material-ism are relevant for Marx. Nothing in his corpus commits him to any view about metaphysical theses such as reductive or elimina-tive materialism (the reductive materialist claims that all apparently non-material entities [e.g., thoughts] are reducible to material ones; the eliminative materialists says any entities that are not reducible to material ones are to be "eliminated" from our picture of what the world is like). The *materialism* of historical materialism is a thesis only about how to explain social and economic change. It posits that the best way to do so is by looking at the material or economic conditions of people's existence: how did they procure food and shelter, what productive activity did they engage in, who controlled their productive activity, what technology did their society have? The essence of historical materialism is the claim that *these kinds of material or economic* facts explain social and economic development. It is opposed to the view Marx associates with Hegel (described ear-lier) that one can understand history in terms of people's ideas— for example, their moral, political, and religious beliefs—without regard to the "material" or economic conditions of their existence.

More precisely, historical materialism posits an "explanatory asymmetry" between the material conditions of existence (i.e., how people produce what they need and want) and the other character-istics of society: historical materialism "assigns a primary role to so-called material conditions in explaining social phenomena" (Railton

1986: 233). It is easy to see how the Orthodox Functionalist model of historical materialism honors the commitment to explanatory asymmetry: it claims that only changes in productive power (in technology and modes of cooperation) result in changes to relations of production and ideology. Relations of production and ideology never bring about, *ex nihilo*, new developments in technology, even if they play a crucial functional role of sustaining, facilitating, or legitimizing the utilization and development of existing productive power. The same explanatory asymmetry also holds in the case of the Causal Theory of historical materialism: what explains why one class is able to prevail over a competitor is precisely the level of development of technology. As Railton puts it (1986: 237):

> When the terms of competition … shift [due to new technologies], individuals or groups who happen to be so situated or so to act as to take differential advantage of these changes … will acquire increased resources, power, and so on. The result may be the emergence into prominence of new groups at the expense of those groups who previously commanded resources, power, and so on.

Nascent bourgeoisie prevail over the remnant classes of the feudal order because they are able to exploit new technologies in a way that feudal lords and guild-masters cannot.[26] Once again, it is the level of development of the forces of production that is crucial to explaining historical change. Here again is how Railton, a defender of the Causal Theory of historical materialism, puts it:

> [O]nce we have the protoforms of capitalist relations of production [out of the earlier feudal relation], we need to explain why they came to predominate … Marx's explanation of this may appropriately be called materialistic because he posits a tendency of individuals with similar 'material interests'— similar relations to the means of production [i.e., the same class interests]—to coalesce in social competition. Further, he claims that the deciding factor in this struggle is the extent to which such classes possess a distinctively material kind of power, a power that stems in the first instance more or less directly from

their relation to the forces of production. Moreover, their maintenance of this power in the long run depends upon the ability
of a now-dominant class to consolidate its position by relative
effectiveness at exploiting the possibilities inherent in existing
forces of production.

(Railton 1986: 238–239)

In class struggle, the class prevails that is best at making use of the
available productive power (technology): that is the crux of the
materialism on this view. Classes do not prevail because they have
the best philosophical systems, the best moral arguments, the best
religious values: they prevail because they are best at producing
things to meet people's basic needs and their wants.[27]

6. Is Historical Materialism True?

The connection between class struggle and Orthodox Functionalism
is crucial to responding to one kind of familiar critique of Marx's
historical materialism. Political theorist Jon Elster put the challenge
succinctly:

Marx owes us an account of how the less than optimal character of the existing relations of production motivates individual
men to collective action for the purpose of ushering in a new
set of relations ... From the point of view of the individual economic agent, the benefits of a change in the property regime are
remote in time, subject to uncertainty and independent of his
participation in the collective action. Even when there is a 'need'
for new relations of production, one cannot assume without
further argument that it will be fulfilled. Men are not the puppets of history; they act for goals and motives of their own.

(Elster 1986: 108)[28]

Men, however, can be both the "puppets of history" and "act for
goals and motives of their own." As a psychological matter, individuals have particular goals and motives; but, according to historical materialism, many of the goals and motives they have are
shaped by their material circumstances (in particular, technological

developments) beyond their control. The rising bourgeoisie want to exploit the productive potential of new productive technologies (e.g., power looms in our earlier stylized example). Why? They want to do so because they see that wealth and its benefits would accrue to them. The remnants of the feudal order resist the changes to labor relations that would be required by the changes the bourgeoisie seek. Why? Guild-masters and the former feudal landlords see that their whole way of life will be destroyed, their wealth and status destroyed, if these changes occur, if they lose control over their serfs, their rent-paying peasants, their tightly regulated journeymen.

Marx assumes, quite plausibly, that people want to satisfy their basic needs and their wants; but he also assumes, again plausibly, that how different "classes" of people will do that depends on their relationship to the existing forces of production, both labor power and its organization, and technology.[29] "Class struggle" is the name for this phenomenon, in which one class—that wants to exploit new productive power or technology to satisfy its own needs and wants—tries to change the existing relations of production that, as currently constituted, benefit a different class. The crucial point is that Marx's underlying view of human motivation is that human beings are instrumentally rational in trying to satisfy their desires, but what would suffice for satisfying those desires is shaped by their material circumstances.[30]

Even if Elster's kind of objection can be met,[31] there are other doubts one might have about historical materialism. No one, after all, has developed a general explanatory and predictive theory of historical change that is completely successful—not Vico,[32] or Hegel, or Braudel,[33] or Marx. This is partly due to the sheer difficulty of explaining the evolution of complex phenomena like human societies, which are (1) made up of individuals with their own complex and often mysterious motivations—motivations often unknown to the individual actors themselves, whose (2) interactions often have unintended and surprising effects, and which are also (3) subject to natural calamities and forces. Still, among theories of social and economic change over history, historical materialism has been far more successful than most: many of the best and most influential accounts of societal transformations in history adopt Marx's framework,[34] and many others have adopted an essentially "materialist" framework to make sense of cultural and social practices—that is, an effort to understand human culture and behavior as a response to the economic (or "material") circumstances of existence.[35]

The philosopher G.A. Cohen's influential defense of Orthodox Functionalism (Cohen 1978) emphasized that there must be a *tendency* for the productive forces to grow throughout history, one presumably rooted in human material interests (i.e., in being able to produce more, have more, enjoy more material goods[36]): the growth of productive power is the motor of history (as it were) on this account, and the key to explaining changes in forms of social and economic organization. Some of the counterexamples to this supposed tendency of the productive forces to grow are now well-known: for example, the long period of stagnation (i.e., no growth in productive power) in China from roughly the 14th century until around 1900;[37] or the "genuine regression in agricultural productivity [in Poland] resulting from the 'second serfdom,' i.e., from the imposition of substantial labor services on the Polish peasantry" (J. Cohen 1982: 267 and note 16).

What can we conclude about historical materialism from such cases? Both cases suggest there are significant exceptions to any assumption that productive forces necessarily grow over the course of history. That latter fact is still compatible with the possibility that *when productive forces grow*, their growth explains changes in the relations of production and the ideological superstructure of society, which we take to be the most plausible core of Marx's theory (*contra* G.A. Cohen). One might think of historical materialism as being, in this regard, a bit like Darwin's theory of evolution by natural selection. For natural selection to work, there must be random genetic mutations that produce changes in the phenotypic features of organisms, features that then affect reproductive success (e.g., making proto-cheetahs run faster). Darwinian theory does not explain why genetic mutations occur;[38] but it does explain what happens when certain mutations affecting phenotypic features occur: those that are conducive to reproductive advantage come to dominate in a population.

So, too, Marx may not be entitled to assume (if he did) that productive forces always grow everywhere and at all times; but when technological innovations occur that enhance productive power (the analogue of genetic mutations in the Darwin case), Marx's theory of historical materialism offers an explanation of how the relations of production and ideological superstructure will change (they will change to accommodate and support the exploitation of those productive forces), and those changes will predominate in the population affected by the technological advance. That aspect of historical materialism fares rather well on the evidence.

Even here, however, there are exceptions to the generalization, ironically in societies that claimed a Marxian lineage. In the late 1920s, the Soviet dictator Stalin adopted centralized control of an economy that was essentially pre-industrial and pre-capitalist, and propelled massive development in the productive forces to the point that the Soviet Union was competitive technologically with the capitalist world. Yet, according to historical materialism, capitalist relations of production are essential for the maximal development of productive power in human societies: this is why an orthodox Marxist in Russia in 1917, or China in 1949, or Cuba in 1959 would have demanded the institution of some kind of capitalist relations of production in order to insure the maximal development of productive power.[39] Stalin did nothing of the kind, and yet propelled the agricultural economy of Tsarist Russia into the 20th century. Marx did not anticipate, to be sure, how effective the modern tools of tyranny could be in compensating for a lack of capitalist relations of production to produce technological growth and innovation.[40] Here, again, the complexity of human societies defeats an attempt to offer an exception-less generalization about how societies change.

By contrast, counting in favor of Marx is the fact that the massive growth in productive power in communist China only occurred after Mao's death and the "market" reforms of Deng Xiaoping. Mao persecuted Deng for having capitalist sympathies, and he was correct that Deng did. Fortunately for hundreds of millions of Chinese, Deng assumed power after Mao. Marx's theory of historical materialism would have sided with Deng, since China, given the state of its productive forces, desperately need capitalist relations of production.

We will return in later chapters on class and ideology to some other objections to the claims of historical materialism related to the role those notions play in Marx's theory.

7. Conclusion

History, according to Marx, is the history of class struggle, the history of groups of individuals with similar material interests (in virtue of their relationship to the existing technology and methods by which society reproduces itself) competing for control of the wealth or surplus that existing technology can produce. Most people have only their own labor power to sell; but in every historical epoch some individuals control other forms of technology: the machine, the computer software, the assembly line. Some interpreters of Marx have read him as offering a "functional" explanation of the role of growth in productive power in historical change; but this, as we have argued, is not quite right. Marx's explanation of historical change is a quite familiar kind of causal explanation: those classes that make more successful use of technology acquire wealth and power, and triumph over their competitors. Indeed, the fact that they can acquire wealth and power in the struggle motivates individuals to act as they do. This is still a "materialist" theory in the sense that the ultimate explanation for any historical transformation is the level of development of technology in the broad sense we have emphasized throughout.

Notes

1 Later writers in the Marxist tradition, such as Theodor Adorno, Max Horkheimer, and Herbert Marcuse, were especially concerned with how "wants and desires" are shaped by capitalist markets, a topic we return to in Chapter 7. Other writers in the Marxist tradition have tried to argue that there are no basic, biological needs, which seems to us implausible. Some have suggested, more plausibly, that in his early work (see Chapter 6), Marx thought that humans have basic needs beyond their physical/biological ones, such as the need to engage in productive activity unrelated to securing the means of survival ("freedom from necessity"). See Chitty (1993) for one discussion and Leopold (2007: 227–241) for careful documentation of "physical" and "social" needs recognized by Marx in his early writings of 1843–1844. We return to the topic in Chapter 3, Section 4C.

2 The importance of "modes of cooperation" in production is correctly emphasized by Miller (1984: 188–195). See also MECW 35: 327–331 on the importance of forms of "cooperation" for productive power.

3 Other non-Marxist, but nonetheless "materialist," historians have explored similar ideas: see, e.g., Morris (2015).

4 Feudal lords can exercise *de facto* ownership of the labor power of serfs insofar as the serfs are unable to work anywhere else but for the lord.

5 In wealthy capitalist societies, those who sell their labor power for wages also sometimes acquire ownership of some of the technology, often through investments that are part of retirement plans. This is a very recent development in these capitalist societies.

6 The status of serfs in Russia was often an exception to this generalization.

7 Marx sometimes speaks of "law" as part of the ideological superstructure, which presents some complicated issues since parts of "law" are clearly constitutive of the relations of production. Marx himself writes a bit loosely on this topic. For discussion, see Leiter (2015a).

8 See, for example, Finkelman (2019).

9 Those skeptical of religious interpretations of Hegel will still concede that his view of historical evolution is exceptionally optimistic.

10 See Forster (1993: 132–133).

11 One exception for Hegel concerns the regress from certain aspects of the Greek beginning, when the pernicious "dualisms" that concerned Hegel were less prevalent.

12 This passage continues by cautioning against treating later historical events as the "goal" of earlier ones (his example is treating the French Revolution as the "goal" of discovering America, which is obviously absurd). As we will see, elsewhere he does endorse a teleological interpretation of history, although not in the crude form of his example. (Thanks to Vanessa Wills for calling this to our attention.).

13 Recall the discussion of Hegel's dialectical method from Chapter 1, and see Forster (1993).

14 Ironically, this style of Left Young Hegelian critique was revived in the 20th century by the Hungarian Marxist Georg Lukács in *History and Class Consciousness* (1972 edition).

15 *Die selbständige Philosophie verliert mit der Darstellung der Wirklichkeit ihr Existenzmedium.*

16 This reading received a well-known defense and articulation by the late philosopher G.A. Cohen (1978). The issue has also been debated among historians: cf. Aston and Philpin (1985: 7–8).

17 Or, similarly, from *The German Ideology*: "an earlier form of intercourse [relations of production], which has become a fetter [*Fessel*], is replaced by a new one corresponding to the more developed productive forces and, hence, to the advanced mode of the self-activity of individuals—a form which in its turn becomes a fetter and is then replaced by another. Since these conditions correspond at every stage to the simultaneous development of the productive forces, their history is at the same time the history of the evolving productive forces taken over by each new generation" (MECW 5: 82).

18 Cf. *Capital*, volume I, Ch. XXXII for similar thoughts (MECW 35: 749–750).

19 See Dobb (1946) and Sweezy's (1976) critique of Dobb for more nuanced discussion. See, e.g., Marx and Engels in *The Communist Manifesto* (MECW 6: 485) for

a similarly stylized account: "The feudal system of industry, under which industrial production was monopolised by closed guilds, now no longer sufficed for the growing wants of new markets. The manufacturing system took its place. The guild-masters were pushed on one side by the manufacturing middle class." As Engels sums up the transformation: "The spinning-wheel, the hand-loom, the blacksmith's hammer, were replaced by the spinning-machine, the power-loom, the steam-hammer; the individual workshop, by the factory implying the co-operation of hundreds and thousands of workmen" (MECW 24: 308).

20 By the time the power loom was invented in the late 18th century, of course, feudalism had been vanquished in much of Europe, although there remained many peasant farmers, mostly paying money rent to landlords. The feudal system of production proper—a system of "production-for-use" (i.e., producing what the producers needed to live)—dominated some or all of Europe from the Middle Ages into the 16th century, although it was in severe decline in Western Europe during the 14th and 15th centuries. There emerged in Western Europe then, and especially in England, a kind of post-feudal/pre-capitalist system (cf. Sweezy 1976: 49–51) which did not involve any dominant relations of production: "There were still strong vestiges of serfdom and vigorous beginnings of wage-labor, but the forms of labor relation which were most common in the statistical sense were pretty clearly unstable ... This holds especially of the relation between landlords and working tenants paying a money rent" (Sweezy 1976: 51).

21 Again, the actual transition was far more complex, and has been treated at length by Marxist historians and economists. See again Dobb (1946) and Sweezy (1976) for competing views; and, more recently, the debates arising from Robert Brenner's work in Aston and Philpin (1985).

22 Most important is the way in which technological progress increasingly makes human labor power superfluous. Since most humans have only their labor power to sell, if no one buys it, they will be both immiserated and unable to buy the products of capitalism, producing a crisis of "underconsumption" in Marxian lingo.

23 See Wright (1976) and Railton (1986).

24 So, for example, in *The Eighteenth Brumaire*, the "June Insurrection" is described in class struggle terms (MECW 5: 46); so too "the defeat of the June insurgents" (MECW 5: 47), the "threshold" period before the February Revolution (MECW 5: 47), the ultimate account of Bonaparte's triumph (MECW 5: 49), and so on.

25 See, for example, Brenner (1976) or Thompson (1968). Orthodox Functionalism would be hard to recognize in the work of these Marxist historians.

26 Again, this is a simplification, omitting in particular the role of what Marx calls "primitive accumulation"—"conquest, enslavement, robbery, murder, briefly, force" which "play[s] the great part" in the initial accumulation of capital by the nascent bourgeois class (MECW 35: 705).

27 G.A. Cohen, the leading defender of the Orthodox Functionalist version of historical materialism, arguably sees the complementary of the "class struggle" interpretation. He writes, for example, that:

Classes are permanently poised against one another, and that class tends to prevail whose rule would best meet the demands of production. But how does the fact that production would prosper under a certain class ensure its dominion? Part of the answer is that there is a general stake in stable and thriving production, so that the class best placed to deliver it attracts allies from other strata in society. Prospective ruling classes are often able to raise support among the classes subjected to the ruling class they would displace. Contrariwise, classes unsuited to the task of governing society tend to lack the confidence political hegemony requires, and if they do seize power, they tend not to hold it for long.

Sometimes, too, as in the gradual formation of capitalism, the capacity of a new class to administer production expresses itself in nascent forms of the society it will build, which, being more effective than the old forms, tend to supplant them. Purposive and competitive elements mingle as early growths of capitalism encroach upon and defeat feudal institutions that would restrict them. There is also adaptive metamorphosis. For example: a pre-capitalist landed ruling class in an epoch of commercialization requires finance from a not yet industrial bourgeoisie. When landlords cannot meet the commitments engendered by their new connections, they lose their holdings, so others, in fear of a similar fate, place their operations on a capitalist basis. Some see what is required for survival, and undergo an alteration of class character; others fail to understand the times, or, too attached to an outmoded ideology and way of life, fight against the new order, and disappear.

(1978: 292–293)

In other work, however, Cohen says that "it is true that for Marx the immediate explanation of major social transformation is often found in the battle between classes. But that is not the fundamental explanation of social change" (2000: 148). It is not fundamental because we must still ask: "why does the successful class succeed? Marx finds the answer in the character of the productive forces" (149). But Railton accepts this too: it is the basis on which he says the Causal Theory preserves the explanatory asymmetry essential to a materialist theory of historical change.

28 Elster (1986) applies a "rational choice" framework to his analysis of Marx. According to rational choice theory, individuals are instrumentally rational in trying to satisfy their desires, and individuals are assumed to have a desire to expend as little effort as possible and take as little risk as possible in satisfying their other desires. This makes collective actions difficult, since instrumentally rational self-interested actors will try to "free ride" on the efforts of others whenever possible. Robert Paul Wolff (1990: 472) notes that, in fact, "collective action is the norm in human affairs," which is a reductio of the rational choice assumption. We return to this topic in Chapter 4. Elster's challenge, discussed in the text, is still relevant even if one rejects his rational choice framework.

29 In his more nuanced account of the transition from feudalism to pre-capitalism to capitalism, Sweezy notes that some serfs were able to flee the old feudal estates because of "the rise of towns, which were the centers and breeders of [the new] exchange economy," and thus offered "the servile population of the countryside the prospect of a freer and better life" (1976: 43). Notice that the motivation for serfs abandoning the old feudal estates and moving to the towns is easily assimilated to the explanatory framework of neoclassical economics, in which individuals are instrumentally rational in trying to satisfy their desires, including, most importantly, their desire for better material circumstances.

30 What their desires are can also be shaped by their material circumstances: if the most the productive power of a society offers is sustenance, then people will desire sustenance; but if the productive power can offer far more, then, unsurprisingly, many people will desire more too. This point is independent of the question of central importance for the Frankfurt School about how capitalism also manufactures desires it can then satisfy in the market.

31 We return to the "collective action" worry Elster expresses (i.e., the worry that, even if everyone would be better off if things were different, individuals would rather "free ride" on the efforts of others to change things than risk everything by taking action) in Chapter 4.

32 Giambattista Vico (1668–1744) was an Italian philosopher, rhetorician, and historian. He is best known for his work *The New Science*, in which he sought to provide a philosophical foundation for the study of human society, history, and culture. Vico's ideas are often regarded as a precursor to modern anthropology and the philosophy of history, emphasizing the role of language, myth, and custom in the development of cultures and civilizations.

33 Fernand Braudel (1902–1985) was an influential French historian, leader of the *Annales* school of historiography, according to which geographic and demographic facts are crucial to explaining historical developments. Like Marx's historical materialism, individual agency is accorded a subordinate role.

34 See, e.g., Hobsbawm (1989, 1996a, 1996b) and Thompson (1968).

35 See, e.g., Harris (1989) and Morris (2015).

36 For a critique of this assumption, Brenner (1977) is quite interesting. (Thanks to Ben Laurence for calling this to our attention.).

37 See Perkins (2017).

38 To be clear, Darwin himself knew nothing about the genetic mechanisms of natural selection. His theory of natural selection was based on an abductive inference over the observable evidence—that is, animals with similar phenotypic features that evolved without contact with each other in distant lands but shared similar environments. One might worry that technological growth is not an exogenous variable in Marx's account, since classes in conflict have motivations to produce it: in this regard it would not be wholly exogenous. This is a possibility, although Marx himself was not very clear on why technological

advances occur: arguably, chance plays a role there too. (Thanks to Pascal Brixel for pressing us on this.)

39 The Bolsheviks did this, briefly, with the "state capitalism" proposed by Lenin after the October (1917) Revolution, but it was soon derailed by the Russian Civil War, in which Britain, France, and other capitalist powers lent financial and military support to opponents of the Bolshevik regime.

40 Arguably, though, the Soviet Union collapsed for reasons consistent with historical materialism: the economic stagnation that afflicted the Soviet Union surely had something to do with the fact that centralized planning of the economy did not enable the effective use and development of technology.

Further Reading

Aston and Philpin (1985) is an excellent collection of historical papers on Marxian interpretations of the evolution of capitalism out of feudalism, with particular attention on the seminal work of the decidedly non-orthodox Marxist historian Robert Brenner.

Cohen (1978) is the most important defense of the Orthodox Functionalist interpretation of historical materialism.

Miller (1984) presents a sharp challenge to Cohen (1978), esp. in Chapter 5.

Railton (1986) proposes a succinct way of reconciling the Class Conflict and Orthodox Functionalist understandings of historical materialism.

3

Class Conflict, the State, and the Communist Revolution

Classes and the role that their conflicts with one another play in propelling historical transformation was the central thread running through Marx's writing across his decades-long career, and is central to the Causal Theory of historical materialism we defended in Chapter 2. He expresses his general view, recall, in the famous opening of the first chapter of the *Communist Manifesto*:

> The history of all hitherto existing society is the history of class struggles. Freeman and slave, patrician and plebeian, lord and serf, guild-master and journeyman, in a word, oppressor and oppressed, stood in constant opposition to one another, carried on an uninterrupted, now hidden, now open fight, a fight that each time ended, either in a revolutionary reconstitution of society at large, or in the common ruin of the contending classes.
>
> (MECW 6: 482)

Several years later, reflecting in a letter to a friend on what was most distinctive about his view, Marx wrote:

> I do not claim to have discovered either the existence of classes in modern society or the struggle between them ... My own contribution was 1. to show that the *existence of classes is merely bound up with certain historical phases in the development of production*; 2. that the class struggle necessarily leads to the *dictatorship of the*

DOI: 10.4324/9781315658902-3

proletariat;[1] 3. that this dictatorship itself only constitutes no more than a transition to the *abolition of all classes* and to a *classless society*.

(MECW 39: 62–65)

The present chapter will examine these ideas, and in roughly the order Marx outlines above: we will present his general characterization of classes, what distinguishes them, and the nature of their conflicts; his account of the ways each epoch's dominant economic class monopolizes state power and employs it to its advantage; and his claim that the emerging proletariat is the historically unique class that will carry out a revolution that will finally end class conflict once and for all. We return in Chapter 4 to Marx's economic explanation for the supposedly inevitable collapse of capitalism.

1. Class in General

Given the centrality of the concept of class in Marx's writing, we might hope to begin with his own definition. Unfortunately, he never provides a precise one, leaving us to infer what he means on the basis of broad characterizations, various enumerations, discussions of particular instances, and negative definitions. He appears to come close in his most explicit consideration of the question when writing, "The first question to be answered is this: What constitutes a class?; and the reply to this follows naturally from the reply to another question, namely: What makes wage labourers, capitalists and landlords constitute the three great social classes?" (MECW 37: 871). However, in what follows, he only takes the time to reject one seemingly plausible contender before the manuscript breaks off. Nevertheless, we can work out the main current of his thought. Marx thinks it is obvious that people have material (economic) interests, and that the prevailing economic system sorts them into different groups whose members are similarly situated with respect to realizing these. For example, the most central players in Marx's Europe are those who own the factories (the capitalists), those who own vast tracts of land (the landlords), and those who work in the factories (the wage laborers). In this vein, Marx suggests that classes can be distinguished from one another in virtue of their "common situation, common interests" (MECW 6: 211). Moreover, and of crucial importance to his account, the common interests of one class are typically opposed to the interests of another (capitalists seek lower wages while workers seek higher; landowners seek higher rents while tenants [who are sometimes capitalists!] seek lower). It is this opposition of interests that manifests in ever-present social tensions and occasionally erupts into the revolutionary conflicts that result in epochal shifts.

The difficulty begins when we try to specify more precisely what this "common situation, common interests" consists of. Those writing in the Marxist tradition often emphasize ownership of the means of production (or lack thereof) as the defining feature of class. On this view, the landowners are a class in virtue of their ownership of land, the capitalists in virtue of their ownership of factories and machines, and the working class in virtue of the fact that they own nothing but the labor power they sell for a wage. This view, which we can call the "simple ownership" definition of class, initially seems to comport well with much of what Marx says: for example, "the various stages of development in the division of labour are just so many different forms of ownership ... [which] determines also the relations of individuals to one another with reference to the material, instrument, and product of labour" (MECW 5: 32).

The main problem, however, is that a strict application of the simple ownership definition fails to distinguish sets of individuals in the way Marx clearly intends to do. Suppose we collect together everyone who has a stake in the ownership of the means of production beyond their own labor power. In that case, our collection includes people in very different situations and with disparate interests: for example, the billionaire tycoon who owns the controlling interest in a Fortune 500 company, together with a desk clerk who owns a few shares of stock via a retirement plan or the salaried mechanic who brings her own tools to work. We might try to preserve the simple ownership definition by demarcating the various "owners" in virtue of the amount of the means of production they own. However, unless we are to draw these boundaries arbitrarily, we will need to modify the simple ownership view in some way. Marx explicitly rejects other definitional contenders on similar grounds, such as the "common sense" idea that class is determined by one's income level, which he rejects as a "purely quantitative distinction" that places everyone on a large continuum without specifying where or in virtue of what we should draw distinctions between them (MECW 6: 330).

A better way of sorting individuals into groups sharing common situations and common interests, following a suggestion by Jon Elster (1986: 126–127), is to do so based on which activities in the prevailing economic system they are compelled to perform in order to best realize their material interests, given the extent of their effective control of the various means of production. In other words, what can someone do with what they own? A paradigmatic member of the capitalist class possesses a controlling share of the means of production in a particular company, employs workers to use these means to produce commodities for exchange on the market, and is in a position to live off of the generated profits. To best succeed, they will be compelled to maximize their profits by lowering workers' wages, increasing worker productivity, or replacing their labor through automatization. A paradigmatic member of the working class will be someone who has the capacity to work for a wage and who owns either nothing or too meager a share of anything besides to do otherwise, and so will be compelled on pain of hunger and homelessness to find paid work where they can while lobbying for better wages and conditions whenever possible. This amended view preserves the central role that ownership clearly plays in Marx's thought, while helping to distinguish the tycoon from the desk clerk and mechanic as he certainly intends.

There will continue to be classes that may seemingly include disparate members (for example, a capitalist employing 50 workers and another employing 50,000). Yet, as economic actors, they will be united by the fundamental aims they share and in opposition to other classes (maximizing profit at the expense of the workers, since profit goes up as wages go down[2]). There will also continue to be marginal cases (the highly paid salaried employee considering going into business for themself). Marx himself emphasized that such cases frustrate conceptual precision,[3] yet he was untroubled by this fact. His aim was not to give necessary and sufficient conditions of class membership but to identify paradigmatic cases and their conflicts. Marx's project remains viable if he can successfully identify such paradigmatic cases while demonstrating that their members are sufficient in number and their interests sufficiently at odds to

generate the sorts of class struggle that he thinks explain historical changes (as we discussed in Chapter 2), and ultimately explain
revolutionary conflict.

The amended definition of class helps to articulate the "common
situation, common interests" that individual members of a class in
fact share, at least in paradigmatic cases. However, this does not yet
entail that the individuals are "class conscious"—i.e., aware of this
fact (their common situation and common interests) or its significance. Marx considered the small-holding peasants in France in the
mid-19th century to be a case in point. This class consisted of millions of people in a common situation sharing similar material interests; yet they were isolated from each other geographically due to
rural distances, and isolated economically due to the relative self-
sufficiency of farm life. As a result of this isolation, "the identity of
their interests begets no community, no national bond and no political organization among them … They are consequently incapable of
enforcing their class interests in their own name, whether through a
parliament or through a convention" (MECW 11: 187). In contrast,
when members of a group come to recognize their common situation and band together in pursuit of their collective interests, a pursuit that Marx believes inevitably brings them into conflict with other
classes, they develop class consciousness, becoming what he calls a
"Class for itself." Marx at times describes the protagonists of his writings, the industrial proletariat of the 19th century, to have already recognized their common cause, and thereby to have developed a class
consciousness,[4] while at other times it seems that he views his own
project as one of proletariat consciousness raising.[5] It is the fact that a
class of individuals shares a common situation and common interests
together with their consciousness of this fact that is the essential condition of their collective action—that is, their acting to change society.

2. The Ruling Class

On Marx's account, as we have seen, the prevailing economic system sorts people into different classes of individuals similarly situated with respect to realizing their material interests and in conflict
with those of others. He adds that in every particular epoch the
economically dominant class typically attains a "ruling-class" status,

monopolizing state power that it employs to secure its interests. Marx claims, for instance, that just as the landed nobility had ruled politically during feudal times, the industrial capitalists had come to rule politically after the Industrial Revolution: "the bourgeoisie has at last, since the establishment of modern industry and the world market, conquered for itself, in the modern representative state, exclusive political sway" (MECW 6: 486).

His thoughts on the nature of this monopolization certainly evolve, and his actual case studies of the historical events unfolding around him highlight and attempt to explain variations of the ways in which this monopolization manifests; yet the fact that economic elites monopolize political power remains a conviction of his throughout his writing. The monopolized state, on this view, is a partisan agency that prioritizes securing the preferred outcomes of the dominant economic class. This means securing the dominant class's preferred economic policies, as well as managing non-economic policy in a way that complements, or at least does not disrupt, these economic aims. Thus Marx's view, to put it in terms of contemporary political science,[6] is an early exemplar of "elite domination" and stands in stark contrast to "majoritarian theories of power" that see the state as the impartial coordinator of a power that is distributed fairly evenly across a range of different organizations and interest groups representing the citizenry ("majoritarian pluralism"), or of a power that is distributed evenly amongst the citizens themselves who represent their interests directly through democratic processes ("majoritarian electoral democracy").

What does this economic elite monopolization of political power look like in practice, according to Marx? His earliest formulations, expressed throughout most of the 1840s, are his boldest: the ruling class seizes direct control of the state and uses it simply as a means of managing its interests. In *The German Ideology*, Marx and Engels write:

> [T]he bourgeoisie ... organise[s] itself ... nationally, and to give a general form to its average interests ... the state ... is nothing more than the form of organisation which the bourgeois are compelled to adopt ... for the mutual guarantee of their property and interests.
>
> (MECW 5: 90)

A year later Marx reemphasizes his commitment to the bold claim: "Legislation ... never does more than proclaim ... the will of economic relations" (MECW 6: 147). And another year later still, the Communist Manifesto, having asserted that the capitalist class has seized political rule, adds: "The bourgeoisie has conquered for itself in the modern representative state exclusive political sway. The executive of the modern state is a committee for managing the common affairs of the whole bourgeoisie" (MECW 6: 486). These passages suggest an economic elite that has already completed its monopolization of political power and of a state that simply follows the orders that this ruling class hands down concerning economic affairs, and that lacks any other apparent purpose or purview.

Marx, however, soon modified his view in light of an empirical reality that suggested the situation was more complicated. After 1848, he continues to see the capitalist class as the overwhelming beneficiaries of political rule throughout Europe; yet he also recognizes that the capitalists themselves seem to disengage from direct political action. In England, the Anti-Corn Law League, an organization Marx considered to be the political arm of the capitalist class, had dissolved itself shortly after having achieved significant legislative victories. The British Parliament would continue to be governed for decades by Whigs and Tories, two competing factions of the landed aristocracy that the capitalists were supposed to have displaced. Events in France similarly challenged the account. According to Marx, the capitalists had been steadily securing behind-the-scenes power throughout the early decades of the 1800s; and, with the revolution of 1848, under the moniker "the Party of Order," had succeeded in taking direct control of the government. However, the Party of Order's rule quickly faltered, and in 1851 Louis Bonaparte staged a broadly supported coup d'état that marketed itself explicitly as a rejection of the Party's despotic economic and political aims. Throughout most of the rest of Europe, the revolutions of 1848, which early in the year had seemed to reshape Europe, had failed completely by the fall, and ended with the reinstatement of the very same feudal regimes that had briefly retreated.

Marx responds to these events by claiming that the capitalist class recognized that its interests were better served by stepping back from direct political rule:

> [This class] committed itself to quiescence, while it declared the political rule of the bourgeoisie to be incompatible with the safety and existence of the bourgeoisie … It declared unequivocally that it longed to get rid of its own political rule in order to get rid of the troubles and dangers of ruling.
>
> (MECW 11: 172)

Here, however, we must be careful. It is not that the capitalist class, reflecting from a position of power, realized that it is always and everywhere better for economic elites to relinquish direct political rule. Marx notes that in France, for instance, it is not that the capitalists stepped aside but rather that "the Executive, in the person of Louis Bonaparte, turned them out" (MECW 22: 330).

Marx's revision to his earlier account is that he now recognizes that the capitalists had attained a measure of political power before they had actually become the dominant economic class, and that their political power was consequently tenuous: "French industry," Marx writes, was "more developed and the French bourgeoisie more revolutionary than that of the rest of the Continent"; but most of France had not yet been industrialized, and, consequently, "the industrial bourgeoisie did not rule France" (MECW 10: 56). The capitalist class was internally divided into financial and industrial factions (that is, those who made money from lending money and those who made money from running factories), and externally threatened by a not yet vanquished aristocracy and an emerging working class. This left them vulnerable to having their political power usurped, and even relieved at the prospect so long as they could hope that the new regime would protect their commercial interests. Marx suggests a similar revision with respect to England, where capitalism was more advanced, and hence the capitalist class more secure, but still only one of the two ruling classes alongside the aristocracy.[7]

Although the capitalist quiescence of the 1840s may not have been wholly voluntary, Marx suggested that there were several immediate benefits. First, relinquishing direct control gives the government an appearance of neutrality: "State power," he writes, now "apparently soar[s] high above society and the very hotbed of all its corruptions" (MECW 22: 330). The capitalist class continued to receive immense advantages from the state, but this arrangement now seemed less obviously self-serving. Second, it enabled the capitalist class to misdirect the ire of the working classes away from themselves and on to the state, since it was no longer clear exactly what the source of their domination was, whereas when the capitalist class ruled directly they were required to "confront the subjugated classes and contend against them without mediation, without the concealment afforded by the crown, without being able to divert the national interest by their subordinate struggles ... with the monarchy" (MECW 11: 129). Third, a semi-autonomous government would be better positioned to act as an impartial judge looking after the interests of the capitalist class (that is, impartial between the different factions of the capitalist class). Such a government could serve this function by curbing any deleterious effects one faction might have on the system as a whole (by curbing monopoly power, for example). It could also help ensure that the short-term interests of capitalists do not undermine their long-terms goals (by enforcing standard practices, for example).

In *Capital*, Marx suggests the passage of the Ten Hours Bill, which limited the hours that teens and women could work to ten per day, was a necessary means of ensuring that competing capitalists would commit to preserving for future exploitation a workforce that was in danger of being prematurely exploited to death (MECW 35: 247).[8] Marx claims that the long-term benefits of quiescence were immense: "Under its sway, bourgeois society, freed from political cares, attained a development unexpected even by itself" (MECW 22: 330).

Marx's talk of quiescence after the 1848 revolutionary period does not mean that he thinks the capitalist class settled on a strategy of long-term retreat from political rule. Reflecting from the 1870s on the subsequent trajectory of European politics, he writes:

> Its political character changed simultaneously with the economic changes of society. At the same pace at which the progress of modern industry developed, widened, intensified the class

antagonism between capital and labor, the state power assumed more and more the character of the national power of capital over labor, of a public force organized for social enslavement, of an engine of class despotism.

(MECW 22: 548)

In the aftermath of the mid-century upheavals, the reactionary governments embarked on a project of rapid industrial development, which increasingly strengthened the political position of the capitalist class. As it continued to amass wealth and increase its central role in the economy, the capitalist class reasserted direct political influence. Beginning already by the 1860s, Marx was once again speaking of an economic ruling class that was in control of state power: "the parliament of the ruling classes" (MECW 35: 497), English officials "ever complaisant in the service of the ruling classes" (MECW 35: 730), and so on. At this stage the capitalists still largely exercised their power behind the scenes while the rulers of a fading era continued to govern nominally (the aristocratic in England and the Napoleonic in France). Nevertheless, Marx had long predicted that the capitalists would complete their economic domination by sweeping away these mediators and reasserting direct control:

They cannot avoid fulfilling their mission, battering to pieces Old England ... the very moment when they will have conquered exclusive political dominion, when political dominion and economical supremacy will be united in the same hands, when, therefore, the struggle against capital will no longer be distinct from the struggle against the existing Government—from that very moment will date the social revolution of England.

(MECW 11: 333)

Throughout his political analysis, the key idea is that the economically dominant class will tend to monopolize political rule, and the extent of the latter will depend on the extent of that class's economic dominance.

Marx's commentators, despite their numerous and often virulent disagreements over other matters, have been notably united in taking Marx to have underestimated the degree of the state's autonomy.[9]

The state, according to this general trend of thinking, is admittedly both incentivized and constrained by the capitalist class; yet it is also responsive to broader pluralist concerns and has interests of its own that it pursues independently. First, members of the state (e.g., prime ministers, elected members of the legislature, ministers, or heads of various state agencies) have an interest in defending the state bureaucracy in order to maintain the power, income, and status that their position within it brings them.[10]

Second, it is said, the state has an interest in promoting the national interest, and it is overly "cynical" to insist instead that the state aims to promote the interests of the capitalist class alone. Of course, these critics allow, the state's interests typically coincide very nicely with the promotion of the capitalist class's interests. The state depends, after all, on the capitalist class for its financing, and it depends on a generally functioning economy for its popular support. However, as the argument continues, the state also has interests of its own that can come into direct tension with the capitalist class, and these highlight its autonomy especially well.[11] The financing of the state comes through taxation, something that is typically opposed as far as possible by the capitalist class. Moreover, many of the state's actions aimed at protecting the long-term health of the markets are opposed by capitalists at the time.[12]

Finally, the state occasionally sides with other classes in society against the capitalist class (for example, by establishing minimum wages, limiting working hours, and enacting workers' compensation laws). For its part, the capitalist class tolerates these aggravations because it recognizes that it ultimately benefits from the stability the state generally insures, while also seeing that the costs it endures do not outweigh the costs of seizing power themselves.[13] So, this line of argument concludes, instead of seeing the state as a mere instrument of the capitalist class, it should be seen as an autonomous actor that generally shares a mutually beneficial relationship with the capitalist class, but which is additionally tasked with handling spheres of activity that are of no concern to the capitalists, as well as a willingness to challenge them when their different aims come into conflict.

In contrast to these Marx commentators whose assessments reflect the pluralist orthodoxy at the time they wrote, many contemporary scholars of politics have shifted in support of the sort of theory of elite domination Marx himself offered. For example, the American scholar Jeffrey Winters has argued that the United States, which has been the most advanced capitalist country in the world for the last century, is an oligarchy, dominated by "actors who command and control massive concentrations of material resources that can be deployed to defend or enhance their personal wealth or exclusive social position" (Winters 2011: 6). The French economist Thomas Piketty concurs. Having argued that increasing inequality is an inherent feature of unchecked capitalism, he warns that "the risk of a drift towards oligarchy is real and gives little reason for optimism about where the United States is headed" (Piketty 2014: 514).

In a monumental study, Martin Gilens (2012), comparing decades of surveys of people's policy preferences against whether or not these policies were subsequently enacted, found that the policy preferences of the affluent and of business-based interest groups overwhelmingly prevail when in conflict with those of other members of the population: "The central point that emerges from our research is that economic elites and organized groups representing business interests have substantial independent impacts on U.S. government policy, while mass-based interest groups and average citizens have little or no independent influence" (Gilens & Page 2014: 565).[14] The only factor that appears to inhibit the affluent and business-aligned groups from getting what they want is a status quo bias that results in a degree of legislative inertia.[15] Gilens observes, however, that the affluent are increasingly overcoming even this obstacle, as policy-responsiveness to their preferences has increased steadily over the forty years that the data documents. Gilens takes these findings to provide decisive reasons for rejecting majoritarian theories of either the pluralist-interest group or the electoral-democratic variety[16] in favor of a theory of elite domination—precisely the sort Marx proposed (although he is not mentioned for ideological reasons, as we will discuss in Chapter 5).[17]

It is not difficult to see how the elite economic class secures the outcomes it desires from the state. There are four obvious mechanisms. First, the affluent and the government have shared membership. As of the last counting, more than half of the members of the U.S. Congress, for example, are millionaires, and the median net worth of all of the members is itself over a $1 million, roughly ten times that of the average American family.[18] Moreover, there is a well-documented "revolving door" through which individuals move between careers in American government and careers in business, particularly as advocates for firms they previously regulated (Lazarus et al. 2016).

Second, the affluent act as patrons of individual government actors. Campaigns in the U.S., in particular, are extremely costly, and most candidates need to raise significant amounts of money from outside interests. This shows up in two ways: money acts as a gatekeeper, determining which candidates are eligible to run (Christiano 2012); and money can be used in a more targeted way, such as ensuring that a particular agenda is set or a particular vote is cast (Mayer 2016).

Third, the affluent are patrons of the state itself. The state, in all capitalist countries, is primarily funded through revenue raised through taxation, and thereby heavily reliant on the economic elites. This is a point Marx emphasizes:

> To this modern private property corresponds the modern state, which, purchased gradually by the owners of property by means of taxation, has fallen entirely into their hands through the national debt, and its existence has become wholly dependent on the commercial credit which the owners of property, the bourgeois, extend to it.
>
> (MECW 6: 90)

Fourth, the capitalist class is typically perceived by legislators as a source of a general economic stability that supports a well-functioning society (as in the famous American slogan, "What's good for Wall Street is good for Main Street"). The state perceives itself to be dependent on the capitalist class, not only as a direct source of patronage via taxation but also as the source of enough employment and material goods to keep the general population satisfied.

Here we should note an additional mechanism by which the ruling class influences the state, one which we will detail in Chapter 5—namely, that of ideological domination. According to Marx, the dominant class also monopolizes the ideological channels through which social and political ideas are produced and disseminated throughout society (the media, political parties, advocacy groups, universities, the church, and so on). As he puts the point:

> The ideas of the ruling class are in every epoch the ruling ideas ... The class which has the means of material production at its disposal, consequently also controls the means of mental production, so that the ideas of those who lack the means of mental production are on the whole subject to it ... [They rule] as thinkers, as producers of ideas, and regulate the production and distribution of the ideas of their age.
>
> (MECW 5: 59)

On Marx's view, we should expect these ideas to valorize the prevailing economic system and vilify opposing views, or, at the very least, suggest nothing that would disrupt the system's operation. Both the dominant class and those they dominate will be subject to this messaging from cradle to grave and, as a century of social science research suggests, to great effect.[19] This means that the population will be primed to be accepting of government policy drafted to favor the interests of the economically elite class, including both elites and non-elites who attain positions of political power. General popular support of elite policy will also help ensure that the elite class is able to rally the general public against any critic of the system who did manage to attain a position of power and was committed to significant restructuring of the economy.

3. The Proletariat and Revolution

We now turn to the protagonists of Marx's writings—the proletariat, those who sell their labor power for wages in order to live. We have seen that individuals sort into classes based on the extent of their effective control over the means of production and the economic activity they are compelled to carry out in virtue of this fact. The attempt to make the most of their positions brings the different classes into conflict with one another, with classes becoming dominant politically to the extent that they dominate economically. Marx claims that this has been a fact of social structures since the time that a division of labor resulted in a productive surplus that enables some members of society to effectively live off the labor of the others.

The classes that filled the role of dominant actor have changed as the mode of production transitioned from slave societies to feudalism, and then to capitalism. However, the fact that society is structured around some dominant class and those they dominate ("oppressor and oppressed") has remained a constant. Marx identifies the proletariat, the urban industrial working class emerging with the industrial revolution, as a world-historically unique class that will eventually bring about a revolution that will finally end this cycle of class conflict once and for all. We now turn to a consideration of why Marx believed they are uniquely positioned to carry out this revolution, when and where they will do so, and how they will carry it out.

The proletariat, for Marx, has four features that, taken together, enable it to carry out such a revolution.

First, it is organized, and hence capable of collective action. This is the result of the capitalist process of industrialization itself, whose factory system required large workforces laboring together in close contact on highly collaborative processes. Thus, as Marx notes with some irony, the capitalist class—in constructing a proletariat work force "always increasing in numbers, and disciplined, united, organised by the very mechanism of the process of capitalist production itself" (MECW 35: 750)—in fact "produces, above all ... its own grave-diggers" (MECW 6: 496).

Second, the proletariat will consist of a large majority of the population, and hence have sufficient numbers to carry out successful collective action. As the *Communist Manifesto* emphasizes, "All previous historical movements were movements of minorities ... The proletarian movement is the self-conscious, independent movement of the immense majority, in the interest of the immense majority" (MECW 6: 495). Numbers alone, of course, do not guarantee successful collective action. We know, in fact, that smaller populations have successfully dominated larger ones in the past. However, Marx's expectation here, taking the two points above together, is that a vast and effectively organized majority of the population will be positioned to do so.

Third, the proletariat will become increasingly immiserated, while at the same time the system itself achieves a level of material productivity that makes this immiseration completely and obviously unnecessary, and hence the proletariat will be motivated to take collective action. Capitalism is achieving a level of production few could have imagined before the onset of the industrial revolution; yet capitalists themselves remain compelled by market forces to continue to extract as much profit as possible from working-class labor and to replace this labor with the use of automation wherever possible. As this process reaches its zenith and capitalism has "rendered the great mass of humanity 'propertyless', and produced, at the same time, the contradiction of an existing world of wealth and culture," the tension between what is possible and what is actual will become palpable to a working class that faces destitution, and Marx expects that this will compel them to act (MECW 5: 48). (We return in Chapter 4 to what it is about the economic logic of capitalism that guarantees, according to Marx, this development, and some possible reasons for skepticism about it.)

Fourth, the proletariat will be able to correctly identify the capitalist class as the source of its unnecessary immiseration, and hence know where to effectively direct its collective action. According to the *Communist Manifesto*, as the worker sinks deeper into immiseration,

> it becomes evident, that the bourgeoisie is unfit any longer to be the ruling class in society ... It is unfit to rule because it is incompetent to assure an existence to its slave within his slavery ... Society can no longer live under this bourgeoisie ... its existence is no longer compatible with society.
>
> (MECW 6: 495–496)

One can, of course, suffer deprivation even in times of relative abundance without recognizing where the fault lies. Elites have long been expert in deflecting the blame away from themselves for the suffering of those they dominate, encouraging people to blame themselves or scapegoat others, and we will see below that Marx details several ways the capitalists attempt this exact thing. However, he also clearly thinks the proletariat will recognize the source of its immiseration, in part because of its proximity to the productive process[20] and in part because communists will educate the proletariat about how capitalism really works and about the unique historical opportunity that capitalism presents to the vast majority.

The conditions that explain why the proletariat is well positioned to carry out a successful revolution are the same ones that indicate when we should expect them to do so. An organized mass movement of workers will be motivated to act once they are sufficiently immiserated, realize that this immiseration is unnecessary, and clearly identify the capitalist class as responsible for their plight. At this point, as the *Communist Manifesto* puts the point, it becomes clear that "the proletarians have nothing to lose but their chains. They have a world to win" (MECW 6: 519).

Marx was personally subject to bouts of wishful thinking, and his writings from the revolutionary 1848 period often suggest the proletariat revolution itself was imminent. After these upheavals abated and a reactionary period set in, Marx tempered his expectations. In 1850, recognizing the working class was still relatively small and unorganized, and that the capitalist conditions themselves had not fully matured, Marx argued against fellow communists who advocated for immediate revolution in Germany:

> We say to the workers: "You will have to go through 15, 20, 50 years of civil wars and national struggles not only to bring about a change in society but also to change yourselves" ... we are at pains to show the German workers in particular how rudimentary the development of the German proletariat is.
>
> (MECW 11: 403)

Seventeen years later, in an 1867 Preface to *Capital*, Marx notes various remarks from political leaders expressing growing alarm over a re-emerging working class, and he concludes, with cautious optimism: "These are signs of the times ... They do not signify that tomorrow a miracle will happen. They show that, within the ruling classes themselves, a foreboding is dawning, that the present society is no solid crystal" (MECW 35: 11). This post-1848 cautiousness does not reflect a change to his basic theory, but rather that in his revolutionary exuberance he had not himself taken his theory seriously enough.

There are several revolution-delaying factors that Marx himself highlights, though whose effect even the more temperate Marx of later years seems to have underestimated.

First, capitalism drives the process of globalization, which greatly extends the life cycle of capitalism itself, and hence delays the conditions that precipitate the proletariat revolt against it. Marx himself was among the very first theorists to identify this phenomenon and recognize its significance. Capitalism presses beyond national borders in order to secure raw materials, cheaper labor, and new markets for its goods. Marx expects that capitalism will continue its reign until it has completed its natural cycle on an international scale, which will give rise to an international mass movement of organized and immiserated workers ready to revolt.[21]

It is also in this context that we must understand his commentary on various imperialist enterprises, such as the British in India. On the one hand, Marx considered imperialism in general to be the "ultimate form of the state power" that capitalists had devised for "the enslavement of labor by capital" (MECW 22: 330); and in British exploitation of India in particular, he said that the "inherent barbarism of bourgeois civilization lies unveiled before our eyes, turning from its home, where it assumes respectable forms, to the colonies, where it goes naked" (MECW 12: 221). On the other hand, Marx also hopes to see this process hasten, insofar as "communism is only possible as the act of the dominant peoples 'all at once' and simultaneously, which presupposes the universal development of productive forces and the world intercourse bound up with them" (MECW 5: 49). However, just as Marx occasionally overestimated the development of the capitalist process within the industrialized nations of Europe, he seems to have quite significantly overestimated its rate of international development, which even now has yet to reach the level his theory expects.

Second, capitalists are able to grant marginal improvements to the lives of workers, which allays their immiseration and hence their motivation to revolt. In his lifetime, Marx witnessed European governments offer various concessions to the working class—extending the vote, regulating working hours and factory conditions, and increasing wages. Looked at narrowly, the trajectory of the working class in the last decades of the 19th century seemed exactly the opposite of the ever-increasing immiseration Marx had predicted.[22] This encouraged many in the labor movement to focus on improving life through subtle reforms to the system rather than a full-scale revolt against it. Marx and Engels, however, noted that the European governments were in a position to make concessions painlessly precisely because of the bounty they enjoyed as a result of their imperialist endeavors around the globe. Engels, in a letter to Marx, explains the reformist tendency within the British working class as due to "the fact that the English proletariat is actually becoming more and more bourgeois," adding sardonically, "In the case of a nation which exploits the entire world this is, of course, justified to some extent" (MECW 40: 344).

Marx saw the reformist tendency take root within his lifetime; but it was Engels who lived long enough to see it flourish, and much of his later writing aims to combat it. In 1891, Engels cautioned the SPD, Germany's newly powerful socialist party, against "forgetting of the great" in favor of "the principal considerations for the momentary interests of the day, this struggling and striving for the success of the moment regardless of later consequences, this sacrifice of the future of the movement for its present" (MECW 27: 227). Marx and Engels alike supported political activism within government-sanctioned channels, both for the concessions it might win and for the training in political action it afforded, but they cautioned against being lulled by this activity into settling for short-term reforms to the system rather than a revolution against that system.

Third, the proletariat can be distracted by various social antagonisms beyond its conflict with the capitalist class, and hence distracted from the actual source of its felt misery and its effective remedy. Marx detailed numerous instances of this sort throughout his writing; but he was especially struck by the case of the British working class, the most organized working class in the most advanced industrial nation, and its hostile attitude toward the Irish working class. In an 1870 letter, Marx details the way in which the British ruling class cultivates this hostility and its deleterious effect on the working-class movement. British exploitation of Irish land had resulted in a wave of displaced Irish laborers coming to England to seek work. This extra supply of labor subsequently forces down the wages and living standards of the English working class, which, quite predictably, generates hostility among them: "The ordinary English worker hates the Irish worker as a competitor who forces down the standard of life." Moreover, this motivates a more general cultural animosity: "In relation to the Irish worker, he feels himself to be a member of the ruling nation ... He harbours religious, social and national prejudices against him" (MECW 43: 474).

Since this antagonism keeps the British working class focused on the Irish working class as a material and cultural threat, rather than its near mirror image with whom it should join in solidarity against the capitalists, all of these resentments are encouraged by the capitalists, who ensure that "this antagonism is kept artificially alive and intensified by the press, the pulpit, the comic papers, in short by all the means at the disposal of the ruling class" (MECW 43: 475). Consequently, the English worker, the portion of the international working class best positioned to be in the vanguard of the revolution, instead,

> makes himself a tool of his aristocrats and capitalists ... strengthening their domination over himself ... This antagonism is the secret of the English working class's impotence, despite its organisation. It is the secret of the maintenance of power by the capitalist class. And the latter is fully aware of this.
>
> (MECW 43: 474–475)

As we have just seen, Marx notes ways that intra-class antagonisms can distract the proletariat from its more fundamental conflict with the capitalist class. Some argue, however, that Marx greatly underestimates the significance of these intra-class antagonisms more generally, particularly with respect to race, gender, and religion. At times this takes the form of the claim that Marx downplays the harm caused by racism, sexism, and religious discrimination; at other times it is the claim that he downplays the ability of non-class-based social movements to effect historical transformation.[23]

The first charge, about ignoring intra-class antagonisms, is largely unfounded, as Marx (and Engels even more so) highlights many of the cruel effects of pernicious attitudes and practices related to gender and race.[24] The second claim, about the need for class-based movements, is largely accurate, as Marx would gladly acknowledge.

We can glean his general outlook on this issue as early as "On the Jewish Question," an essay that emphasized a crucial distinction between "political emancipation" and "human emancipation."[25]

Political emancipation is primarily concerned with extending the realm of civic and political rights (e.g., the right to vote or to hold office) to all citizens regardless of other facts about their status or identity (race, religion, gender, etc.). Marx welcomed the establishment and extension of these political rights as "a big step forward" that was "the last form of human emancipation within the prevailing scheme of things" (MECW 3: 155). However, he thinks that this sort of political emancipation remains compatible with continued widespread oppression and degradation (for instance, those dying sick and hungry in the streets may still technically retain the right to vote or run for office).

Human emancipation, or "real, practical emancipation," by contrast, requires ensuring that people enjoy conditions that enable human flourishing more generally. In a capitalist society increasingly dividing into the "haves" and "have nots," there is no doubt that there can be real progress in overcoming non-class-based discrimination. This will result in greater numbers of those who have suffered such discrimination making it into the ranks of the "haves," and it will result in improved treatment of those who have suffered discrimination within the ranks of their fellow "haves" or "have nots." However, despite this progress within the framework of capitalist society, this society itself remains dependent on the continued existence of "haves and have nots"; and it is this fact that makes it incompatible with human emancipation and destined to be toppled by the mass movement of the immiserated, as we have outlined. This "emancipation of the producing class is that of all human beings without distinction of sex or race" (MECW 24: 340).

Where does Marx expect this proletariat revolution to begin? Throughout his writings he emphasized that the proletariat revolution will first occur in the most advanced industrial nations. He considered England to be the prime candidate, but thought Germany and the United States were viable contenders. This is for the reasons we have already seen: the most industrially advanced nations will be the first to achieve the jointly necessary conditions of having created material abundance and a mass movement of immiserated workers.

Throughout most of his writing he considered less-developed nations to be the next in line for capitalist exploitation, but not themselves in a position to serve as main instigators of revolutionary action. Later in life, Marx increasingly took note of growing socialist movements on the margins of the industrialized nations, particularly in Russia, which remained a rural, agricultural, peasant society at the time. At least when writing to his supporters in those countries, he would express support for their efforts. In 1882, one year before his death, Marx (with Engels) could write in the preface to the Russian edition of the *Communist Manifesto*: "Russia forms the vanguard of revolutionary action in Europe" (MECW 24: 426).

Perhaps the struggles in the industrialized centers and the radicalized margins could complement each other? They saw the possibility, for instance, that a revolt in Russia could become "the signal for a proletarian revolution in the West" (MECW 24: 426). The then revolutionized industrialized countries could return the favor by sponsoring industrial advances in the not yet industrialized revolutionary vanguard nations that would enable them to bypass the stage of bourgeois industrialization that had been requisite in the industrialized center, providing a sort of historical shortcut through which "the present Russian common ownership of land may serve as the starting-point for communist development" (MECW 24: 425–426). Again, as Engels emphasizes elsewhere, this is a real possibility, but one that "can only happen if ... a proletarian revolution is successfully carried out" in industrialized nations first, since only the industrialized nations will be able to offer "the Russian peasant the preconditions requisite for such a transition, particularly the material things he needs, if only to carry through the revolution, necessarily connected therewith, of his whole agricultural system" (MECW 24: 48).

What form will the proletariat revolution take? Most often, Marx envisioned the revolution as an armed uprising. This should come as little surprise, since most revolutions throughout history have involved taking up arms, including those that loomed most large in Marx's thinking—the July Revolution of 1830 in France, the French Revolution of 1989, the revolutions of 1848 throughout Europe, and the Paris Commune of 1871. Given that he considered the governments of advanced industrial countries to be firmly under the control of the capitalists, he fully expected this class to fiercely resist their own ouster, and this would almost certainly require taking up arms against them. The following sample of passages, which roughly bookend his life as a political agitator, indicate the general tenor of his thought: In *The Poverty of Philosophy* of 1847, Marx writes:

> The antagonism between the proletariat and the bourgeoisie is a struggle of class against class, a struggle which carried to its highest expression is a total revolution ... on the eve of every general reshuffling of society, the last word of social science will always be: "Combat or death, the bloody battle or nothing. That is how the question is irresistibly posed."
>
> (MECW 6: 212)

The *Communist Manifesto* of 1848 is equally explicit that the proletariat revolution will be an armed uprising:

> In depicting the most general phases of the development of the proletariat, we traced the more or less veiled civil war, raging within existing society, up to the point at which the war breaks out into open revolution, and where the violent overthrow of the bourgeoisie lays the foundation for the sway of the proletariat.
>
> (MECW 6: 495)

Nearly a quarter of a century later, in an 1871 address to the First International in which he reflects on the military defeat of the Paris Commune, the workers' government that had just briefly ruled in Paris, Marx says that the proletariat required a "proletarian army" because "the working classes would have to conquer the right to emancipate themselves on the battlefield" (MECW 22: 634); and in an address the following year to this same body, he said:

> we must also admit that in most countries on the Continent it is force which must be the lever of our revolution; it is force which will have to be resorted to for a time in order to establish the rule of the workers.
>
> (MECW 23: 255)

Marx does entertain the possibility of a peaceful path to proletariat power under certain conditions. As he notes in his 1872 First International address,

> We know that the institutions, customs and traditions in the different countries must be taken into account; and we do not deny the existence of countries like America, England ... where the workers may achieve their aims by peaceful means.
>
> (MECW 23: 255)

He reiterates this idea eight years later in a letter to the left-wing political activist Henry Hyndman, in which he states that a revolution in England is "not necessary, but ... possible," and spells out some of the reasons why England might be the exception (MECW 46: 49). Marx notes that England has had a history of labor organizing that has secured concessions from the British government to improve working conditions. Moreover, England was continuing to extend voting rights, which Marx consistently encouraged the working class to see as a means to securing more power: "[Proletariat aims] must be striven for, using all the means at the disposal of the proletariat, including universal suffrage, thus transformed from the instrument of deception which it has been hitherto into an instrument of emancipation" (MECW 24: 340).

This said, it is not entirely clear why Marx sees England to be especially distinct in these regards. At the same time that he wrote to Hyndman, both Germany and France had working-class movements and enjoyed even broader voting rights than England. Regardless, Marx's optimism for the peaceful path is directed at the British working class, who have not yet learned how to fully "wield their power and use their liberties, both of which they possess legally," adding that, "If the unavoidable evolution turn into a revolution, it would not only be the fault of the ruling classes, but also of the working class" (MECW 46: 49).

However, even in this best-case scenario in which the working class comes to power through peaceful and legal means, it must still expect to take up arms in response to an inevitable armed revolt of the displaced ruling class. Engels emphasizes this point in the 1886 Preface to the English edition of *Capital*:

[Marx was] a man whose whole theory is the result of a lifelong study of the economic history and condition of England, and whom that study led to the conclusion that, at least in Europe, England is the only country where the inevitable social revolution might be effected entirely by peaceful and legal means. He certainly never forgot to add that he hardly expected the English ruling classes to submit, without a "proslavery rebellion", to this peaceful and legal revolution.

(MECW 35: 36)

Thus, whether the proletariat takes power through legal means or through revolutionary means, Marx fully expects that there will be a violent conflict. Despite all of his disdain for the ruling class, nowhere does he celebrate this fact. He simply underscores how seriously he is committed to the claim that the ruling class monopolizes political power and employs it as a means of securing its aims while dominating others, and that this is not a power that it will relinquish without a fight. At the same time, Marx fully expects that an organized mass movement of immiserated workers, having nothing but their chains to lose and the world to win, will prevail.

4. The "Classless" Society

Marx, the world's most famous communist and a theorist who wrote tens of thousands of pages, had very little to say about what a post-revolutionary communist world would be like, except, of course, that it would be "classless." This is a deliberate stance reflecting his view that, although we can grasp the general principles of historical development in basic outline (those expressed with historical materialism), we cannot anticipate in very great detail distant future material developments and the ways that social life will evolve in response to these. In light of this commitment, Marx clearly relished the criticism he received from a reviewer of *Capital*—that he had "confine[d] [him]self to the mere critical analysis of actual facts, instead of writing receipts [recipes] ... for the cook-shops of the future" (MECW 35: 17). He does, however, offer some predictions about how events will proceed immediately following the proletariat's seizure of effective political control. That moment itself will not mark the beginning of full communist emancipation. Rather, he anticipates events unfolding through two phases, a "first phase" and a "higher phase," each with its own political character and economic principle.

A. The Two Phases of Communism

At the outset of the first phase, immediately after the proletariat has seized effective political control, it will need to set about securing it. This means establishing what Marx called the "dictatorship of the proletariat." In the aftermath of brutal 20th-century dictatorships, this term is likely to provoke alarm; but, as noted earlier, Marx is clearly taking over the concept from ancient Roman law, which provided for time-bounded dictatorial rule in the event of emergencies. Indeed, he offered the Paris Commune as an exemplar of proletariat dictatorship. As Marx saw it, among its other virtues, the Commune was radically democratic:

> The Commune was formed of the municipal councillors, chosen by universal suffrage in the various wards of the town, responsible and revocable at short terms … Instead of deciding once in three or six years which member of the ruling class was to misrepresent the people in Parliament, universal suffrage was to serve the people.
>
> (MECW 22: 331–333)

In order to secure political power, Marx also emphasized that the proletariat would need to secure the army: "The communal organization once firmly established on a national scale, the catastrophes it might still have to undergo, would be sporadic slaveholders' insurrections" (MECW 22: 491). And, of course, to begin the transition to communism, "The proletariat will use its political supremacy to wrest, by degrees, all capital from the bourgeoisie, to centralise all instruments of production in the hands of the State, i.e., of the proletariat organised as the ruling class" (MECW 6: 504).

In this first phase, with respect to economic structure specifically, Marx expects that the proletariat dictatorship will begin to abolish private ownership of the means of production and of rental lands. However, he suggests that this emerging collective economy will continue to be shaped for a time by the attitudes and expectations of the bygone capitalist epoch:

> What we are dealing with here is a communist society, not as it has developed on its own foundations, but on the contrary, just as it emerges from capitalist society, which is thus in every respect, economically, morally and intellectually, still stamped with the birth-marks of the old society from whose womb it emerges.
>
> (MECW 24: 85)

In particular, Marx expects that this will be manifest in what is called the "contribution principle," according to which a worker will expect to be paid for the work that they have done—no more, nor less. This means that more productive workers (whether because they are stronger, more efficient, or whatever) will receive more than those who are less so. Marx sketches what this might look like in practice:

> The individual producer receives back from society … exactly what he gives to it … For example … He receives a certificate from society that he has furnished such and such an amount of labour … and with this certificate he draws from the social stock of means of consumption as much as the same amount of labour costs. The same amount of labour which he has given to society in one form he receives back in another.
>
> (MECW 24: 86)

This arrangement is free from the wage exploitation that characterized capitalism (which we will discuss in Chapter 4), but the individuals continue to be motivated by the fixation on meritocracy that it had long cultivated.

Gradually (how gradually, Marx does not say) this first phase will transition to a higher one. As the dictatorship of the proletariat increasingly democratizes the political process and socializes the economic system, the state itself will grow obsolete. In *The Poverty of Philosophy*, Marx writes:

> the working class, in the course of its development, will substitute for the old civil society, an association which will exclude

classes and their antagonism, and there will be no more political power properly so-called, since political power is precisely the expression of antagonism in civil society.

(MECW 6: 212)

Engels spells this idea out at greater length in *Anti-Dühring*, where he adds the caveat that this does not imply the end of social planning:

> As soon as there is no longer any social class to be held in subjection; as soon as class rule, and the individual struggle for existence based upon our present anarchy of production, with the collisions and excesses arising from these, are removed, nothing more remains to be repressed, and a special repressive force, a state, is no longer necessary … State interference in social relations becomes, in one domain after another, superfluous, and then withers away of itself; the government of persons is replaced by the administration of things.

(MECW 25: 268)

It is clear Marx and Engels expect that a highly productive society will still require planning and coordinating activity. We also know that they expect this transition from a "state" to an "administration of things" to signify more than a nominal change, since the current state, in addition to simply administrating things, is tasked with securing the advantages of the economic elites against the class-divided and often-frustrated masses. What remains unclear, however, is everything else about the nature of this "administration of things." Will it be overseen by a centralized body or is it a purely local affair? How much administration will the "higher stage" require, and hence how large will this administrative apparatus need to be? What exactly is its mandate? Who will staff it? How much will it differ in its operations from what we now think of as "states"?

Marx sketches an account of economic life corresponding to the political transformation of this higher phase. Society will gradually transcend the economic conditions "of the slavery of labour by the conditions of free and associated labour" (MECW 22: 491). At this point, "the narrow horizon of bourgeois right [will] be crossed in its entirety" and society will adopt a new principle of distribution, "inscrib[ing] on its banners: From each according to his abilities, to each according to his needs!" (MECW 24: 87). In contrast to the contribution principle of the first phase, in which the worker receives no more and no less than the value of the labor she contributes, in this higher phase citizens will contribute what labor they can and receive the goods they require. Marx suggests that people will be happy to work, going so far as to say that "labour ... become[s] not only a means of life but life's prime want (MECW 24: 87),[26] and he expects that they will not begrudge helping those who are less able to contribute labor to produce the goods that will be available to everyone. These claims, as Marx himself makes clear, are premised on the crucial expectation that the higher phase of communism will enjoy relative material abundance: "after the productive forces have also increased with the all-round development of the individual, and all the springs of common wealth flow more abundantly" (MECW 24: 87).

B. Skepticism about the "Higher Phase" of Communism

How plausible are the conditions that characterize Marx's "higher phase" of communism? Taking the political dimension first, it must be said that it is difficult to evaluate the plausibility of "the state" withering away to be replaced by the mere "administration of things" given the fact that Marx's account is so underdescribed. Given what he does say, however, we can identify two central concerns.

First, it is difficult to imagine how a society advanced enough to produce the relative abundance that communism requires could achieve this without a fairly robust organizational apparatus, unless we are to imagine that we have finally constructed manna-from-heaven machines that run on their own in perpetuity. Marx does not deny this. He does, however, argue that we overestimate the need for a class of specialists managing the workers from above to oversee such an apparatus. Here, he took inspiration from the Paris Commune:

> [Gone is] the Delusion as if administration and political governing were mysteries, transcendent functions only to be trusted to the hands of a trained caste, state parasites, richly paid sycophants and sinecurists, in the higher posts ... The whole sham of state mysteries and state pretensions was done away by a Commune, mostly consisting of simple working men, organizing the defence

of Paris … securing the approvisionment of that immense town … doing their work publicly, simply, under the most difficult and complicated circumstances, and doing it … for a few pounds.

(MECW 22: 488–490)

Marx, therefore, does not deny that the communist society will require planning and organization, only that such organization would require specialization beyond what the communists would be able to offer in drawing from their own ranks. One might, of course, remain skeptical whether the complexity of the modern world and technology makes this supposition plausible.

Here, however, a second sort of worry arises—namely, what is to prevent people in positions of any authority from asserting that authority in a way that reestablishes class divisions? This possibility poses a problem both in the transition from the first to the higher phase of communism and within the higher phase insofar as the administrators, though supposedly drawn from proletariat non-specialists, threaten to coalesce into a new class of administrative specialists. This is sometimes presented as a problem for Marxists considering the way in which the autocrats that ruled nominally Marxist 20th-century regimes clung to power; but it was already a worry put to Marx himself by his occasional collaborator and frequent adversary, the Russian anarchist Mikhail Bakunin:

> From whatever point of view we look at this question, it always comes down to the same dismal result: government of the vast majority of the people by a privileged minority. But this minority, the Marxists say, will consist of workers. Yes, perhaps of former workers, who, as soon as they become rulers or representatives of the people will cease to be workers and will begin to look upon the whole workers' world from the heights of the state. They will no longer represent the people but themselves and their own pretensions to govern the people. Anyone who doubts this is not at all familiar with human nature.
>
> (Bakunin 2012: 178)

Marx is not naïve about the evils humans are capable of inflicting on one another (as anyone who reads *Capital* recognizes), yet neither does he share Bakunin's wholly pessimistic assessment of human nature, rightly or wrongly. He also thinks that there are reasonable checks we can place on ourselves, such as the democratic structure of the Paris Commune, whose popularly elected administrators were drawn from the working class to serve short and revocable terms. Perhaps structuring the roles of those tasked with the "administration of things" along similar lines could prevent the reestablishment of pernicious class dynamics, though this is admittedly far from certain.

How plausible is the economic principle of the higher phase of communism, "From each according to his abilities, to each according to his needs"? We have seen that the principle depends crucially on relative material abundance. Marx was understandably awestruck by the remarkable advances in productivity brought on by the industrial revolution, and he did not see any reason to doubt that such exponential progress might continue into the future. He, obviously, could not foresee the climate change crisis, which may raise fatal obstacles to the spectacular productivity that would make a classless society viable.[27] Of course, technological innovation may yet solve the climate crisis; but even more important is that the global population will start declining some time in the next forty to sixty years, making it more realistic, within environmental constraints, that immense productivity sufficient for genuine freedom will be a possibility.[28]

C. *After Capitalism: Freedom from Necessity*

Whatever its prospects, the most striking fact about the post-capitalist and classless society is that no one would be reduced to selling their labor power for wages to survive. It is important to emphasize what a dramatic change that alone would be in the lives of almost everyone reading this volume. Most people survive by selling their labor power for wages; most people (except a lucky few) would rather do something else with their time, except that they need wages to survive. If capitalism's great gift to humanity is, as Marx points out, an extraordinary development of productive power such that life choices need not be structured around the question, "How much will I earn?", then almost all human lives would be utterly different than they are now. Being "competitive on the job market," choosing a "practical college major," making oneself "marketable": all these considerations would be bygones of an earlier, primitive era. In a passage from *The Germany Ideology*, Marx and Engels write that,

> in communist society, where nobody has one exclusive sphere of activity but each can become accomplished in any branch he wishes, society regulates the general production and thus makes it possible for me to do one thing today and another tomorrow, to hunt in the morning, fish in the afternoon, rear cattle in the evening, criticise after dinner, just as I have a mind, without ever becoming hunter, fisherman, herdsman or critic.
>
> (MECW 5: 48)

Even if that may seem an extravagant fantasy,[29] it does capture the ideal of communism: to make people free, in the sense that they can expend their productive and creative energies on the work they want to do, not on the work they must perform for a wage in order to survive. Late in his life, Marx observes that "the realm of freedom actually begins" when "labor which is determined by necessity [i.e., the need to survive] and mundane considerations ceases" (MECW 37: 807). This ideal of "freedom" as productive activity *not* necessitated by the need to survive is one Marx embraced throughout his intellectual career. In his unpublished 1844 *Manuscripts*, Marx laments that most people's labor is "not the satisfaction of a need; it is merely a *means* to satisfy needs external to it.[30] Its alien character emerges clearly in the fact that, as soon as no physical or other compulsion exists, labor is shunned like the plague" (MECW 3: 275). Wage slaves only work to earn a wage (to "satisfy needs external" to their work, such as their need for food, shelter, etc.), not because they want to do that work. The wage slave's "labor is … not voluntary, but coerced; it is *forced labor*" (MECW 3: 275): forced in the precise sense that they would not choose to perform it if they did not need the wages to survive. Communism, as Marx conceived it, had as its fundamental aim *freedom*—more precisely, to enable people to engage in productive activity because they want to do so and not simply out of necessity.

To a contemporary reader, especially one exposed to substantial amounts of anti-communist propaganda, this may seem ironic (or even perverse) given the unhappy association of Marx's name with regimes (like that in the former Soviet Union or Maoist China) which were very far from free and which Marx would certainly have condemned.[31] Marx, however, would not have been surprised by this. As he observed in a passage from *The German Ideology*: "[T]his development of productive forces ... is an absolutely necessary practical premise [for communism] because without it *want* is merely made general, and with *destitution* the struggle for necessities and all the old filthy business would necessarily be reproduced" (MECW 5: 49). "Want" was indeed made general in both the Soviet Union and in Mao's China, since neither country was in a position to abandon capitalism: Russia in 1917 and China in 1949 were both essentially agricultural economies that had not undergone industrialization under pressure of capitalism.[32] They were countries whose productive output was so meager that they could not possibly render their citizens free from the necessity of laboring to survive. A communist society, as Marx thought of it, would be the first in the history of the world in which people were free to engage in productive and creative activities without worrying about survival. Any university student, facing an uncertain future, can well appreciate the appeal of that ideal.

5. Conclusion

Class struggle was the central focus of Marx's writings throughout his career. In every epoch, societies are divided within themselves over the production and distribution of material goods, and it is this conflict that motors history (i.e., the class struggle discussed in this chapter is the causal mechanism of historical materialism that was the focus of Chapter 2).

   Given the centrality of class struggle to Marx's account, it can be surprising that he never precisely defines the concept of "class," leaving us instead to infer what he means on the basis of his enumerated lists of the various classes and detailed discussions of particular cases of class struggle. Moreover, even a careful reconstruction of his meaning will not issue in a concept of class with necessary and sufficient conditions, since borderline cases will always appear to frustrate precise analysis, as Marx himself acknowledged. Nevertheless, Marx thinks that we can quite clearly identify paradigm instances of the various classes; and his project succeeds if he can show that the membership of the various classes is sufficient, and that their relative interests are sufficiently divergent to give rise to the kind of class struggle that he claims accounts for historical shifts. The paradigm cases of classes are demarcated based on which activities in the prevailing economic system they are compelled to perform in order to best realize their material interests, given the extent of their effective control of the various means of production. In other words, what can someone do with what they own? It is this criterion that determines which class someone belongs to, whether they realize it or not. If and when members of a group come to recognize their common situation and band together in pursuit of their collective interests, a pursuit that Marx believes inevitably brings them into conflict with other classes, they develop class consciousness, becoming what he calls a "class for itself."

In every epoch, Marx adds, one class typically attains ruling-class status through securing an economic dominance, which it leverages to monopolize political power that it employs to further entrench its own status. Marx's most focused analysis of this general phenomenon was his various accounts of the emerging capitalist class's seizure of the aristocratic power of the nobility. In his early accounts, Marx wrote as if the capitalists had already come to rule directly in England and in France in the early decades of the 1800s. However, Marx modified this view in light of the unfolding events of his time, noting that countervailing forces had pushed back some of the capitalist classes' political gains, which they had achieved before thoroughly securing their economic dominance. As the century wore on, however, the capitalists were to extend this economic dominance, and thus to reassert their political dominance along with it.

In this account of class struggle unfolding across history, the proletariat, the protagonists of Marx's work, plays an extraordinary part. According to Marx, it will be the class that finally ends the process by bringing about a classless society. The proletariat has four features, according to Marx, that position it to successfully revolt against the capitalists:

1. Its work in the factory has required it to act as an organization; and, now organized, its members are capable of collective action.
2. The proletariat constitutes the majority of the population, and so has the numbers necessary to carry out a successful revolution.
3. The proletariat will become increasingly immiserated, while at the same time the system itself achieves a level of material productivity that makes this immiseration completely and obviously unnecessary, and hence the proletariat will be motivated to take collective action.
4. The proletariat, in virtue of its direct contact with the capitalist system, will be able to correctly identify the capitalist class as the source of its unnecessary immiseration, and hence know where to effectively direct its collective action.

Although Marx identified a number of factors that could impede the revolution (globalization would extend the lifecycle of capitalism, and capitalists could mollify the working class for a time with modest improvements to their standard of living, as well as distract them by fostering intra-class conflicts), he never ceased anticipating the revolution to come. Here we note that, while a capitalist ruling class clearly still remains, the industrial proletariat is at most a distinct minority of the working force in the most advanced capitalist countries.

Marx was reserved in his predictions of what would come after the revolution (to some, his account is maddeningly vague). Whether or not the revolution was initially violent (Marx was open to the idea that the revolution could be brought about electorally), he expected that it would turn violent as the capitalists clung to power. Having been suppressed, Marx expected that there would be a period where the proletariat ruled politically (what he called "the dictatorship of the proletariat") and the economic principles of this time would still be shaped by the attitudes of the capitalist era (characterized by the "contribution principle" according to which people would expect to be paid for work they had done—no more and no less). As time moved on, however, Marx suggested that society would transition to a "higher" form, with the economic principle "from each according to his abilities, to each according to his needs" and the gradual withering away of the state.

Crucially, we have not yet addressed the question why Marx believes that capitalism will produce the immiseration of the vast majority, one of the preconditions for communism. That requires us to turn our attention to Marx's economic analysis of capitalism in his mature work, especially *Capital*, which is the subject of Chapter 4. As we will see, consideration of the details of Marx's economic analysis of capitalism provides additional grounds for skepticism about what will *really* come after the end of capitalism.

Notes

1 The term "dictatorship" has its origins in the classical Roman Republic's *dictatura*, which referred to a magistrate or ruler who was granted extended (though not unlimited) powers for a period of up to six months during times of emergency or crisis. It was this sense of the term that Marx had in mind, not the connotation that emerged in the 20th century of a form of government in which absolute power is concentrated in the hands of a single individual or a small group, often maintained by force and characterized by the absence of democratic practices like free elections and civil liberties. For an extensive discussion, see Draper (1986).

2 We return to this topic in Chapter 4.

3 "In England, modern society is indisputably most highly and classically developed in economic structure. Nevertheless, even here the stratification of classes does not appear in its pure form. Middle and intermediate strata even here obliterate lines of demarcation everywhere" (MECW 37: 870).

4 "Economic conditions had first transformed the mass of the people of the country into workers. The domination of capital has created for this mass a common situation, common interests. This mass is thus already a class as against capital, but not yet for itself. In the struggle … this mass becomes united, and constitutes itself as a class for itself. The interests it defends become class interests" (MECW 6: 211).

5 Marx and Engels's famous injunction at the conclusion of the Communist Manifesto might be seen in this light: "The proletarians have nothing to lose but their chains. They have a world to win. Working men of all countries, unite!" (MECW 6: 519).

6 See Gilens and Page (2014).

7 "The time just before the repeal of the Corn Laws threw new light on the condition of the agricultural labourers. On the one hand, it was to the interest of the middle-class agitators to prove how little the Corn Laws protected the actual

producers of the corn. On the other hand, the industrial bourgeoisie foamed with sullen rage at the denunciations of the factory system by the landed aristocracy, at the pretended sympathy with the woes of the factory operatives, of those utterly corrupt, heartless, and genteel loafers, and at their 'diplomatic zeal' for factory legislation. It is an old English proverb that 'when thieves fall out, honest men come by their own,' and, in fact, the noisy, passionate quarrel between the two fractions of the ruling class about the question, which of the two exploited the labourers the more shamefully, was on each hand the midwife of the truth" (MECW 35: 667).

8 Marx is not wholly consistent on this point, however, since at other times he treats the passage of this Bill as a major achievement of the labor movement in contrast to the wishes of the capitalists: "the Ten Hours' Bill was not only a great practical success; it was the victory of a principle; it was the first time that in broad daylight the political economy of the middle class succumbed to the political economy of the working class" (MECW 20: 11).

9 Consider, for instance, the following three representative claims from across the Marxist spectrum. First, Elster (1986 143): "The state is an independent actor in the social arena and ... the interests of the capitalist class serve as constraints rather than goals for its actions ... Marx held a narrow, prestrategic conception of power that prevented him from recognizing that the states he observed had autonomy in a real sense and not only as a fief from the capitalist class." Second, Miliband (1983: 58): "A distinction had to be made between the state autonomously acting on behalf of the ruling class, and its acting at the behest of that class ... What I was rejecting there was the crude view of the state as a mere 'instrument' of the ruling class obediently acting at its dictation." Third, Poulantzas on what he calls the "relative autonomy" of the state:

> The state is not a class instrument ... the capitalist state's particular characteristic feature of representing the general interest of a national-popular ensemble is not simply a mendacious mystification, because within these limits it can effectively satisfy some of the economic interests of certain dominated classes. Furthermore, it can do this without however allowing its political power to be affected.
>
> (1978: 191–192)

10 Miliband (1983: 63): "Thousands of people in the upper reaches of the state are involved, whom the state provides with high salaries and all that goes with state service at this level, not only in government departments, but also in innumerable boards, commissions, councils and other public bodies. Such people constitute a 'state bourgeoisie', linked to but separate from those who are in charge of corporate capitalist enterprise. Their first concern is naturally with their jobs

and careers. Capitalist interests are in no danger of being overlooked; but they are not the sole or primary concern of these office holders."

11 Elster (1986: 153): "A state that can consistently impose policies very different from what capitalists would prefer and promote interests very different from theirs is a paradigm of autonomy. It does not become less so by the fact that the capitalist class may prefer this state over any feasible alternative."

12 Block (1977: 9): "[I]nstrumentalism fails to recognize that to act in the general interest of capital, the state must be able to take actions against the particular interests of capitalists. Price controls or restrictions on the export of capital, for example, might be in the general interest of capital in a particular period, even if they temporarily reduced the profits of most capitalists. To carry through such policies, the state must have more autonomy from direct capitalist control than the instrumentalist view would allow."

13 Elster (1986: 151): "To go into politics is like a costly investment that bears fruit only after some time while requiring outlays in the present. If one's interests are reasonably well respected in the present, the prospect of a future in which they might be even better respected need not be very attractive, considering the costs of transition."

14 This result echoes findings by Larry Bartels (see especially, 2016).

15 Status quo bias is a psychological tendency to prefer maintaining the current state of affairs over making a change. This bias can manifest in various contexts, such as decision-making, where individuals may opt for familiar options even if better alternatives exist. The preference for the status quo can lead to suboptimal choices and hinder progress or adaptation; but it can also serve as a protective mechanism against moving to worse alternatives, as in the case above. We will return to a detailed discussion of this phenomenon with respect to ideology in Chapter 5.

16 Majoritarian theories, whether of the electoral-democratic or pluralist-interest group variety, focus on how the majority's will is translated into public policy, but they differ in mechanisms and inclusivity. In electoral-democratic theories, the emphasis is on the role of elections, where representatives are voted into office to enact the majority's will; the assumption is that elected officials will generally reflect public opinion. Pluralist-interest group theories, on the other hand, argue that public policy is shaped by a multitude of competing interest groups, suggesting that even minority groups can have significant influence through lobbying, advocacy, and negotiation.

17 See Schakel (2021) for a study that largely replicates Gilens's findings in the Netherlands.

18 See Choma (2014).

19 This general thesis is exemplified in the two enormously influential works on public opinion that bookend the 20th century. Walter Lippmann's *Public Opinion*

(1922) argued that the average citizen has neither the time, interest, nor expertise to inform themselves of the details of the social and political issues affecting them, and so depend on a class of specialists (political elites, the media, etc.) who present the issues they deem relevant in a manner that is easy to comprehend and react to—reducing complex issues to yes-or-no positions, or translating them into symbol-laden principles. Consequently, elites have a nearly unlimited ability for what Lippmann termed "the manufacture of consent"—the ability to direct public opinion by deciding which information to present, and in which light to present it. Concurring, John Zaller, in his study *The Nature and Origins of Mass Opinion* (1992: 311), concludes that most citizens "pay too little attention to public affairs to be able to respond critically to the political communications they encounter; rather, they are blown about by whatever current of information manages to develop the greatest intensity. The minority of citizens who are highly attentive to public affairs are scarcely more critical: they respond to new issues mainly on the basis of the partisanship and ideology of the elite sources of the messages."

20 The proletariat labors under brutal conditions producing the abundance enjoyed by a small minority without having any share of it themselves: it is a class that "has to bear all the burdens of society without enjoying its advantages … a class which forms the majority of all members of society, and from which emanates the consciousness of the necessity of a fundamental revolution" (MECW 5: 52).

21 "The mass of workers … cut off from capital or from even a limited satisfaction [of their needs] … their utterly precarious position … presupposes the world market" (MECW 5: 49).

22 The problem with Marx's prediction continues into the 20th century. We return to the topic in detail in Chapter 4, Section 7.

23 Elster, for example, notes that "Marx argued that this is the central problem in understanding social change." He adds, "in the light of the persisting importance of religious, ethnic, nationalistic, and linguistic social movements … the centrality of class struggle in social change cannot be defended as a general proposition" (1986: 123).

24 See, e.g., Marx and Engels's discussion of the plight of sex workers in *The Holy Family* (MECW 4: 168–176); Marx's discussion of the familial oppression of upper-class women in "Peuchet: On Suicide" (MECW 4: 597–612); Engels's extended discussion of modern female servitude throughout *The Origin of the Family, Private Property and the State* (MECW 26: 129–276); and Marx's remarks on the degradation of slavery in the American South in his "Letter to Abraham Lincoln" (MECW 20: 19–21), his enthusiastic support for slave uprisings in an 1861 letter to Engels (MECW 41: 4), as well as his documentation of British cruelty and his support for an Indian uprising in his 1857 *New York Tribune* article "Investigation of Tortures in India" (MECW: 336–341).

25 See the more extended discussion in Chapter 6.

26 Marx takes a more measured attitude towards work elsewhere in his writings. For example, in the third volume of *Capital* he says that work "remains a realm of necessity. Beyond it begins that development of human energy which is an end in itself, the true realm of freedom, which, however, can blossom forth only with this realm of necessity as its basis" (MECW 37: 807).

27 Cohen (2000) drew the conclusion that environmental limitations were fatal to Marx's predictions about capitalism, and thus recommended turning to moral critique of capitalism instead. Some recent writers have argued that Marx was, in fact, prescient about these issues. Saito (2016) is a useful article-length representative of this so-called "eco-Marxism." Saito shows, persuasively, that in his notebooks and letters Marx was alert (starting in the late 1860s) to sustainability problems for capitalist production posed by deforestation, soil depletion, and 19th-century analogues of factory farming starting, although he never developed these issues systematically before he died in 1883. There is no evidence, of course, that he understood the problems posed by climate change for the level of productivity necessary to free people from wage slavery.

28 See, e.g., https://www.nytimes.com/interactive/2023/09/18/opinion/human-population-global-growth.html?smid=nytcore-ios-share&referringSource=articleShare.

29 Terrell Carver (2008) notes that this passage may not have been taken seriously by Marx.

30 See the more extended discussion in Chapter 6.

31 As we noted earlier, and discuss further in Chapter 6, Marx recognized the progress represented by the legal recognition of individual rights (e.g., freedom of expression) in the late 18th century, even if he thought it was only an incomplete liberation.

32 Deng, Mao's successor in China in the late 1970s, introduced capitalist reforms that produced massive economic growth—as Marx would have predicted—but China retained an authoritarian government. Unlike ideologists of capitalism like Milton Friedman, Marx never suggested that a politically free society had any relationship to capitalist relations of production, and contemporary China is a striking example of the point, as was Chile under the dictator Pinochet, the alliance between the capitalist class and Hitler in the 1930s, or the "soft" authoritarianism of Singapore.

Further Reading

Draper (1977–1990) is a five-volume survey of Marx's ideas about classes, the state, and revolution. See, especially, volume III (1986).

Elster (1986), Chapters 7 and 8, provides a helpful overview and characteristically critical discussion of Marx's writings on class and politics.

Gilens (2012) is a sobering work of political science detailing the relationship between economic status and political influence.

Miliband (1977) is an accessible overview of Marx's political writings and of many of the subsequent debates these inspired within the Marxist tradition.

Miller (1984) provides, among other things, a philosophically sophisticated exploration of the idea of a "ruling class" informed by then contemporary debates in political science.

4
Marx's Economics and the Collapse of Capitalism

1. Introduction

Marx devoted much of his later work (from the *Grundrisse* in the 1850s to the uncompleted three-volume *Capital* of the 1860s and after[1]) to developing an economic analysis of capitalism, one that complements but is independent of the historical materialism that we discussed in Chapter 2. The centerpiece of this economics is his version of a "labor theory of value": crudely, the idea that the value (and, ultimately, price) of a product depends on the amount of labor time required to produce it—an idea that prior economic theorists like Adam Smith (1723–1790) and David Ricardo (1772–1823) had also suggested (Smith) and developed (Ricardo). Marx's labor theory of value and the analysis of capitalism that depends on it have come in for withering criticism (Elster 1986: 60–78 is representative[2]), not all of it fair. More recently, however, it has attracted revisionist defenders, who often understand the economic theory differently (e.g., Heinrich 2012).[3]

We shall hue to a traditional understanding of Marxian economics, articulated and defended by the major American Marxist economist Paul Sweezy (1970 [originally published 1942]). We shall argue in particular that, while Marx's version of a labor theory of value has serious problems when understood as a theory of price, in fact many of his economic insights into how capitalism operates, and why communism would be an appropriate solution to its problems, remain intact. Moreover, the core ideas of historical

DOI: 10.4324/9781315658902-4

materialism (discussed in Chapter 2) are not affected at all by any deficiencies of the labor theory of value.

One can think, somewhat crudely, of the labor theory of value as addressing two questions that would occur naturally to anyone familiar with a modern economy. The first has to do with the dramatically different prices at which items are available for purchase: why, for example, does a dress cost several times more than the cloth from which it is made? An intuitive answer would seem to appeal to the fact that the labor that went into turning the cloth into the dress has increased its value, thus explaining (in some sense) the higher price. The second puzzle has to do with how it is that, in the economic system as a whole, any capitalist comes out ahead, in the sense of making a profit. As Sweezy puts the problem (1970: 60):

> If everyone were to attempt to reap a profit by raising his price, let us say by 10 per cent, what each gained as a seller he would lose as a buyer, and the only result would be higher prices all around from which no one would benefit.[4]

Where, in short, does the "surplus" come from if there are "competitive markets, where each factor [in the productive process] is paid its true 'value', and no one makes a windfall profit by cheating his partner in exchange" (Roemer 1990: 257)?

Once again, an intuitive solution to the puzzle starts with the idea that labor adds to the value of the commodities produced. More precisely (and in a sense to be explained in more detail below), if the work done on the cloth that turns it into a dress increases the value of the dress, a profit could be made if the capitalist (the owner of the dress factory) did not pay the workers for all the value they added to the dress through their labor on it. As we will see, this simple idea plays a large role in Marx's analysis of capitalism. First, however, we must begin with some background that was important to Marx.

2. The Origins of the Labor Theory of Value in Smith and Ricardo

Adam Smith, a major figure in the Scottish Enlightenment of the 18th century, made significant contributions to both moral and political philosophy and to economics, essentially establishing the latter discipline in its "classical" form.[5] In his famous work of 1776, *An Inquiry into the Nature and Causes of the Wealth of Nations*, Smith identified the annual labor of every nation as:

> the fund which originally supplies it with all the necessaries and conveniences of life which it annually consumes, and which consist always, either in the immediate produce of that labour, or in what is purchased with that produce from other nations.
>
> (Smith 1976: 10)

Smith distinguished three primary economic classes: workers (those who live off of wages); entrepreneurs (or capitalists) who produce wealth through their utilization of land, tools, machines, and workers, and who then sell the goods produced in the marketplace and live off the profits; and, finally, those who own land (the gentry, the aristocrats), who make their money from renting out their lands, and who are mostly an impediment to economic growth on his view.

Entrepreneurs are the real engines for the growth of the wealth of nations on Smith's account, so he wants to understand, in particular, how the commodities they produce are exchanged in the marketplace. In an important passage in *The Wealth of Nations*, Smith writes:

> The word VALUE, it is to be observed, has two different meanings, and sometimes expresses the utility of some particular object, and sometimes the power of purchasing other goods which the possession of that object conveys. The one may be called "value in use" and the other "value in exchange." The things which have the greatest value in use have frequently little or no value in exchange; and, on the contrary, those which have the greatest value in exchange have frequently little or no value in use. Nothing is more useful than water: but it will purchase scarce anything; scarce anything can be had in exchange for it. A diamond, on the contrary, has scarce any value in use; but a very great quantity of other goods may frequently be had in exchange for it.
>
> (Smith 1976: 44–45)

Smith then distinguishes the "natural" price or value of a commodity from its "market" price. The former is the "centre of repose … to which the prices of all commodities are continually gravitating"

(Smith 1976: 75)—that is, around which market prices revolve. As one scholar puts it: "natural price is simply the price to which a commodity will fall where a free market in that commodity operates over any considerable time. Today we would call it the 'equilibrium price'" (Fleischacker 2021: 270). The "market price," by contrast, will vary with supply and demand: if few diamonds are being mined and demand for them is high, then the market price of diamonds will rise; if diamonds flood the market, the market price will fall. But, in a perfectly competitive market, the natural price will tend to prevail: enough diamonds will be mined by producers to meet consumer demand for them.

So what then determines the natural price? In Chapter 6 of Book I of *The Wealth of Nations*, Smith suggests the natural price, at least in a very primitive economy, is determined by the labor that went into the production of the commodity. In his famous example, if it takes two hours to hunt a beaver and one hour to hunt a deer, then the natural value of one beaver is two deer (Smith 1976: 65). Why, however, should the market price gravitate towards the natural price so determined? Smith's idea is that if beaver hunters cannot get two deer for their beavers, then they will switch to hunting deer; and if deer hunters have to deliver three deer to get a beaver, they will switch to hunting beavers. As long as hunters can easily switch their trade, the market price will tend to gravitate towards the natural price.

One immediate problem with trying to apply this explanation to modern economies is that changing trades is not so simple. A manufacturer of microchips for computers cannot just start making automobiles tomorrow, and vice versa. So, too, a plumber cannot just become an electrician, or a chemist a lawyer. Given that, why think the market price (affected by supply and demand) will gravitate towards the natural price? Yet there is a further difficulty for the labor theory of natural value: namely, that the work of the deer hunter and the work of the beaver hunter are both made possible by the labor of others. Someone labored to produce the bow and arrow or the beaver trap; someone else labored to produce the clothes the hunter wears in the woods, and so on. How is that supposed to affect the natural value of the resulting commodity? Smith did not attempt to solve these problems.[6]

The British political economist David Ricardo, in his 1817 *On the Principles of Political Economy and Taxation*, presents a solution to the latter problem: "Not only the labour applied immediately to commodities affects their value, but the labour also which is bestowed on the implements, tools, and buildings, with which such labour is assisted" (Ricardo 2004 [1817]: 22). Returning to Smith's example of the two hunters, Ricardo observes:

> Suppose the weapon necessary to kill the beaver, was construed with much more labour than that necessary to kill the deer … [O]ne beaver [then] would naturally be of more value than two deer, and precisely for this reason, that more labour would, on the whole, be necessary to its destruction [i.e., killing of the beaver]. Or suppose that the same quantity of labour was necessary to make both weapons, but that they were of very unequal durability; of the durable implement only a small portion of its value would be transferred to the commodity, a much greater portion of the value of the less durable implement would be realized in the commodity which it contributed to produce.
>
> (Ricardo 2004 [1817]: 23)

The first example is clear enough: if beaver traps require more labor to produce than the bow and arrow used by the deer hunter, then that should be reflected in the natural price of beavers compared to deer (in addition, of course, to the greater amount of time required to hunt beavers than deer). So, let us say it takes four hours of labor to produce a beaver trap but only two hours to produce the bow and arrow. If, then, per Smith's example, it takes two hours to hunt a beaver and one to hunt a deer, then it seems the natural value of a beaver should be *two times* that of a deer.

Ricardo's second example, however, shows why the latter conclusion would be incorrect, for the tools used by the hunter may last different amounts of time: each arrow used by the deer hunter is good only once—so the labor that went into making an individual arrow is utilized all at once. But the bow itself may have a longer life, perhaps longer than that of the beaver trap, which presumably can be used more than once but may wear out after ten or fifteen kills.

(One suspects the bow might last through dozens of kills.) So, the indirect contribution of the labor that went into the tools ("weapons") used by the hunters will have to be apportioned to the resulting commodity (the beaver or the deer) depending on how long those tools last. Ricardo grappled with the mathematical difficulties this analysis presents, but the details need not concern us here (see Wolff 1984: 46–74 for a discussion).

3. Marx's Labor Theory of Value

In volume I of *Capital*, Marx takes over the distinction between use-value and exchange-value from the classical economic tradition initiated by Smith and continued by Ricardo.[7] A thing "that by its properties satisfies human wants of some sort or another" is a thing with a "use-value" (MECW 35: 45, 46), as Marx puts it—that is, something that has "utility" for people. Water satisfies our thirst, bread our hunger; a dress, our desire to be clothed; a pretty dress, our desire to be clothed and look attractive to others; a car, our desire for efficient transport; a "fancy" car, our desire for efficient transport *and* to impress others, and so on. Marx effectively agrees with Smith that "material wealth" consists in a large "quantity of use-values" (MECW 35: 56).

That something is useful for some person does not yet make it a "commodity," a crucial term of art for Marx. A person who sews cloth into a dress at home in order to wear it has not yet produced a commodity. A commodity is an item that is produced in order to be *exchanged* to someone else for whom it is a use-value (MECW 35: 51). The dressmaker who turns cloth into a dress and then exchanges the dress for three pounds of venison (deer meat) has produced a commodity; the deer hunter has done the same. Note that the existence of commodities entails the existence of a "division of labor" [8]: some produce dresses from cloth, some hunt deer and produce venison. (It is more than that, of course, as we learned from Ricardo: some produce cloth for dressmakers; some may be producing tools for deer hunting or processing deer meat into saleable venison, and so on.)

The "exchange-value" of commodities is "the proportion in which values in use of one sort are exchanged for those of another sort" (MECW 35: 46). One dress gets the maker three pounds of venison: that is the exchange-value of the dress measured in pounds of venison. But why is one dress "worth" three pounds of venison? As Marx puts it: "there exists in equal quantities something common to both ... Each of them, so far as it is exchange-value, must therefore be reducible to this third" (MECW 35: 47). In other words, we can only explain this exchange ratio in terms of the fact that the proportions of exchange represent something of *comparable* value: "the exchange-values of commodities must be capable of being expressed in terms of something common to them all, of which thing they represent a greater or less quantity" (MECW 35: 47). That something will be for Marx, as for Smith and Ricardo before him, labor. More precisely, Marx refers to "Value" as "the common substance that manifests itself in the exchange-value of commodities, whenever they are exchanged," and says that "the magnitude of this value" is determined by "the quantity of the value-creating substance, the labor" (MECW 35: 48).

Non-Marxian economics need not disagree with Marx's basic supposition: something should explain why one dress garners three pounds of venison rather than one pound or twenty pounds. In the 1870s, and unknown to Marx, there emerged the foundations of what became known as "neoclassical" economics, which explained the prices of commodities not in terms of their utility, *simpliciter*, but instead by their "marginal utility"—that is, how much they add to the utility or happiness of particular consumers, and thus influence what they are willing to pay for them. Water is *very* useful (high utility), but generally easily available; wine is less easily available, but still useful. The marginal utility of one glass of wine (at least for someone who enjoys wine) is greater than the marginal utility of one glass of water (since wine is harder to acquire and water is plentiful), which is why wine costs more than water (at least when water is readily available).

So the neoclassical economist says that what explains the exchange ratio is the marginal utility of dresses and venison for consumers, subject to the pressures of supply and demand: labor inputs, in other words, are not the sole determinant of price.[9] Marx, however, claims that "the exchange of commodities is evidently an act characterized by a total abstraction from use-value" (MECW 35: 47). Marx, of course, is not thinking of marginal utility, but utility, *simpliciter*, and his claim is that it is not relevant to understanding the ratios at which commodities are exchanged (e.g., one dress for three pounds of venison). If we disregard the use-values of commodities, then there is only one thing they have left in common, as Marx observes: namely, "being products of labor"—that is, of "human labor in the abstract" that is abstracted away from the particular kind of labor involved (e.g., sewing or hunting).[10] Each commodity embodies "a mere congelation of homogeneous human labour, of labour power expended without regard to the mode of its expenditure" (MECW 35: 48); this is, in Marx's terminology, "their Value". So, the exchange-value of commodities is to be explained by the abstract labor each commodity represents. Marx writes:

> [T]he coat is worth twice as much as the ten yards of linen. Whence this difference in their values? It is owing to the fact that the linen contains only half as much labor as the coat, and consequently, that in the production of the latter, labor power must have been expended during twice the time necessary for the production of the former.
>
> (MECW 35: 55)

This simple idea from volume I of *Capital* requires several immediate clarifications and qualifications in order to forestall misunderstandings.

First, the value of a commodity is determined by the (abstract) labor time "socially necessary ... to produce an article under the normal conditions of production, and with the average degree of skill and intensity prevalent at the time" (MECW 35: 49). Obviously different workers are more or less efficient, more or less talented; different workplaces (factories, offices, etc.) are also more or less efficient, and so on. According to the labor theory of value, the exchange-values reflect the "socially necessary" labor time—that is, the amount of time needed to produce the commodity "under the normal conditions of production, and with the average degree of skill and intensity prevalent at the time." That means, of course, that, as the "normal conditions of production" and "average degree of skill and intensity" change over time (for example, with technological advances), the exchange-values of commodities will change.

Second, and very importantly, the exchange-value of a commodity is not equivalent to its market price (e.g., the price in a store for the commodity).[11] Smith recognized this with his distinction between "natural" and "market" price; and so does Marx, although he does not use Smith's terminology. Marx understood that "market" prices reflect "supply and demand," which we will discuss momentarily. Marx did devote large sections of volume III of *Capital* (which he himself never completed) to the "transformation problem"—the problem of how exchange-values (reflecting socially necessary labor time) are transformed into what he called "production" prices, a term of art for Marx: the production price is the price of a commodity given the costs of production (raw materials, technology, and labor), and assuming some rate of profit for the capitalist. Like Ricardo, Marx recognized that one had to account for the indirect labor contributions to the production of a commodity; he also recognized that industries differed in the skills and technologies required (ours is not a world in which most workers—unlike Smith's beaver hunters and deer hunters—can switch jobs relatively easily).

A technical literature has arisen in subsequent Marxist economics trying to solve this problem.[12] The technical details do not matter for our purposes, although readers should note that the consensus view among Marxist economists is that there is no solution to Marx's transformation problem (i.e., the labor theory of value fails). We can agree with Sweezy that if what we want to understand is only "the behavior of the disparate elements of the economic system (prices of individual commodities, profits of particular capitalists, the combination of productive factors in the individual firm, etc.)," then neoclassical "price theory [marginal utility theory] … is more useful in this sphere than anything to be found in Marx or his followers" (1970: 129). We may, in short, adjudge the Marxian attempt to solve the "transformation problem" a failure: the labor theory of value cannot explain the production prices of commodities. How much this really matters for Marx's other theoretical purposes is a topic to which we return below: in fact, we will argue, Marx's most important claims about capitalism survive.

Third, contrary to many critics, Marx is fully aware of the role of "supply and demand" in setting *market* prices (as opposed to production prices); indeed, it is important to his own account of what Smith would have called the "market price." Marx even adopts Smith's metaphor of the value (the "natural price") of a commodity as the "centre of gravitation" (Smith 1976: 75) around which the market prices revolve:

> The assumption that the commodities of the various spheres of production are sold at their value merely implies, of course, that their value is the centre of gravity around which their prices fluctuate, and their continual rises and drops tend to equalise.
>
> (MECW 37: 176–177)

This is what Marx calls "the law of value," which, as Sweezy observes, "is essentially a theory of general equilibrium" (1970: 53): in a well-functioning marketplace, commodity prices gravitate towards their values—i.e., the socially necessary labor time to produce them. Marx writes in volume III of *Capital*:

> Since [individual capitalist producers] confront one another only as commodity owners, and everyone seeks to sell his commodity as dearly as possible ... the inner law [of value] enforces itself only through their competition, their mutual pressure upon each other ... Only as an inner law, vis-à-vis the individual agents, as a blind law of Nature, does the law of value exert its influence here and maintain the social equilibrium of production amidst its accidental fluctuations.
>
> (MECW 37: 866–867)

Recall that Smith assumed that his beaver hunters and deer hunters could simply change occupations if, in fact, the exchange value of beavers and deer changed in a way not commensurate with the labor necessary to catch them. That assumption, as we noted earlier, is implausible in a modern economy with higher degrees of worker specialization and investment in commodity-specific technologies. Since Marx understood that, what could explain why the "law of value" holds—i.e., that prices gravitate around their true value as determined by the socially necessary labor to produce them?

In a now famous letter of July 11, 1868, Marx wrote to his German friend and supporter Ludwig Kugelmann:

Every child knows that any nation that stopped working, not for a year, but let us say, just for a few weeks, would perish. And every child knows, too, that the amounts of products corresponding to the differing amounts of needs demand differing and quantitatively determined amounts of society's aggregate labour. It is self-evident that this *necessity* of the *distribution* of social labour in specific proportions is certainly not abolished by the *specific form* of social production; it can only change *its form of manifestation*. Natural laws cannot be abolished at all. The only thing that can change, under historically differing conditions, is the form in which those laws assert themselves. And the form in which this proportional distribution of labour asserts itself in a state of society in which the interconnection of social labour expresses itself as the *private exchange* of the individual products of labour, is precisely the *exchange value* of these products.

(MECW 43: 68)

Every society needs to produce what is necessary for its continued survival. This requires an allocation of the labor power in that society to produce the various things that are needed, i.e., the "*distribution* of social labor in specific proportions." Some will grow wheat, others corn; others will raise cattle and sheep; still others will produce dresses, others cars, and so on. So-called "command" economies (e.g., the economy of the Soviet Union under Stalin) involve centralized power dictating what will be produced, in what quantities, and often who will be enlisted in its production. Yet feudal economics also allocated "social labor in specific proportions," with feudal lords playing the primary role in determining the allocations and proportions.

Crucially—and this is Marx's point—capitalist societies are no different: they too require a "*distribution* of social labor in specific proportions"; but there is neither a feudal lord nor a Stalin to make those decisions. In capitalist societies, it is precisely the exchange of commodities in the marketplace that performs this function: the ratio at which commodities exchange is what determines the "proportional distribution of labor." Put differently, and in a lingo more familiar to contemporary economics, the ratio at which commodities exchange is a signal to capitalists about the demand for those commodities, and thus a signal about whether to invest more or less in their production (including, of course, hiring workers to produce them).[13] While this would contribute to explaining the social distribution of labor in a society, it would not explain why the value of commodities is a matter of the socially necessary labor time as opposed to their marginal utility.

Importantly for Marx, "demand" is not an independent variable in this explanation:

> [T]he "social need" [gesellschaftliche Bedürfnis] ... which regulates the principle of demand, is essentially subject to the mutual relationship of the different classes and their respective economic position ... [A]bsolutely nothing can be explained by the relation of demand and supply before ascertaining the basis on which this relation rests.
>
> (MECW 37: 180, translation slightly modified)

Marx elaborates on this point a few pages later, attacking as "mere illusion" the idea that demand (whether by consumers for goods or capitalist producers for raw materials and technology) somehow functions as a force independent of the existing relations of production:

> If the means of subsistence were cheaper, or money wages higher, the labourers would buy more of [the commodities they want or need], and a greater "social need" would arise for them, leaving aside the paupers, etc., whose "demand" is even below the narrowest limits of their physical wants. On the other hand, if cotton were cheaper, for example, the capitalists' demand for it would increase, more additional capital would be thrown into the cotton industry, etc.
>
> (MECW 37: 187)

Suppose factory workers consume a certain amount of leisure commodities (e.g., televisions, movies, dining out at restaurants), but their "demand" for those particular commodities is limited by their wages: a worker who earned 25 percent more than he presently does might buy a better-quality television, or dine out once a week rather than once every two weeks, and so on. Higher wages would change the demand for commodities. Suppose the factory owner was forced, by competition, to pay 25 percent higher wages to the workers; this would cut into the owner's profits, and thus not only his own demand for, say, luxury commodities (e.g., diamonds, boats, fancy cars) but also the factory's demand for more raw materials for increased production, as well as for more workers, who are now a more expensive commodity. (Labor power is itself a commodity under capitalism, a point to which we will return shortly.)

"Demand," in short, is not an independent force at work in the capitalist economy, but is itself determined by the existing class structure of the society, i.e., the existing relations of production. This is an important point about Marx's idea of exchange-value: exchange-values mediate social relations between people. As Sweezy observes: "The exchange relation as such, apart from any consideration of the quantities involved, is an expression of the fact that individual producers, each working in isolation, are in fact working for each other" (1970: 27).[14] Recall the dressmaker and the deer hunter. Although they may never meet, they are, in effect, working for each other insofar as the deer hunter wants dresses and the dressmaker wants venison. That exchange-values, in fact, conceal the social relations between different producers is a central part of what Marx calls the "fetishism of commodities," a concept we return to in Section 6.

4. Where Does Profit Come From?

Recall Sweezy's observation about the mystery of profit in an economy (1970: 60):

> If everyone were to attempt to reap a profit by raising his price, let us say by 10 per cent, what each gained as a seller he would lose as a buyer, and the only result would be higher prices all around from which no one would benefit.

Even if Marx's labor theory of value cannot explain production prices ("the transformation problem," discussed in Section 3), perhaps it offers an explanation responsive to the puzzle posed by the existence of profit.

Marx thinks it does, and he prefaces his explanation in a famous passage in *Capital*, one intentionally evocative of Dante's account of his visit to Hell in the *Inferno*:[15]

> Accompanied by Mr. Moneybags [i.e., the capitalist] and by the possessor of labour power [i.e., the worker], we therefore take leave for a time of this noisy sphere [the marketplace, where the capitalist purchases the labor power], where everything takes place on the surface and in view of all men, and follow them both into the hidden abode of production, on whose threshold there stares us in the face "No admittance except on business". Here we shall see, not only how capital produces, but how capital is produced. We shall at last force the secret of profit making.
> (MECW 35: 186)

The gates of Hell, in Dante's rendering, are inscribed with the sign "Abandon all hope, ye who enter here," which is for Marx an apt metaphor for the 19th-century factory. As Marx puts it, the worker entering "the abode of production" proceeds "like one who is bringing his own hide to market and has nothing to expect but—a hiding" (MECW 35: 186).[16]

Let us now turn to the details of the "secret." Imagine, as Marx does in *Capital* I, a simple economy in which a person who sews cloth into a dress in order to sell it for food (e.g., venison) produces something (the dress) that is a use-value for another person (the deer hunter) and exchanges it in turn for something (the venison) that is a use-value for them. Capitalism changes this kind of simple "barter": some people (capitalists, e.g., factory owners) produce things not simply to acquire other things of use, but in order to acquire profits. Here we need to introduce the idea of money, whose chief function, Marx says, is "to supply commodities with the material for the expression of their values, or to represent their values as magnitudes of the same denomination, qualitatively equal, and quantitatively comparable. It thus serves as a *universal measure of value*"—thus making possible the circulation of commodities without barter (MECW 35: 104). Money, Marx says, "is the first form in which *capital* appears" (MECW 35: 157, emphasis added).[17] This requires further explication before we return to the question of where profit comes from.

Marx observes that there are two kinds of "circulation of commodities". One he calls "C–M–C", or "selling in order to buy" (MECW 35: 158), where C stands for a commodity and M for money. In this kind of commodity circulation, "the money is in the end converted into a commodity, that serves as a use-value; it is spent once for all" (MECW 35: 159). Even under capitalism, this is the kind of transaction most people engage in: someone sells their labor power for money and uses the money to buy the things that they and their family need or want.

Under capitalism, however, there is a very different way in which commodities circulate, what Marx calls "M–C–M'" or "buying in order to sell" (MECW 35: 158): here someone buys a commodity not because it has a use-value for them, but because they can sell it and get even more money for it. *This exchange is distinctive of capitalism, and constitutes its "leading motive, and the goal that attracts it, [i.e.,] mere exchange-value"* (MECW 35: 160, emphasis added). The capitalist expends money to buy various commodities (raw materials, machines, labor power) not because the capitalist wants to enjoy them himself, but because he can generate *more money* from them[18] (M' in Marx's notation): the real exchange is M–C–M'. This is the crucial aspect of the exchange: the goal is not just to get money back, but to get "the original sum advanced, plus an increment" (MECW 35: 161), i.e., the profit.[19] Capitalists seek capital—i.e., money that they can put into circulation in order to acquire more money, and thus begin the cycle of exchange anew. The peculiar feature of capitalism is that "[t]he circulation of money as capital is … an end in itself … The circulation of capital has therefore no limits" (MECW 35: 163); it is a "restless[,] never-ending process of profit-making alone" which the capitalist "aims at" (MECW 35: 164). (This is one of many of Marx's insights that remain true independent of the labor theory of value.)

And now we return to the question of profit, the M'. What is, as Marx puts it, "the secret of profit making" (MECW 35: 186)? The capitalist is someone who is investing money (capital) in order to produce a commodity that he can then sell for a profit (i.e., for more money than he spent getting it produced). The capitalist has various costs that go into production: raw material, tools and machinery, and, importantly, human labor power. Following Ricardo, Marx realizes that each of these has a value that reflects the labor power required to produce them. With respect to the first two categories, Marx observes, the "labour contained in the raw material and the instruments of labour can be treated just as if it were labour expended in an earlier stage," and its value to the resulting commodity factored in accordingly (MECW 35: 198; cf. 188–190).[20]

Human labor power, however, is also a commodity that the capitalist purchases; and the labor that contributes to its availability as a commodity must also be factored into the costs for the capitalist. The value of the human labor power is determined by "the labour time necessary for the production, and consequently also the reproduction, of this special article" (MECW 35: 180–181). In other words, the worker—whose labor power is sold to the capitalist—needs food and shelter, so those are also costs that affect the value of this commodity (i.e., the labor power). "Reproduction," as Marx says, is at issue because the "owner of labour power is mortal," so the worker must be paid enough to enable him/her to produce more laborers for the capitalist (MECW 35: 181).

This is a variation on Ricardo's point about the durability of the tools used by the deer hunters and beaver hunters: if a beaver trap lasts longer than a bow, that must be factored into the indirect costs of the resulting commodity (the beaver or the deer). For the capitalist, the costs of the worker whose labor power is purchased includes not only the costs required to keep the worker alive and functional, but also the costs associated with the "durability" of the labor power: i.e., insuring that the worker has children who can then grow up to sell their labor power.[21] Of course, the commodity resulting from the worker's labor "is the property of the capitalist and not that of the laborer" (MECW 35: 195): that is the only way the capitalist can secure a profit from the exchange.

Where, however, does the "profit" come from in this circulation of commodities? Marx writes as follows (recall the capitalist is "Moneybags"):

> In order to be able to extract value from the consumption of a commodity, our friend, Moneybags, must be so lucky as to find, within the sphere of circulation, in the market, a commodity, whose use-value possesses the peculiar property of being a

source of value, whose actual consumption, therefore, is itself an embodiment of labour, and, consequently, a creation of value. (MECW 35: 177)

Labor power is a "use-value" for the capitalist: he buys it because it is useful for him. However, the commodity "human labor power" has an unusual attribute, namely, that it can create value: the factory workers who turn the cloth into a dress increase the value of the cloth substantially. And this, according to Marx, is the real secret of profit: *human labor is the one commodity whose consumption as "use-value" creates new value*. When someone eats the venison, its use-value is extinguished and nothing of value remains. Human labor is not like this: when the capitalist utilizes, say, twelve hours of human labor power, the labor power expended adds value to the material labored upon by turning it into a new commodity. The latter point follows, of course, from the labor theory of value, although it is not implausible independent of that theory: capitalists, after all, would not employ laborers if they did not add to the value of raw materials. (That latter observation, however, would not be adequate for Marx's purpose: Marx needs the labor theory of value to be true.)

How precisely does this latter fact about labor power's "use-value" explain profit? Remember that human labor also has an exchange-value determined by the amount of labor needed to produce it. Suppose, as in the example Marx uses, that "the means of subsistence that are daily required for the production of labour power, cost half a day's labour" (MECW 35: 203). Thus, six hours of work suffices for the exchange value of what is needed to keep the laborer sustained and reproducing. The capitalist, however, who has purchased the labor power of the worker, can require the worker to labor for twelve hours, six hours more than is needed to keep the worker alive and multiplying.[22] As Marx explains:

Therefore, the value of labour power, and the value which that labour power creates in the labour process, are two entirely different magnitudes; and this difference of the two values was what the capitalist had in view, when he was purchasing the labour power ... What really influenced him was the specific use-value which this commodity [labor power] possesses of being *a source not only of value, but of more value than it has itself* [i.e., the "surplus value"].... The seller of labour power, like the seller of any other commodity, realizes its exchange value, and parts with its use value. He cannot take the one without giving the other. The use value of labour power, or in other words, labour, belongs just as little to its seller, as the use value of oil after it has been sold belongs to the dealer who has sold it. The owner of the money has paid the value of a day's labour power; his, therefore, is the use of it for a day; a day's labour belongs to him. The circumstance, that on the one hand the daily sustenance of labour power costs only half a day's labour, while on the other hand the very same labour power can work during a whole day, that consequently the value which its use during one day creates, is double what he pays for that use, this circumstance is, without doubt, a piece of good luck for the buyer.

(MECW 35: 204)

"Surplus value" results from "nothing [more] but the continuation of [the process of producing value, i.e., laboring] beyond a definite point" (MECW 35: 205)—that is, the point at which the labor has already created enough exchange-value for its own sustenance. Because the capitalist pays the worker for only six hours (the exchange-value), all the additional value (the surplus value) created by the worker and embodied in the commodity now belongs to the capitalist and is the source of the capitalist's profit. Thus *the "secret" is now revealed: labor power is a commodity that, when consumed (by the capitalist), creates value, but the capitalist pays the laborer for only part of the value created.*

5. Exploitation, Justice, and Private Property

Marx refers to the value-creating work done beyond that needed for the worker's sustenance—value that is now owned by the capitalist (who owns and then sells the products of the worker's labor)—as the "exploitation" of the worker. Although the term "exploitation" has a negative valence[23]—which Marx, a skilled polemicist, certainly intended—it is fundamentally a technical notion for Marx: capitalists "exploit" workers in the sense that workers produce more value (according to the labor theory) than they are actually paid for. As the Marxist economist Sweezy correctly puts it: all commodities produced by a society are "the product of human labor." He continues:

> Under capitalist conditions, a part of this social output is appropriated by that group in the community which owns the means of production [i.e., the capitalists]. This is not an ethical judgment, but a method for describing the really basic economic relation between social groups.
>
> (Sweezy 1970: 129)

In short, owners of capital accrue most of their wealth only because of the work of those who only own their labor power: that is the basic fact of capitalist society, quite independent of the labor theory of value.

Marx remarks that exploitation involves "no injustice" [kein Unrecht] to the seller of labor power (MECW 35: 204),[24] by which we take him to mean the following: (1) conceptions of justice, as part of the ideological superstructure of a society,[25] exist only to legitimize the existing relations of production; and (2) unsurprisingly, under capitalism, it is perfectly in accord with the prevailing notions of justice for the capitalist to "exploit" the worker in the way Marx describes.[26] To be sure, Marx has different rhetorical moods about capitalist exploitation, sometimes also characterizing it as "theft" or "robbery" (but never calling it unjust).[27] The latter rhetoric has led some recent academic interpreters to think Marx must believe exploitation is unjust. G.A. Cohen, for example, writes:

> Marx did not think that by capitalist criteria the capitalist steals, and since he did think he steals, he must have meant that he steals in some appropriately non-relativist sense. And since to steal is, in general, wrongly to take what rightly belongs to another, to steal is to commit an injustice, and a system which is 'based on theft' is based on injustice. Did Marx, nevertheless, lack the belief that capitalism was unjust, because he failed to notice that robbery constitutes an injustice? I think the relationship between robbery and injustice is so close that anyone who thinks capitalism is robbery must be treated as someone who

thinks capitalism is unjust, even if he does not realize that he thinks it is.

(Cohen 1983: 443)[28]

Cohen's response makes two undefended assumptions. First, he assumes that Marx was using the language of robbery (or stealing) to make a cognitive judgment: that is, to describe some moral truth about exploitation.[29] There is another possibility, however, one consistent with Marx's polemical talents—namely, that he employs the language non-cognitively: that is, he is not describing any feature of the world, but rather expressing his opposition to capitalism and motivating his readers to feel the same through provocative and emotionally arousing language. To do the latter requires having no theory of justice.

Given Cohen's cognitivist interpretation, however, Marx could only be using the language of "robbery" if he had a theory of justice that would explain why exploitation was *really* robbery.[30] This seems especially implausible given that, as we discuss in more detail in Chapter 6, Marx had no interest in moral theories, including theories of justice, since he viewed such theories as practically useless: capitalism will not change because its basic economic relation is shown to be allegedly "unjust" by philosophers. Marx took it for granted that, to those working 12 hours per day, 6 days per week, it was obvious they were badly off.[31] No theory was required to explain that! Given Marx's lack of interest in moral theory, it seems more plausible to interpret his language in this context in non-cognitivist, rather than cognitivist, terms, and thus to reject the idea that here he has a *sotto voce* theory of justice. To be sure, using moralized language to describe "exploitation" is motivationally effective for those exploited; but that is compatible with the non-cognitivist interpretation of Marx's rhetoric.

Cohen, however, makes a second assumption: that, when Marx accuses capitalists of "stealing," he is making a non-relative judgment. That does not, however, follow from what Marx says. Exploitation is "theft" (and so, maybe, even "wrong") from the standpoint of a moral outlook that is in the interest of the vast majority—that is, the workers. On this reading, it is true that exploitation is wrong *relative to a particular morality*. "Morality" is often criticized by Marx as "ideological" (in the pejorative sense discussed at length in Chapter 5), in part because its moral prescriptions and proscriptions are presented as being generally binding, as not being in anyone's interests; yet, according to Marx, they are really only in the interest of one class—namely, the ruling (economic) class. The contrast, on this account, would be with a set of moral prescriptions and proscriptions that explicitly acknowledge that they represent the interests of a particular class. For example, Marx and Engels say in *The Communist Manifesto* that "the proletarian movement" simply pursues "the interest of the immense majority" (MECW 6: 495), and they deride the German "True" socialists for thinking that socialism reflects "the requirements of Truth; not the interests of the proletariat, but the interests of Human Nature, of Man in general, who belongs to no class, has no reality, who exists only in the misty realm of philosophical fantasy" (MECW 6: 511). On this alternative reading, in declaring exploitation "theft," Marx is not making a judgment that reflects "the requirements of the Truth," but rather one that is relative to "the interests of the proletariat." So exploitation is wrong *relative to the interests of the proletariat*, but it is not wrong *simpliciter* or objectively.[32]

The crucial point, however, remains that, for Marx, the *fundamental* problem with capitalism is not that it involves exploitation.[33] After all, every economic system in the history of the world has involved exploitation, so this objection would have no special force against capitalism: all economic systems involve appropriation of a "surplus" by some groups in society. More importantly, capitalist exploitation is what makes profit possible, and the pursuit of profit is precisely why capitalist relations of production are the most powerful engine for the development of technology and productive power, which is a necessary condition for communism.[34] As Marx and Engels write in *The Communist Manifesto*:

> The bourgeoisie [the capitalist class] cannot exist without constantly revolutionizing the instruments of production, and thereby the relations of production, and with them the whole relations of society … The bourgeoisie, during its rule of scarce

one hundred years, has created more massive and more colossal productive forces than have all preceding generations together. (MECW 6: 487, 489)

And exploitation, in Marx's technical sense, is essential to capitalism: the possibility of profit is what drives capitalists in endless pursuit of technological improvements to production. The problem with capitalism is that, at some point (Marx thought, wrongly, that it would happen imminently in the 19th century), capitalism generates enough productive power to meet all human needs (and thus render them "free" in the sense discussed in Chapter 3, Section 4C), yet fails to meet these needs because this productive power is hostage to the pursuit of profit by capitalists: capitalism becomes an obstacle, in short, to the well-being (including the freedom) of the vast majority.

We emphasize this point now since the technical account of "exploitation" can seem to depend on the particulars of the labor theory of value, whose problems we have already noted. If the source of profit, for example, were really the capitalist's ability to anticipate the marginal utility that will accrue to consumers from certain commodities—rather than only the labor needed to produce commodities—then Marx's technical notion of exploitation deriving from the labor theory of value falls apart.[35] Other senses of "exploitation," however, would remain intact, as suggested by Sweezy's formulation that we noted at the start of this section: all commodities produced by a society are "the product of human labor."

> Under capitalist conditions, a part of this social output is appropriated by that group in the community which owns the means of production [i.e., the capitalists]. This is not an ethical judgment, but a method for describing the really basic economic relation between social groups.
>
> (Sweezy 1970: 129)

Consider that the workers in the auto plant produce cars that sell for much more than the workers are paid: some of that "profit" goes to the "owners" of the factory who do little or no work at all. Indeed, it is a standing feature of capitalism, almost since its beginning, that most of its wealth goes to those who do not do any actual work, while those doing the actual work in the factories and warehouses and service industries are paid only a small portion of the wealth they generate. Jeff Bezos, the founder of Amazon, does not produce any of the daily value of Amazon by his own efforts; the heirs of the founder of the Walmart chain of retail stores in the United States do no work at all, but are "billionaires" because of the work done by employees of the chain of stores their father started. As Marx and Engels joke in The Communist Manifesto,

> It has been objected that upon the abolition of private property all work will cease, and universal laziness will overtake us. According to this, bourgeois [capitalist] society ought long ago to have gone to the dogs through sheer idleness; for those of its members who work, acquire nothing, and those who acquire anything, do not work.
>
> (MECW 6: 500)

The abolition of "private property" for Marx means the abolition of capital—i.e., the money whose entire purpose is to be exchanged for commodities (raw materials, labor power, technology) to produce more commodities that can be exchanged for more money (profit). As Marx and Engels put it:

> in your existing society, private property is already done away with for nine-tenths of the population; its existence for the few is solely due to its non-existence in the hands of those nine-tenths. You reproach us, therefore, with intending to do away with a form of property, the necessary condition for whose existence is the non-existence of any property for the immense majority of society.
>
> (MECW 6: 500)

This is due to exploitation of course. They continue: "Communism deprives no man of the power to appropriate the products of society; all that it does is to deprive him of the power to subjugate the labour of others by means of such appropriation" (MECW 6: 500). For Marx, ownership of one's home, one's clothes, one's furniture, one's books, and so on is compatible with the abolition of capitalism: what needs to be abolished is wealth that derives from the labor of others.[36]

Even if there is a recognizable sense of "exploitation" that is independent of the labor theory of value, it is not one that actually plays an important theoretical role in Marx's critique, even if its rhetorical effect remains important. We return to these issues in Section 7.

6. The Fetishism of Commodities

One of the most famous discussions in volume I of *Capital* concerns "the fetishism of commodities," an idea closely related to a point emphasized earlier (see Section 3): the ratios at which commodities exchange really reflect the way in which different people in society are working for each other, even though they never meet each other—except, as it were, through the exchange-value of the commodities they produce.[37]

"Fetishism" is a term of art for Marx, as it was for other philosophers at the time. To fetishize an entity means to invest it with inherent powers or attributes that it does not really have—indeed, the powers and attributes are entirely derivative from, or dependent upon, human beings.[38] The 19th century was the first time in history that many thinkers were openly atheistic, and the Judeo-Christian God was often held up as a prime example of fetishism in this sense (indeed, Marx got the basic idea of fetishism from Feuerbach, who applied it to God). This God, a non-existent being, is invested with idealized forms of human capacities (knowledge, benevolence, and love—as well as vengefulness!), which humans then imagine this fictional being wields over them. The Greek gods were no different in this regard, and even more obviously so: they were lustful, cruel, and desirous of glory and power—and they intervened in human affairs for all those reasons. As Marx, an astute student of Greek philosophy and culture, writes regarding fetishism in *Capital* I: "[T]he productions of the human brain appear as independent beings endowed with life, and entering into relation both with one another and the human race" (MECW 35: 83).

If supernatural beings, like the Judeo-Christian God, are paradigms of fetishized entities, then in what sense are commodities in the capitalist marketplace also fetishized? Marx's point is that commodities are experienced as having, beyond their physical property, a "value," with no recognition that this value derives from the labor of other human beings—indeed, without any realization that the exchangeability of different commodities in different ratios really conceals the way in which different people are working for each other. "[E]xchange value is a definite social manner of expressing the amount of labour bestowed upon an object," says Marx, rather than an independent property of the commodity (MECW 35: 93). A worker in a poultry factory saves up for a year, even works overtime, in order to buy a new car for his family. In fact, the worker in the poultry factory has just exchanged his own labor for the labor of all the workers in the auto factory (not to mention all the workers that supplied the raw materials to the auto factory). As Sweezy puts it: "The individual producer deals with his fellow men only through 'the market,' where prices and amounts are sold are the substantial realities and human beings merely their instruments" (1970: 36). Or, as Marx puts it in an important passage from *Capital* I:

> A commodity is … a mysterious thing, simply because in it the social character of men's labour appears to them as an objective character stamped upon the product of that labour; because the relation of the producers to the sum total of their own labour is presented to them as social relation, existing not between themselves, but between the products of their labour … [I]t is a definite social relation between men, that assumes, in their eyes, the fantastic form of a relation between things.
>
> (MECW 35: 82–83)

Under capitalism, people believe that value resides in products—this nice car, that pretty dress—not realizing that the value of the products derives from the labor of their fellow human beings, and that when they purchase a car or a dress they are simply exchanging their labor for that of others in society.

Fetishism of commodities is peculiar to capitalism. As Marx explains, even under feudalism, there is no fetishism of the products of labor,

> for the very reason that personal dependence [e.g., of serfs on lords] forms the groundwork of society, there is no necessity for

labour and its products to assume a fantastic form different from their reality. They take the shape, in the transactions of society, of services in kind and payments in kind … [E]very serf knows that what he expends in the service of his lord, is a definite quantity of his own personal labour power … [T]he social relations between individuals in the performance of their labor, appear at all events as their own mutual personal relations, and are not disguised under the shape of social relations between the products of labour [i.e., the exchange-value of commodities in the marketplace].

(MECW 35: 88)

Under capitalism, by contrast, when you enter the supermarket to purchase milk and poultry—paying for those commodities with the wages you earned in the auto factory—you do not encounter the farmer who produced the milk or the chicken, let alone the workers who processed and packaged those items, let alone the capitalists who profited from the work of the others. The social relations are relations between commodities, and the role that individuals have played in creating things of value is invisible.

7. The Self-Destruction of Capitalism

As we saw in Chapter 2, Marx took over from Hegel the idea that history had a teleological structure; but for Marx it was one determined by the development of productive power, rather than philosophical ideas. According to Marx, however, there was still a *materialist* analogue to the "contradictions" that Hegel claimed afflicted all earlier philosophical systems: namely, when a society's existing relations of production "fetter" the further development of the productive forces. Here is how Marx puts the point in volume I of *Capital*:

The monopoly of capital becomes a fetter upon the mode of production, which has sprung up and flourished along with, and under it. Centralisation of the means of production and socialisation of labour at last reach a point where they become incompatible with their capitalist integument [i.e., the relations of production that enclose them]. This integument is burst asunder. The knell of capitalist private property sounds. The expropriators are expropriated.

(MECW 35: 750)

Similarly, before *Capital*, Marx writes in the *Grundrisse*: "Beyond a certain point, the development of the productive forces becomes a barrier to capital, and consequently the relation of capital becomes a barrier to the development of the productive forces of labour" (MECW 29: 133). Capitalists, recall, have only one purpose (on pain of extinction in the capitalist marketplace): to generate profit. The primary form of capitalist exchange is given by the M–C–M′ formula. At some point, capitalist relations of production fail to yield M′, and if capitalists cannot realize M′, then they have no reason to continue utilizing the productive forces they control.

Why should it happen that capitalism collapses because of a supposed "contradiction" between its relations of production and the potential for further development of the productive power of a society?[39] Unfortunately, Marx never gives a single, systematic answer to this question: this is one of several respects in which the influence of Hegelian historical teleology continued to exercise a strong, and unfortunate, influence on Marx's thinking. It is as though Marx, having realized that Hegelian idealism was mistaken as an account of historical change, then assumed that his materialist alternative would nonetheless justify a conclusion about the necessary trajectory of the historical process. As we will argue, the claim that capitalist development has a necessary outcome is far from clear, even though Marx identifies serious pathologies that afflict the capitalist mode of producing what human societies need. Importantly, as we will argue, the fundamental pathology of the capitalist mode of production according to Marx (its tendency, over the long haul, to produce immiseration and underconsumption) does not depend on the truth of the labor theory of value.

We will focus on two major explanations Marx offers for why capitalism should ultimately collapse. The first pertains to the supposed tendency of the rate of profit to fall under capitalism; the second pertains to the immiseration of the vast majority due to the replacement of human labor by technology, and the attendant collapse in consumption of commodities, which would make it impossible for capitalists to realize M′. We take these up in turn.

A. Tendency of the Rate of Profit to Fall

Marx devoted considerable effort in Part III of *Capital III* to explaining why there was a tendency under capitalism for the rate of profit to fall.[40] This matters because, if the rate of profit falls, then capitalists lose their incentive to continue utilizing the productive forces they control. Marx's account is sometimes caricatured by critics as follows: capitalism incentivizes technological development; technological advances replace human labor; but human labor is the source of surplus value; therefore, as technology replaces human labor, there will be less and less surplus value, and thus less profit for capitalists. The critic then observes—correctly—that replacing human labor with technology typically raises profit margins, not reduces them (if it did not, capitalists would not replace human labor with technology, after all). Needless to say, Marx's argument was not so simple, and not so easily refuted—even though it is, as we argue, ultimately unsuccessful, and for reasons not wholly unrelated to the caricature.

We need, first, to introduce some technical concepts that are important to Marx's analysis:

1. "Constant capital" is the amount the capitalist must spend on raw materials and technology.
2. "Variable capital" is the amount the capitalist spends on labor power (i.e., the wages the capitalist pays to the workers).
3. The "organic composition of capital" is the ratio of constant to variable capital—that is, the ratio of expenditures on raw material and technology to labor costs.
4. The "rate of profit" is the ratio of surplus value to the cost of constant and variable capital. (Recall that "surplus value" is the value created by the amount of time the worker labors beyond that necessary for his own sustenance.)

Let us introduce a highly simplified example to make this concrete. Suppose the cost of constant capital is 100 (the particular currency does not matter for our purposes)[41] and the cost of variable capital is 20. The "organic composition of capital" would then be 5 to 1. Suppose, in addition, that the variable capital that costs 20 produces a surplus value of 30. Then the "rate of profit" is 30/120

(1/4)—that is, for every 120 the capitalist lays out, the capitalist comes away with 30 of profit. The "rate of profit" falls if it goes from 1/4 to 1/10, for example: this would happen if, for instance, the cost of variable and/or constant capital increased to 300 while the surplus value remained the same.

Why, then, is there a tendency of the rate of profit to fall under capitalism? Marx's answer is that there is a tendency for the expenses associated with *constant* capital (i.e., technology and raw materials) to increase. Recall that capitalism's great contribution to humanity is to incentivize technological development: the capitalist who can take advantage of a new technology can out-produce his rivals, whether they are late feudal lords (hundreds of years ago) or other capitalists (today). With the demise of feudalism and feudal-like arrangements, any technological innovation will gradually be adopted by all other capitalists, on pain of extinction. If Henry Ford introduces the assembly line with its machines into his factory to mass produce automobiles, then every other capitalist will eventually do the same or they will not be able to compete. Ford's short-term advantage—being the first to add the technology (conveyor belts, machines, etc.) to make assembly line production possible—may increase his rate of profit initially (his workers will produce more cars, more quickly, and maybe more cheaply); but that will not last, as every other automobile manufacturer invests in the same technology. And, with the increase in productivity—the ability of fewer (or the same number of) workers to produce more automobiles—the costs of raw materials will also increase for the capitalist since he will need to supply his more efficient workers with more raw materials for their production process. Thus, the cost of constant capital tends to go up across the whole economy as capitalists compete with each other for short-term advantages through technological advances, and purchase more raw materials given the increased productivity of labor utilizing these new technologies. This is one of Marx's important insights about capitalism that does not depend on the labor theory of value (even though, as we will see, his claim about the falling rate of profit does).

If the rate of exploitation in Marx's technical sense holds steady—i.e., the surplus value remains fixed, as in our initial example, at 50 percent (an outlay on variable capital of 20 produces surplus value of 30)—then the rate of profit will necessarily fall because the constant capital costs increase: let us suppose from 120 to 150, thanks to technological advances and more utilization of raw materials. In that case, the rate of profit is now 30/150, or 1/5, so lower than the earlier rate of profit (1/4). As Marx puts the general point:

> [T]he same rate of surplus value would express itself under the same degree of labor exploitation in a falling rate of profit, because the material growth of the constant capital implies also a growth—albeit not in the same proportion—in its value, and consequently in that of the total capital.
>
> (MECW 37: 209-210)

This all follows straightforwardly from the concepts so defined.

Marx recognizes, however, that the rate of exploitation (the rate at which surplus value is produced) is unlikely to remain constant. Capitalists can increase the length of the working day or reduce wages: both will increase the surplus value produced. (There are limits to both, of course: workers cannot labor 24 hours per day, day after day, for example; and wages must be adequate for the worker to have sustenance adequate to work another day.) What Marx calls the "reserve army" of workers—those who are unemployed or underemployed, often because of prior technological advances, or simply because of population growth—allows capitalists to cut wages while still finding workers (MECW 35: 626). Capitalists can often reduce the cost of constant capital insofar as increased productivity lowers the costs of raw materials and the technology needed: that will affect the rate of profit. The globalization of capitalist markets makes both of these easier: capitalists gain access to cheaper labor power, or laborers who will work longer hours, as well as (often) cheaper raw materials. For all these reasons, Marx says it is only a "tendency" that the rate of profit will fall. He cannot establish that it actually will.[42]

There is another worry looming over this entire analysis. If surplus value does not derive from "surplus" labor (i.e., the labor the capitalist pays for beyond that which is necessary for sustenance of the laborer), then the entire analysis of the tendency of the rate of profit to fall collapses. We have already noted reasons to think the labor theory of value is incorrect. Since this first explanation for the self-destruction of capitalism depends on the labor theory of value, it must be rejected. Marx's second line of analysis, however, fares much better.

B. Immiseration and Underconsumption

Marx's more promising explanation for why capitalism will enter a serious "crisis" (if not *necessarily* lead to communism) does not depend on the labor theory of value at all. It appeals instead to the essential logic of capitalist markets, which we have already discussed at length (and which was presupposed in the discussion of proletarian revolution in Chapter 3). We may summarize the basic problem as follows.

Capitalists are out to make profit from their expenditures on constant and variable capital: their only goal, recall, is M'. Because capitalists compete against each other, they are incentivized to innovate, develop new productive technologies, and reduce their production costs (either by increasing productivity or reducing the cost of constant and/or variable capital) so as to increase their profitability. This accounts for why, as Marx emphasizes, capitalism is unparalleled in its ability to develop technology and increase productivity: individual capitalists live or die on their ability to do this. Capitalists, however, do not provide jobs for people out of altruistic concern for the welfare of workers: they do so only because it is necessary to produce the commodities that are their source of profit. All those whose lives depend upon wages from capitalists work and survive only as long as some capitalist needs them. Because capitalist producers are always locked in life-and-death competition struggles with other capitalists, they must reduce costs where they can and increase productivity where they can, sometimes doing both at the same time: that often means reducing the cost of variable capital. Global corporations in the United States move jobs to India or Mexico for one simple reason: labor costs (variable capital costs) are lower there (thus increasing the rate of profit). Corporations embrace new technologies, such as robots, because they prove cheaper than human labor and/or increase productivity.[43]

A 2019 story in the *New York Times*—one of the most important mouthpieces for the ideology of the capitalist ruling class in the

United States—concerning the annual meeting of capitalist elites in Davos, Switzerland provides (unintentionally) a capsule summary of Marx's argument:

> They'll never admit it in public, but many of your bosses want machines to replace you as soon as possible … [I]n private settings … these executives tell a different story: They are racing to automate their own work forces to stay ahead of the competition, with little regard for the impact on workers.
>
> (Roose 2019, emphasis added)

The suggestion that capitalists might make decisions with "regard for the impact on workers" is, as we will see in Chapter 5, a prime example of ideology: it disguises the actual reality (namely, that capitalists definitely want machines to replace workers as soon as possible) by suggesting that the capitalist class might want to take into account the "impact on workers"—even though the entire logic of the capitalist marketplace forbids that, unless it could contribute to profit.[44] Indeed as the *NewYork Times* article admits, "in private settings … these executives tell a different story: They are racing to automate their own work forces to stay ahead of the competition, with little regard for the impact on workers." The story continues:

> All over the world, executives are spending billions of dollars to transform their businesses into lean, digitized, highly automated operations. They crave the fat profit margins automation can deliver, and they see A.I. [Artificial Intelligence] as a golden ticket to savings, perhaps by letting them whittle departments with thousands of workers down to just a few dozen.
>
> In Davos, executives tend to speak about automation as a natural phenomenon over which they have no control, like hurricanes or heat waves. They claim that if they don't automate jobs as quickly as possible, their competitors will.
>
> (Roose 2019)

The economic pressure to shed workers in favor of machines is not a "natural phenomenon": that is an instance of another ideological mistake, treating as natural and necessary what is in fact the result of a contingent form of economic organization of society (see Chapter 5). Yet, from Marx's point of view, the executives in Davos are not wholly wrong: insofar as they want to remain viable under capitalism, they have no individual control over this. Any "kind-hearted" capitalist who resists automation out of concern for the "impact on workers" will be destroyed in the marketplace by the capitalists who automate, fire the unneeded workers, reduce their variable capital costs, and sell their commodities at lower prices than the kind-hearted capitalist can. The New York Times story concludes: "As to who will buy the products of their operations once all the workers are gone … well, that doesn't seem to occur to any of them" (Roose 2019).[45] That, in a journalistic nutshell, is the problem of underconsumption: in the drive to cut the costs of variable capital, capitalists also eliminate the potential consumers of their commodities.[46]

Let us turn now to Marx's discussion of the phenomenon, before considering objections to his diagnosis. In volume III of Capital, Marx writes:

> Production of surplus value … is the immediate purpose and compelling motive of capitalist production … As soon as all the surplus labour it was possible to squeeze out has been objectified in commodities, surplus value has been produced. But this production of surplus value completes but the first act of the capitalist process of production … The entire mass of commodities, i.e., the total product, including the portion which replaces the constant and variable capital, and that representing surplus value, must be sold. If this is not done, or done only in part, or only at prices below the prices of production, the labourer has been indeed exploited, but his exploitation is not realised as such for the capitalist, and this can be bound up with a total or partial failure to realise the surplus value pressed out of him, indeed even with the partial or total loss of the capital.
>
> (MECW 37: 242–243)

In other words, if the commodities produced are not sold, the capitalist reaps no profit. The realization of that exploitation (i.e., the realization of the profit) depends on the "consumer power of society," which is not a function of what it can actually produce, but rather "the consumer power based on antagonistic conditions of distribution" (i.e., the existing relations of production in which capitalists try to reduce the cost of variable capital), "which reduce the consumption of the bulk of society to a minimum varying within more or less narrow limits" (MECW 37: 243)—that is, the limits imposed by the need to pay workers what is necessary for them to sustain themselves. The limit on what capitalists can expend on wages (variable capital) is exacerbated by

> the drive to expand capital and produce surplus value on an extended scale. This is law for capitalist production, imposed by incessant revolutions in the methods of production themselves, by the depreciation of existing capital always bound up with them, by the general competitive struggle and the need to improve production and expand its scale merely as a means of self-preservation and under penalty of ruin ... But the more the productive power develops, the more it finds itself at variance with the narrow basis on which the conditions of consumption rest.
>
> (MECW 37: 243)

The need for capitalists to endlessly innovate technology (and spend money on constant capital)—the basic imperative of the capitalist marketplace—also increases pressure to either reduce expenditure on labor or extract more work hours from labor for the same wages. In either case, the ability of workers to consume commodities is kept within "narrow limits," assuming it is not eliminated altogether. Marx's frequent collaborator, Engels, expresses the worry even more concisely in 1880:

> [T]he perfecting of machinery is making human labour superfluous. If the introduction and increase of machinery means the displacement of millions of manual, by a few machine, workers, improvement in machinery means the displacement of more and more of the machine-workers themselves ... Thus it comes about, to quote Marx, that machinery becomes the most powerful weapon in the war of capital against the working-class; that

the instruments of labour constantly tear the means of subsistence out of the hands of the labourer.

(MECW 24: 314)

Workers rendered obsolete by technology cannot consume commodities, since they no longer have any income. If no one consumes commodities, however, then there is no profit for the capitalists to realize. And if there is no profit to be realized, then capitalists have no reason to continue engaging in production, since the point of production is to yield profit—that is, M'.

That conclusion may be too hasty. If those who sell labor power to survive can no longer consume commodities when their labor is no longer needed by capitalists, that does not mean that *no one* can consume commodities. Marx was aware of this complication. In *Capital III*, he writes:

> [T]he replacement of the capital invested in production depends largely upon the consuming power of the non-producing classes [i.e., neither capitalists nor workers]; while the consuming power of the workers is limited partly by the laws of wages, partly by the fact that they are used only as long as they can be profitably employed by the capitalist class. The ultimate reason for all real crises always remains the poverty and restricted consumption of the masses as opposed to the drive of capitalist production to develop the productive forces as though only the absolute consuming power of society constituted their limit.
>
> (MECW 37: 482–483)[4/]

In the first sentence of this passage, Marx acknowledges the role played in the realization of profit by "non-producing" classes—i.e., those not involved in producing what a society needs to reproduce itself, but who nonetheless buy commodities. Those classes would include, for example, servants, artists, ministers, and other religious officials, "service" professionals, as well as various employees of the state, such as judges, soldiers, police, and bureaucrats. We might also note that not all commodities are sold to ordinary consumers: many capitalists produce commodities (e.g., computer or automotive parts) for sale to other capitalists, not consumers.

So why then does Marx nonetheless claim, in the preceding passage, that the "ultimate reason for all real crises remains the poverty and restricted consumption of the masses"? As capitalists purge from the payrolls those who have only their labor power to sell, and replace them with technology, consumption by the non-productive classes would continue. Why should a "crisis" ensue? Certainly, in a society where *most people* are selling their labor power to capitalists, the disappearance of that class would result in a massive decline in consumption of commodities. Moreover, insofar as the non-productive classes are dependent on workers who sell their labor power, their consumption power will ultimately be affected as well: this will be especially true of the state, to the extent it depends on taxes not only on the income of those who sell labor power but also of those non-productive people (e.g., service professionals, artists, ministers) who depend on either selling their services to workers or who depend on their voluntary financial support. Even capitalists who primarily sell their commodities (e.g., computer parts or automotive parts) to other capitalists will eventually be affected by a decline in consumption of the downstream commodities aimed at consumers for which those parts are utilized.

As we saw in Chapter 3, Marx thinks that capitalism will collapse only under certain rather extreme circumstances:

> [Capitalism] must necessarily have rendered the great mass of humanity "propertyless", and moreover in contradiction to an existing world of wealth and culture, both these premises presuppose a great increase in productive power, a high degree of development ... [T]his development of productive forces ... is an absolutely necessary practical premise because without it want[48] is merely made general, and with *destitution* the struggle for necessities and all the old filthy business[49] would necessarily be reproduced; and furthermore, because only with this universal development of productive forces is a *universal* intercourse between men established, which on the one side produces in *all* nations simultaneously the phenomenon of the "propertyless" mass ... Empirically, communism is only possible as the act of the dominant peoples "all at once" and simultaneously, which

presupposes the universal development of productive forces and the world intercourse bound up with [communism].

(MECW 5: 48–49)

On this account, there are three necessary conditions for a transition to communism. First, there must be, *mass*, i.e., wide-scale, immiseration. Second, capitalism must have become truly *global* (which is precisely what produces mass immiseration: "the mass of *propertyless* workers ... presupposes the *world market* through competition" (MECW 5: 49)); this is the situation (the world market) we are approaching in the 21st century. Third, and finally, capitalism can only be replaced when there has been an enormous increase in productive power, of a kind that would make meeting human needs (and many, if not all, wants) easy. As G.A. Cohen aptly puts it, the transition from capitalism to communism is brought about by "the problem ... of massive power to produce, alongside massive poverty. As that problem deepens, its solution looms, as and because the problem deepens" (2000: 63). (Note, by the way, that it is not a condition for revolution that people have the correct philosophical theory of justice or fairness!) The "contradiction," in which capitalist relations of production "fetter" the development of the forces of production (see Chapter 2, Section 3), is here described by Marx quite simply:

> The contradiction between the individuality of each separate proletarian and labour, the condition of life forced upon him, becomes evident to him, himself, for he is sacrificed from youth upwards and, within his own class, has no chance of arriving at the conditions which would place him in the other class.
>
> (MECW 5: 79)

Capitalist relations of production evolve, as described in the prior section, so that those who labor for survival wages realize there is no hope of a better future. Such people, unsurprisingly, will revolt, especially if they have a correct understanding of the cause of their situation (i.e., that massive productive power is controlled only by those interested in profit), precisely what Marx aimed to provide them.

The agent of revolutionary transformation in the Marxian view, in short, has something in common with the "rational actor" of economics in the neoclassical tradition: he has certain basic desires (to survive, to live decently), and he is (at least sometimes) instrumentally rational (choosing the appropriate means to realize his ends) in pursuit of their satisfaction. Neoclassical economics, of course, treats instrumental reason as the only kind of thinking that could count as rational; under capitalism, this turns out to be mostly true, since anyone who fails to reason instrumentally will be destroyed in the marketplace. Ironically, the same turns out to be true for the vast majority who sell their labor power to survive: at some point, they too have instrumental reasons to destroy capitalism in order to satisfy their basic desires.[50] In a communist revolution, Marx says, "individuals must appropriate the existing totality of productive forces, not only to achieve self-activity, but, also, merely to safeguard their very existence" (MECW 5: 87). If most people are to survive or live decently, productive power must be wrested from the control of capitalists and utilized to meet the needs of the vast majority.

When writing for a popular audience, in the 1848 Communist Manifesto, Marx (together with Engels) is clear about the relevant motivations of those who revolt:

> The modern labourer ... instead of rising with the progress of industry, sinks deeper and deeper below the conditions of existence of his own class. He becomes a pauper, and pauperism develops more rapidly than population and wealth.[51] And here it becomes evidence, that the bourgeoisie is unfit any longer to be the ruling class in society ... It is unfit to rule because it is incompetent to assure an existence to its slave within his slavery ... Society can no longer live under this bourgeoisie ... its existence is no longer compatible with society.
>
> (MECW 6: 495–496)

The laborer's motivation to revolt under these circumstances is that he works and works, and his life gets worse and worse (or he is unable to work at all). It not only gets worse and worse, but it does so under circumstances in which the productive capacity of humanity is so great that, if things were otherwise, his life would be better in

its material respects.[52] In short, people revolt when they are miserable, see no alternative, and understand that radical action holds out
the promise of an alternative given the level of development of the
productive forces. It is important to see that appeals to altruism and
moral concern for others play no role in Marx's explanation for why
the vast majority will, at some point, be motivated to reject capitalism: the appeal is to the collective self-interest of the vast majority.

The "rational actor" of neoclassical economics—who calculates
the most efficient way to satisfy his desires—is presumed to face
serious obstacles to engaging in collective activities, since he may
always be tempted by the possibility of free riding on the efforts of
others (e.g., letting others overthrow capitalism while he waits to
enjoy the benefits of communism). Some analytical Marxists (e.g.,
Elster 1986) have endorsed this worry. As another Marxist, Robert
Paul Wolff has observed (1990: 473):

> A little reflection will remind us that all of the productive activi-
> ties of human beings are collective in character ... All kinship
> interactions, sexual liaisons, all our activities of eating and war-
> ring, almost all religious activities and activities of artistic cre-
> ation, reproduction, and appreciation, are collective in character.
> Voting, strikes, military campaigns, riots, cocktail parties, family
> vacations—all of these, on Elster's view, are so improbable that
> we can barely understand how they might, on rare occasions,
> actually happen. Clearly, there is something badly wrong with
> a theory of society that concludes that the norm is so abnormal
> that it is almost never likely to occur![53]

Elster's mistake, like the mistake of "rational actor" models generally,
is in assuming that agents who are often instrumentally rational and
self-interested are continuously calculating expected utilities: they
are not, as the examples of riots, in particular, suggests. In this regard,
the Marxian account departs from the idealized assumptions of neoclassical economics and analytical Marxism, but in a most plausible
way: when things are bad enough for people, the calculations of
the accountant cease, and people do what they can in the moment
if they understand their options. Marx's goal was to explain both
the current state of affairs and the possibilities inherent in them for

the benefit of those classes motivated to act. That was surely Marx's realistic picture of revolutionary transformation.[54]

C. Will Capitalism Collapse?

Is Marx correct about the long-term tendency of capitalism to eliminate human labor in favor of technology,[55] and thus, ironically, to eliminate the consumers of commodities on which capitalism relies for profit? Contemporary neoclassical economists would make several objections to Marx's diagnosis.

A first difficulty is that the history of capitalism since Marx wrote contradicts his prediction. While technology frequently displaces human labor (no one denies this phenomenon), productivity gains from technology often result in capital being utilized to employ human labor in other jobs, sometimes jobs that arise precisely because of technology. (Consider: mass production of automobiles reduces the need for workers who service horses, like blacksmiths and saddlers, but increases demand for factory workers. Technology that replaces factory workers creates new opportunities for engineers and those who build the technology.) There are, as some contemporary economists put it, "reinstatement" effects for labor from technological developments (see Acemoglu & Restrepo 2019). In the mid-19th century, this was not as obvious as it has become since.

As we discussed in Chapter 3, Marx's assumptions about the time frame in which capitalism would develop and revolutionary transformation would occur were mistaken. Like many 19th-century utopians, Marx was impressed by the remarkable development of productive power in the first 100 years of the industrial revolution, and thought the era of productive plenty was on the horizon. Perhaps because of the lack of relevant data and information, he was unaware of the extent to which the globalization of capitalism had barely begun, which on his own theory was a prerequisite for the full displacement of labor by technology.

While the displacement of human labor by technology has generally been offset by the reinstatement of human labor in other contexts, something closer to what Marx expected has begun to occur more recently in the developed capitalist economies. As two contemporary non-Marxist economists note, since 2000, there has been "a significant decline in the labor share after more than a century of stability" (Grossman & Oberfield 2022: 94; see also Acemoglu & Restrepo 2019). As some other recent economists write:

> Labor's share of national income has fallen in many countries in the last decades. In the United States, the labor income share has accelerated its decline since the beginning of the new century … While estimates of their long-run trends depend heavily on accounting assumptions and, thus, are subject to debate, they have all gone through a clear fall in the last 20 years.
>
> (Bergholt et al. 2022: 163)

Why has labor's share fallen? Some non-Marxist economists think automation is the primary explanation (e.g., Bergholt et al. 2022: 166), which is what Marx would have predicted. Others cast the net wider in terms of explanatory factors for the decline of human labor's share of income: "[M]any economists appear to believe that further automation, robotization, globalization, market concentration, and aging of the population spell ongoing declines for the labor share. Some even fear that the labor share in national income might fall to zero" (Grossman & Oberfield 2022: 117–118). If the labor share fell to "zero" that would be consistent, of course, with Marx's prediction of eventual immiseration of the vast majority.

Contemporary neoclassical economists, including those just quoted, tend to be more optimistic that the future will be like the past, and that displacement of labor will continue to be offset by reinstatement effects (cf. Grossman & Oberfield 2022: 118–119), despite "the deceleration of labor demand growth over the last 30 years … due to anemic productivity growth and adverse shifts in the task contents of production owing to rapid automation that is not being counterbalanced by the creation of new [human labor] tasks" (Acemoglu & Restrepo 2019: 21). The primary argument they offer involves an inductive inference over the last 150 years of capitalism: since displacement of labor by technology has generally been offset by new demands for human labor in other economic activities, there is no reason to worry. One might wonder whether this is just a different kind of utopian optimism than Marx's.

Marx's best argument for why capitalism will self-destruct is not an inductive one: it is that the logic of capitalism will necessarily eliminate most of the consumers of its commodities. Recall that this is because capitalist producers are always locked in life-and-death struggles in the market. If a technology arises that is cheaper than human labor, then a capitalist must utilize that technology lest his competitors do so. That is the essence of the capitalist "race to the bottom" of trying to cut costs through discarding human labor in favor of technology. Only if one thought that there were certain tasks that human labor could perform more cheaply than the technology of the future would one expect capitalism to preserve any role for human labor. That, in any case, is Marx's argument.

The contemporary labor economist Daron Acemoglu and colleagues have argued for many years that one cannot neglect the role of "institutions and politics that shape markets, prices, and the path of technology" (Acemoglu & Robinson 2015: 6). Marx does not, as we saw in Chapter 3 (Section 3 in particular). Acemoglu is unusual among contemporary non-Marxist economists in recognizing that technological progress does not result in everyone being better off materially in the absence of political interventions (see generally, Acemoglu & Johnson 2023).[56] Marx, although he recognized the ways in which the ruling class might utilize the political system to facilitate the dominance of the ruling class, clearly did not anticipate the extent to which the state would impose compromises between capitalists and labor to secure social peace in the 20th century.

Even acknowledging this clear failure of prophecy on Marx's part, we are still left with the question why, if technology is consistently cheaper than human labor, capitalist markets will not eliminate any role for human labor (i.e., reducing its share of income to "zero")? There are two possible answers. In the view of neoclassical economists, human greed is unbounded; so, if technology replaces most human labor, then human labor will become *very cheap*, and greedy capitalists will want to pay something, even if not very much, for the human labor still available to satisfy new desires and whims. This scenario, however, is clearly compatible with Marx's view that the logic of capitalism will generate immiseration.

A more serious challenge comes from the fact—one Marx grants—that the state under capitalism is "nothing more than the form of organization which the bourgeois are compelled to adopt … for the mutual guarantee of their property and interests" (MECW 5: 90). Yet surely the capitalist class, the argument goes, can see that eliminating its consumers (by rendering them unemployed) would spell doom; and so they will solve, through the state, the collective action problem presented by the market incentives to always replace labor with cheaper technology. They could do so through "universal basic income" or redistributive taxes or regulation requiring human labor and the like. This is certainly a possibility Marx never considered, although it would require some remarkably forward-looking coordination by the capitalist class, of a kind we have not seen before in human history. But Marx also never considered another scenario that would constitute a response to the same state of affairs, in which human labor is displaced by technology but without preserving consumption by the majority.

D. The Elysium Scenario

If, in fact, technology continues to displace human labor, without reinstating labor elsewhere, the capitalist class might enlist the state in solving the collective action problem of preserving its consumers of commodities, as just noted. There is, alas, another possibility, which we will henceforth call the "Elysium Scenario," after a 2013 science fiction film about a world in which the ruling class lives in luxury in a space station hovering above Earth, while those still on the planet live in poverty and misery. The Elysium elite, now controlling extraordinary productive power (thanks to technology), can produce everything they need and want; but, having no need for human labor power (or not very much human labor power), they do not produce the commodities that everyone else needs. In the movie, the elite retreat to a luxurious space station hovering above the destitute planet Earth.

The phenomenon of the capitalist class walling itself off—often literally—from the rest of the population is certainly familiar today, even without the science fiction component. The final difficulty for Marx's diagnosis is that it is unclear why underconsumption, economic depression, and resulting immiseration should result in communism rather than an Elysium Scenario? To be sure, the Elysium

Scenario marks the end of capitalism as we have known it, involving as it does a kind of localized communism for those who control productive power—they utilize productive power for their benefit—but it is certainly not a case of the "expropriators [being] expropriated" (MECW 35: 750), as Marx envisioned the end of capitalism.

Marx's account of capitalism seems fully compatible with the possibility that at some point the capitalist class will simply utilize its immense productive power on its own behalf, with some wages (and consumption) going to those who protect their Elysium. Indeed, the problem may be worse in the 21st century. In the 19th century, laborers were congregated in urban centers, making mass action easier to organize, as Marx himself emphasized (see Chapter 3, Section 3). Technological innovations (plus the migration of capital to sites of low-cost labor, often outside urban areas) mean the advantage of the social proximity of the victims is lost.[57]

In short, nothing in Marx's theory rules out that the choice between "socialism and barbarism"—as Rosa Luxemburg (1871–1919), a leading Marxist theorist and revolutionary, framed it more than a century ago—will not be decided in favor of barbarism, as the immiserated majority is suppressed by force (or consigned to the destitute planet Earth, as in Elysium), and barbarism protects the capitalist elite and their control of productive power.[58] Marx's Hegelian optimism about how history must necessarily unfold is not warranted. "Socialism," in Marx's and Luxemburg's sense, would, of course, be the more humane response: that is, utilization of massive productive power to meet human needs and liberate human beings from wage slavery. There is, alas, no guarantee that will be the point to which human societies evolve.

8. Conclusion: Marxian Economics without the Labor Theory of Value

Even if it is false, as we have argued, that the socially necessary labor time to produce a commodity explains production prices, this does not matter for Marx's most important insights into capitalism. Certain familiar Marxian ideas—"the falling rate of profit," "the transformation problem"—must be put to one side, and rightly so;

but what matters in Marx's diagnosis of capitalism remains intact.[59] We can summarize those surviving claims—all discussed above—as follows.

First, capitalists have only one aim: profit, the *raison d'être* of all capitalists. They lay out money for raw materials, technology, and labor power in order to produce commodities that they can sell for purposes of acquiring more money. Here Karl Marx and well-known ideologists of capitalism like Milton Friedman fully agree: any capitalist who decides to put other goals before profit—concern for their workers or the community—risks destruction in the marketplace. Only when such concerns enhance profitability are such considerations colorable for the capitalist.

Second, capitalists employ human laborers only because their labor on raw materials increases the value of the resulting commodities; if it did not, capitalists would not employ humans at all. This remains true even if it is false that the socially necessary labor time of human beings explains the "center of gravity" around which price revolves. Given that Marx and Friedman are right about the *raison d'être* of capitalists (the first point), it follows that capitalists would only employ workers if in fact they added to the market value of the commodities.

Third, capitalists make money because of the work others do. Jeff Bezos may figure out how to use the Internet as a sales platform ("Amazon"), and Bill Gates may figure out how to design computer software ("Microsoft"); but these innovations are worthless, and generate no profit, without the work of tens of thousands of other people: programmers, technicians, warehouse workers, sales people, drivers, factory workers, secretaries, accountants, and on and on. Other capitalists, such as the heirs to vast capitalist fortunes (e.g., Walton, Mars, Pritzker, etc.), have done nothing at all but still enjoy the value created by the work of others, including their forebears.

Fourth, competition in the capitalist marketplace requires all capitalists to reduce their costs in order to sustain their profit margins. Investments in technology (generally) allow capitalists to replace costly human labor (variable capital) with technology that costs less over time. Since all other capitalists will invest in the same technology, the pressure to reduce labor costs (either by eliminating the labor with yet newer technology or getting the same human labor to work more for the same wages) continues. As capitalists increasingly shed human labor, consumption of commodities will decline since its consumers will be destitute. Unable to sell commodities, capitalists will employ even less human labor. At the extreme, capitalists, having invested mightily in technology, will control enormous productive power but have no reason to utilize it, since the only reason to utilize it would be to generate profit. At that moment, human societies face the choice between "socialism and barbarism": use the productive power that the merciless capitalist marketplace generated so that it meets human needs and permits people to finally be free (socialism); or let all those whose existence depended on wage slavery, and who are no longer needed, be damned, while capitalists use their productive power to sustain themselves and protect themselves from the disposable and increasingly immiserated former wage slaves.

None of the preceding claims about capitalism depend on the labor theory of value, which has received so much attention in Marx scholarship and the history of Marxism. Marx, like all of us, was a thinker of his times and an inheritor of the accumulated "wisdom" of his predecessors, whether Hegel or Ricardo (even though he was highly critical of both). As we have argued throughout the book, Marx also transcended his times, and the limitations of his intellectual influences.

Notes

1 The *Grundrisse* was written in 1857–58, and *Theories of Surplus Value* in 1861–63. These works anticipate many ideas and arguments in *Capital*. Volume I of *Capital* appeared in 1867 (a revised version appeared in 1872); volumes II and III appeared after Marx's death, under the editorship of Engels since Marx never completed these volumes.

2 Elster wrote a much longer book, *Making Sense of Marx* (1985), full of polemics against Marxists and other Marx commentators; he then excised most of the polemics in a much more concise volume (Elster 1986). Our references are to the latter volume, which is more useful for those new to Marx.

3 It is a curious feature of Heinrich's account that it must treat the "transformation problem" (how exchange values are transformed into production prices [discussed later in the chapter])—to which Marx devoted a large portion of Volume

III of *Capital*—as based on confusion or misunderstanding on Marx's part (cf. Heinrich 2012: 148, 230 n. 10, 234 n. 40). On many important points, however, Heinrich agrees with Sweezy (1970), though we generally find Sweezy to be clearer. The key dispute between the revisionist and traditional interpreters of Marx's economics concerns the extent to which Marx really took over Ricardo's framework, even allowing for Marx's explicit criticisms of and departures from it. Heinrich and other scholars think that Marx breaks decisively from Ricardo's paradigm, while others (including Sweezy) disagree. We cannot attempt to settle the exegetical question here, although we note that we agree with the revisionists this far: what is important in Marx's economics does not depend on any version of the labor theory of value. We return to this topic in the conclusion of the chapter. (Thanks to Daniel Burnfin for useful discussion and guidance on these issues.).

4 Marx makes a similar observation in *Capital* I (MECW 35: 173-174).

5 Newton's discovery (in the 17th century) of laws governing the movement of physical objects inspired many others to try to ascertain the "laws" governing human beings and human affairs: this was true of David Hume, another major figure in the Scottish Enlightenment; and of Smith, who was the first to suggest that the economic activities of disparate people in a society might, in fact, be explicable in terms of economic laws.

6 For doubts that Smith was ultimately committed to a "labor theory of value" in order to explain prices, see Fleischacker (2021: 271–275.) For a more technical discussion, see Blaug (1985: 38–39).

7 He disagrees quite substantially with Ricardo on many issues: Marx's ideas of abstract labor, socially necessary labor time, and the essential role of money in a capitalist economy (all discussed below) have no analogue in Ricardo.

8 As Marx notes, the converse does not hold: a division of labor does not mean commodities are exchanged (MECW 35: 52). In a modern factory, there is a division of labor (one person puts in the bolts, another turns the screws, etc.), for example, but no exchange of commodities.

9 As one economist puts the central neoclassical criticism of Marx on this score: "the marginalist revolution in the 1870s shows that neither labor nor any other input determined price because it was not cost of production that was crucial, but the utility of the output to the consumer, which determined whether or to what extent the consumer would be willing to pay to cover those costs" (Sowell 2006: 184).

10 Ricardo focused on actual or concrete labor, *not* abstract labor in Marx's sense.

11 As Roemer (1990: 257) puts it, "the labor theory of value was not a theory of price," although Marx thought it had implications for production price, as we discuss in the text.

12 Foley (1982) is an important example; Sweezy (1970: Chapter VII) discusses the problems with Marx's own attempt to solve the transformation problem, and explores some other Marxian solutions. Heinrich (2012: 50–51) denies that socially necessary labor time is supposed to explain the exchange-value of

commodities, and so side-steps the transformation problem. He claims instead that the socially necessary labor time is only determined in market exchanges. What this alternative explanation amounts to (and what it explains) is, unfortunately, somewhat obscure; and, as we noted at the start, it requires discounting the enormous effort Marx himself invested in the transformation problem, presumably because he thought labor explains value, which then stands in some explanatory relation to prices.

13 It is a distinctive contention of Michael Heinrich's revisionary account of *Capital* that the social necessary labor time is only determined by the act of exchange in the market (2012: 50–51), and thus cannot explain the exchange values. Whether Heinrich's real point is the one we note in the text is less clear to us.

14 The Marxist economist Heinrich concurs: "Marx sees the individual exchange relation as part of a *particular social totality*—a totality in which the reproduction of society is mediated by exchange—and asks what this means for the labor expended by the *whole society*" (2012: 46–47).

15 Roberts (2016) offers a novel reading of volume I of *Capital* as modelled on Dante's *Inferno*, although this sheds little light on Marx's economic theory as a whole, including volumes II and III of the work (as Roberts admits [2016: 14], his focus is a reading of volume I, the one volume Marx himself completed). Roberts's ultimate aim is to present Marx as a normative theorist of "republican freedom," i.e., freedom as non-domination. That Marx thought capitalism rendered people unfree seems right; that he was offering a "republican theory" of freedom, however, seems implausible. After his very early writings, Marx had no interest in normative theory, and thought it an irrelevant exercise; moreover, what he actually says about freedom as involving "spontaneous activity" is much more demanding than what republican theories of freedom require. (Thanks to Kate Petroff for pressing the latter point on us.) On the general topic of normative theory in Marx, see Chapter 6, and Section 4C of Chapter 3.

16 The German here is: *der seine eigne Haut zu Markt getragen und nun nichts andres zu erwarten hat als die – Gerberei*—that is, someone bringing his own skin to a tannery (*Gerberei*), a place where animal skin is processed and turned into saleable leather products. So, too, the value added by the laborer to the products he works on is taken from him and turned into a commodity on Marx's view.

17 This represents a major break from the theories of Smith and Ricardo, and also many later economists. Money is essential to capitalism for Marx.

18 What is really at issue for the capitalist is what Marx calls "surplus value," to which we return below.

19 To be clear, not all profit is realized this way, just the distinctive profits of capitalist production.

20 Most (but not all) "raw material[s]" must be "filtered through previous labor"; and tools and machines, as well as "workshops, canals, roads, and so forth" that "are necessary for carrying on the labor process" must be factored in (MECW 35: 188, 190).

21 We elide an important complication—namely, that, while the capitalist class *as a whole* requires that the sellers of labor power reproduce so that there are future workers, no individual capitalist has reason to pay for that.

22 Marx assumes that the bargaining position of the capitalist is always sufficiently strong that the person selling their labor power cannot, in fact, secure the full value of their work in wages. This is related to his supposition that there will always be a "reserve army" of the unemployed (and underemployed). See MECW 35: 623–634.

23 Marx often uses the French word *exploitation*, although he sometimes uses the German *Ausbeutung*. The French word certainly had that negative connotation, but Marx "tried to wrest the word away from these [French] origins and to give it an entirely new sense" (Roberts 2016: 109). On the history of the term and Marx's usage of it, Roberts (2016: 108–121) is illuminating. As Roberts notes, Marx's account of exploitation, by emphasizing the impersonal logic of the capitalist marketplace, rejects the earlier French understanding of "individualized and moralized" exploitation (i.e., one person wrongfully taking advantage of another) (2016: 133). See also Raekstad (2022: 232) for related discussion.

24 Cf. Marx's comments about the "fair distribution" in his *Critique of the Gotha Programme* (MECW 24: 84).

25 See the discussion in Chapter 2, Sections 1, 3, and 4.

26 On behalf of Marx, one might observe that the most famous philosophical account of justice in the 20th century—that of John Rawls in *A Theory of Justice* (1971)—presupposes that there will be "exploitation" in Marx's technical sense, and argues only for some degree of redistributive taxation as a requirement of justice. On a Marxian critique of Rawls, Buchanan (1982) is illuminating.

27 Geras (1989: 225–227) is a useful survey. Geras writes: "Does [Marx] say, in fact … that the real and exploitative content of the wage relation is *unjust* or is in violation of anyone's rights? In so many words he does not"—although Geras (225) thinks it is implied, for reasons similar to those offered by G.A. Cohen.

28 Cohen here argues against the view defended by Wood (1981) that Marx could not have thought capitalism was unjust since, as Cohen puts it, "Marx thought all non-relativist notions of justice and injustice were moonshine" (1983: 444). Our view is closer to that of Wood.

29 "Cognitive" judgments are ones that can be true or false: "There is a cat on the mat" is either true or false depending on whether there is a cat on the mat. "Non-cognitive" judgments are ones that express attitudes or feelings that are neither true nor false: e.g., "Yuck, that food is disgusting" or "Ouch" after stubbing one's toe.

30 Alternatively, one might surmise that Marx thinks it is "obvious" that it is robbery; but that of course would beg all the questions against his opponent, so would be rather uninteresting, as most claims about what is "obvious" are.

31 People can adjudge themselves "badly off" without any comparative case in mind; but, for the 19th-century working classes, the comparison case was all

around them in the form of the luxurious living of the landed aristocracy and their own capitalist employers.

32 On how this could count as a conception of moral wrongness, see Leiter (2024).

33 Recall that the supposed moral wrongness of exploitation was a feature of the earlier French approach to exploitation that Marx rejected. See n. 23, above.

34 Marx is entirely "consequentialist" in his thinking: he has a conception of human well-being, and the only question is what set of economic circumstances would maximize well-being.

35 Recall Sowell (2006: 184): "the marginalist revolution in the 1870s shows that neither labor nor any other input determined price because it was not cost of production that was crucial, but the utility of the output to the consumer, which determined whether or to what extent the consumer would be willing to pay to cover those costs." Scholars, writing in a Marxian spirit, have proposed alternative accounts of exploitation in terms of the putative moral wrong involved (e.g., Cohen 1979; Roemer 1985). Whether exploitation is "wrong" is for Marx, as we suggested in the text, an irrelevant and ahistorical question of no significance.

36 Marx devoted significant space to analyzing the subject of land rent. Already in *The 1844 Manuscripts*, he takes extensive notes on Smith's discussion of the topic and endorses his disdain for the landowning class (MECW 3: 259–270). In his mature works, Marx devotes substantial parts of his economic writing to the subject, particularly in volume III of *Capital*, where he spends roughly two hundred pages (see especially, MECW 37: 608–800). Nevertheless, despite this attention, he always regarded the central issue to be the way in which surplus value is generated by the proletariat working for the capitalists, and land rent as a secondary issue concerning one of the various ways this surplus is then doled out to different unproductive classes: "The analysis of landed property in its various historical forms is beyond the scope of this work. We shall be concerned with it only in so far as a portion of the surplus value produced by capital falls to the share of the landowner" (MECW 37: 608).

37 Marx takes it up again in a well-known discussion in volume III of *Capital*, Chapter 48 ("The Trinity Formula"). Lukács (1972 [1923]: 83) gives a famous and apt formulation: "a relation between people takes on the character of a thing and thus acquires a 'phantom [spectral] objectivity,' an autonomy that seems so strictly rational and all-embracing as to conceal every trace of its fundamental nature: the relation between people." (He calls this "reification," although later acknowledged this was an inapt label.) We return to the topic in Chapter 7.

38 The popular notion of a "sexual fetish" preserves the basic idea: someone with a "foot fetish," for example, invests the foot with sexually arousing features it does not possess inherently, but only in the mind of the fetishist.

39 This is different from, although related to, the question in Chapter 2, Section 6 about why people would be motivated to act because the relations of production fetter further development of the forces of production.

40 The ideas were first sketched in the *Grundrisse*.

41 Technology, a key component of constant capital, lasts for an extended period of time. We ignore that complication here. We also ignore an even more technical complication—namely, that the unit of measurement (e.g., *money* or *value*) affects the analysis as well, and yields different conclusions. This has been shown by Roemer (1981).

42 For a more technical analysis of the problem with Marx's analysis, from a sympathetic economist, see Chapter XI in Sweezy (1970).

43 Here is how one Marxist economist makes the same point: "Individual capitalists are *forced* into this movement of restless profiteering (constant accumulation, expansion of production, the introduction of new technology, etc.) by competition with other capitalists: if accumulation is not carried on, if the apparatus of production is not constantly modernized, then one's own enterprise is faced with the threat of being steamrolled by competitors who produce more cheaply or who manufacture better products" (Heinrich 2012: 16).

44 In a 1970 article in the *New York Times*, the economist Milton Friedman, an important ideologist of American capitalism, generated much controversy in the capitalist press by suggesting that businesses should only have as their goal the maximization of profit—which, as Marx would have agreed, is their only possible goal under capitalism. An interesting aspect of ideological illusions is that they sometimes require denying even the most basic facts about the economic system. Other ideologists, like those at the *New York Times*, apparently recognized the danger inherent in correctly describing what American businesses must do if they are to survive, and devoted a special issue in 2020 to revisiting Friedman's article and denouncing it. See "Greed Is Good. Except When It's Bad," *New York Times* (2020, September 13), https://www.nytimes.com/2020/09/13/business/dealbook/milton-friedman-essay-anniversary.html.

45 A widely repeated bit of labor union folklore claims that Walter Reuther, leader of the United Auto Workers labor union in Detroit, toured a new Ford automotive factory that utilized robots to do tasks previously performed by human laborers. The Ford Company executive leading the tour said to Reuther, "Try to get these robots to pay dues to the labor union!" Reuther replied: "Try to sell them your cars!" That is the problem of underconsumption.

46 In the intra-Marxist literature there is a vigorous debate about underconsumption that is somewhat orthogonal to our concerns. Are crises in capitalism caused by the misallocation of production to particular areas of the economy or to falling demand by consumers? We are only interested in the conditions under which capitalism is supposed to collapse according to Marx, and on either account of "crises" that supposes there will be immiseration of the majority.

47 Marx makes a similar point in *Capital II* (MECW 36: 83–84). Credit also complicates this story, in ways that we ignore here. See Evans (1997) for a useful overview, esp. pp. 16–18.

48 Literally, *Mangel* (dearth, lack, shortage).

49 Literally, *Scheisse* (shit).

50 This also marks one of the dramatic breaks from Marx in the writings of the Frankfurt School theorists. As Anton Leist aptly observes: "Horkheimer early on (and in contrast to Marx) favoured a Kantian rationality that was to be held as an ideal over and above the instrumental rationality present in existing society" (2008: 335). This break is then exacerbated by Habermas. We return to this topic in Chapter 7.

51 In later work, Marx allowed that the immiseration of the working class might be "relative" rather than "absolute": in the former case, workers were poor relative to the wealth society as a whole was capable of producing (MECW 9: 216).

52 Much Marxist theory after Marx, including importantly the Frankfurt School theorists, was devoted to trying to understand why communism has not overtaken capitalism in a "more timely" fashion, as it were. The worry, of course, has been that the immiserated, due to false consciousness, are quite tolerant of their misery. Ideological delusion is real, to be sure, and it is part of the task of Marxist political advocacy to shatter it. But the basic mistake of much Marxism after Marx was failure to realize that capitalism had yet to run its course: there is both more productive power and more misery in the offing. And the misery must be sufficient to motivate the counterfactual thought that, if things were otherwise, everything would be better. We return to this topic in Chapter 7.

53 Wolff overstates his case slightly: rational actor models do not deny that collective actions can take place when there are structures of authority and rules that ensure a high degree of compliance, as in military campaigns or voting, and, in a different way, many kinship activities.

54 Buchanan (forthcoming), in Chapters 2 and 3, correctly calls attention to the way in which an "ideology" (in a non-pejorative sense) can also help motivate revolutionary action, as well as help overcome collective action problems.

55 Chapter 5 of Srnicek and Williams (2015) makes the case that he is. Frey and Osborne (2017: 265) give a high-end estimate that 47 percent of U.S. jobs (as categorized by the Bureau of Labor Statistics in 2010) are at "high risk" of automation (just in the decades after 2010—a century hence no one knows). Benanav (2022) is a nuanced, popular account that suggests massive underemployment rather than unemployment is the likely outcome. When the media trumpet "low unemployment" rates, as often happens in the United States, they neglect to mention that the figures exclude those who have given up trying to find work, while including those who work part-time (including just a couple of hours per week), as well as the "underemployed" and those earning poverty wages.

56 It is revealing about the ideological blinders of contemporary neoclassical economics that it had to even be pointed out, by other economists, that technological progress does not necessarily benefit everyone in society.

57 The same technology that makes the dispersal of labor possible may make other forms of collective organization possible, perhaps through the Internet, although there is not much evidence of that to date.

58 It is possible, as noted in the prior section, that mass immiseration will lead the capitalist class to decide to provide the means of subsistence to those whose labor is no longer needed. The recent popularity of "Universal Basic Income" proposals in the Western media is a symptom of the realization of the trajectory of labor markets under capitalism. We may note, in favor of Luxemburg's grim diagnosis, that the capitalist classes have never before in the modern era been charitable on the scale that mass immiseration due to the displacement of human labor by technology would actually require.

59 "Fetishism of commodities" can also be salvaged without the labor theory, if the emphasis is on the way in which commodities become objects of worship and veneration in capitalist societies.

Further Reading

Roemer (1981) is a detailed, technical treatment of Marxian economics.

Sweezy (1970) remains the best overall treatment of Marx's economics.

Wolff (1984), Chapters 2 and 3, offers a helpful introduction to the economic theories of Smith and Ricardo, as well as a more technical treatment of Marx's economic theory.

5
Ideology

As we saw in earlier chapters, Marx frequently claims that moral, religious, philosophical, and economic ideas are "ideological." In Chapter 2, we introduced the idea that ideology functions to legitimize the existing relations of production, part of Marx's theory of historical materialism. In Chapters 3 and 4, we highlighted some of the ways that ideology functions in class conflict in general and under capitalism in particular. However, while this provocative idea is widely considered one of Marx's most distinctive contributions, in his various remarks on ideological belief across his decades-long career he never specifies precisely what he means by the concept, and he employs it in a number of different ways at different points in his work. Moreover, the concept has been extended by others working in the Marxist tradition beyond how Marx himself used it. Consequently, though the term "ideology" itself has entered the common vernacular, commentators have remained divided on what Marx himself really intended by it and whether he had one view or several.

Here we trace Marx's various uses of the concept in more detail than we have done so far, identify what we take to be the essential characteristics of ideology across Marx's different applications, and distinguish his own account from those of subsequent accounts of ideology with which it is often misleadingly equated. We begin with what we call Marx's "Narrow Account"—his critique of all Hegelian-like idealism that treats ideas as the motor of history. This is not the sense of ideology that has dominated in the post-Marxian

DOI: 10.4324/9781315658902-5

traditions. The critique of the Narrow Account of ideology is most prominent in Marx's criticism of the Young Hegelians in the *German Ideology*, though he maintains skepticism about this sort of idealism throughout his career.

We then examine what we will call the "Extended Account" of ideology found throughout his political and economic writings. This is a critique of ideology as the expression of ruling-class interests more generally, whether idealist as in the narrower sense or (mostly) not. Common to both the Narrow and Extended Accounts, we argue, is a general understanding of an ideology as a cluster of inferentially related *beliefs* (and also *causally* related *attitudes*[1]) that have three characteristics:

1. At least some of the ideology's central beliefs are false.
2. The ideology is the product of ideologists (economic, religious, and philosophical "theorists") who systematically make claims underdetermined (or even contradicted) by evidence (typically due to shared biases that undermine their theorizing).
3. The ideology supports the interests (in a sense to be explained) of the ruling class, and harms the interest of the vast majority, most often by misrepresenting how the existing state of affairs affect their interests. This puts the concept of "interests" at the center of the critique of ideology, a point to which we will return.

Thus, an ideological critique aims to unmask false beliefs that harm the interests of those who hold them, while also explaining their genesis in a way that simultaneously explains their prevalence and intractability.

1. The Narrow Account: Ideology Critique as a Critique of "Sociological Idealism"

Though made prominent with Marx's writings, the term "ideology" predates him. It was introduced by Antoine Destutt de Tracy (1754–1836), a member of the school of French empiricist theoreticians influenced by the English philosopher John Locke. De Tracy's project was a "sociology of knowledge," which he termed ideology.

His central claim was that all our ideas (understood to include perception, memory, judgment, and volition) could be traced to the senses; and, since changes in social circumstances lead to changes in sensory stimuli, different circumstances produce people with quite different ideas. With Napoleon, however, ideology became a term of abuse. He charged these same French empiricists, who were emerging as his political opponents, with pursuing hopeless abstractions instead of focusing on practical reality. As we will see, Marx borrows something from both of these applications of the term in tracing out the way in which consciousness stems from material reality, while also castigating the abstract thinking that fails to engage practically with this reality.[2]

In introducing Marx's critique of idealism as an ideology, we should distinguish two senses of idealism. Marx occasionally discusses the term "idealism" in the traditional sense, as an ontological claim that the universe is constituted by minds. In one of his earliest philosophical writings, of course, he had critiqued Hegel as an idealist in just this sense. The protagonist of Hegel's philosophy is *Geist* (spirit or mind), the self-conscious and self-determining subject who posits the objects and institutions of the world in its quest for self-realization. Accordingly, the chief explanatory factor and proper object of study is *Geist* itself, not that to which it gives rise (i.e., the world) and which remains essentially a property of it.

However, typically when Marx criticizes theorists for being idealists, he is not critiquing their ontological commitments about the fundamental nature of reality. Instead, the charge is that they treat ideas as not being the product of the social and economic contexts that gave rise to them, while also granting ideas explanatory pride of place in their accounts of social transformation. Following Charles Mills (1992), we will call this view "sociological idealism." Marx also emphasizes that in critiquing ideology he is not concerned with all theoretical claims in general (e.g., the claims of physics or biology are not his target), but instead with our understanding of human beings and society. He writes, for example, that "natural science, does not concern us here … we will have to examine the history of men, since almost the whole ideology amounts either to a distorted conception of this history or to a complete abstraction from it" (MECW 5: 29). His critique of sociological idealism then is a critique of any theory that thinks ideas can be used to explain social and historical developments without regard to the economic circumstances in which those ideas arise.

This sense of idealism animates Marx's first explicit and sustained discussion of ideology in the *German Ideology* of 1845. This work critiques the Young Hegelians, the left-wing philosophers whose criticisms had recently scandalized Europe and exerted an enormous influence on Marx himself, but whose persisting sociological idealism he now found theoretically misguided and an obstacle to social and political progress. Marx begins by articulating the paradigmatic Young Hegelian thought:

> Hitherto men have always formed wrong ideas about themselves, about what they are and what they ought to be. They have arranged their relations according to their ideas of God, of normal man, etc. ... They, the creators, have bowed down before their creations. Let us liberate them from the chimeras, the ideas, dogmas, imaginary beings under the yoke of which they are pining away.
>
> (MECW 5: 23)

The Young Hegelian solution to this problem is to exhort people to *think differently*: they are to abandon their superstitious beliefs and finally see themselves aright. As Marx describes the Young Hegelian "solution": "[They] consider conceptions, thoughts, ideas ... as the real chains of men" and consequently take it to be "evident that [they] have to fight only against these illusions of consciousness" (MECW 5: 30). Marx rejects this strategy, and warns that the change both he and they desire will not be realized simply by encouraging people to reinterpret the world through a different philosophical lens: "they themselves are opposing nothing but phrases to these phrases, and ... are in no way combating the real existing world when they are combating solely the phrases of this world" (MECW 5: 30). The attempt to change the world by changing one's thinking without addressing the material conditions that give rise to this thinking in the first place is a hopelessly ineffectual endeavor rooted in sociological idealism.

This conception of idealism in the sociological sense underwrites Marx's claim to find idealism in theorists of all kinds, not only in

Hegel's philosophical heirs who have yet to free themselves from his idealism: "There is no specific difference between German idealism and the ideology of all the other nations. The latter too regards the world as dominated by ideas, ideas and concepts as the determining principles" (MECW 5: 24). It also underwrites Marx's claim that ideologists "give a sort of theoretical independence" to "the conditions of existence of the ruling class" by expressing them in legal and moral theories that appear independent of the conditions that gave rise to them, noting,

> here, as in general with ideologists … they inevitably put the thing upside-down and regard their ideology both as the creative force and as the aim of all social relations, whereas it is only an expression and symptom of these relations.
>
> (MECW 5: 419–420)

In other words, sociological idealism afflicts any sort of theorizing that considers ideas about human relations independently of the social conditions that give rise to them, and which accords these ideas explanatory priority with respect to social transformation. (This is one of the main reasons Marx does not produce normative moral and political philosophy.) Philosophy is guilty; but so too religion, which explains the human world as a creation of the supernatural realm instead of the reverse, as well as the "superannuated idealism" of legal and political thinking "which considers the actual jurisprudence as the basis of our economical state, instead of seeing that our economical state is the basis and source of our jurisprudence," and so on (MECW 43: 490).

Marx attempts not only to critique sociological idealism as erroneous but also to explain the genesis of this error in order to explain its pervasiveness. Why, then, do social theorists almost universally succumb to this sort of idealism? Again, sociological idealism involves both a failure to recognize the social origins of one's thinking and an overestimation of thought's influence on social transformation. Marx suggests the first failure stems from a theorist's diminished contact with the basic material conditions resulting from the division of labor—that is, from the fact that ideologists labor only in the domain of ideas (think of university professors or opinion writers at newspapers). Their overestimation of the causal power of ideas Marx attributes to a bias resulting from their own professional status and its preoccupations.

Ideologists in general make the mistake of believing that ideas govern social reality, and the ideologists working within each particular "ideological subdivision" come to view social reality as largely governed by their areas of specialty. The cleric believes that social reality is ultimately governed by spiritual forces; legal theorists believe it is legal ideas; and the same with ethicists, metaphysicians, economists, political theorists, and so on. Theorists systematize thinking within their respective domains, and this "exclusive, systematic occupation with these thoughts on the part of ideologists and philosophers" encourages the valorization of their particular domain of research (MECW 5: 446–447). This is "why the ideologists turn everything upside-down"—that is, why they imagine the explanatory relationship between material conditions and theoretical ideas to be the reverse of what it actually is:

> everyone believes his craft to be the true one [and] illusions regarding the connection between their craft and reality are the more likely to be cherished by them ... The judge, for example, applies the code, he therefore regards legislation as the real, active driving force.
>
> (MECW 5: 92)

This is an illusion owing to social position, and Marx's suggestion is that it can be explained both as a result of what we would now call a cognitive bias (a theorist overestimates the significance their particular specialty plays in the world because of the significance it plays in their own life), as well as what we would now call a motivational bias (a theorist comes to "cherish" their role and desires it to have a greater significance than it truly does).

In addition to identifying the error of idealism and explaining its genesis, Marx highlights the way that sociological idealism functions to bolster the prevailing social structures and the norms to which these give rise. Both Marx and the Young Hegelians criticized Hegel's idealism on these grounds. As we discussed in Chapter 1, Hegel's dictums—such as "the state is the divine idea as it exists on earth" (Hegel 2004: 39) and "what is rational is actual; and what is actual is rational" (Hegel 1991: 20)—were taken to be philosophically cloaked defenses of the Prussian state of his day. The "Left" Young Hegelians rejected Hegel's perceived glorification of the prevailing social order and were outspoken critics of it. Marx notes that these criticisms were "received by the German public with horror and awe" and the Young Hegelians viewed themselves as radical social critics unleashing "world-shattering danger and criminal ruthlessness" on society, as Marx puts it sarcastically (MECW 5: 23). However, Marx argues that the sociological idealism still at the core of their thinking ensured their criticisms would be ineffective.

In failing to address the material relations that are the source of social domination, the Young Hegelian philosophy does nothing to combat it. In fact, it does worse than nothing since it *distracts* attention away from the actual means of doing so. "The Young-Hegelian ideologists", Marx concludes, "in spite of their allegedly 'world-shattering' phrases, are the staunchest conservatives ... they are in no way combating the real existing world when they are combating solely the phrases of this world" (MECW 5: 30). They are deluded about the efficaciousness of their social theorizing, and their projects amount to nothing more than a distraction from addressing the material conditions that actually determine the social domination they seek to challenge. Consequently, the Young Hegelian project contributes to protecting the prevailing social order, despite its intention to do otherwise.

In sum, Marx's critique of the Young Hegelians and other sociological idealists faults them for their idealist presuppositions, and labels them "ideologists" in virtue of these. They treat social and political ideas as though their full significance can be comprehended independently of the social contexts that give rise to them, and they grant these ideas explanatory pride of place in their accounts of social transformation. This is an illusion on both counts, and it is owing in part to the fact that theorists work at a distance from the material conditions that give rise to the social relationships that structure their thinking, as well as working in specialized enclaves, which leads them to overestimate the role their particular area of thought plays in determining the social world.

Finally, the idealist emphasis on changing people's ideas distracts attention away from changing the material conditions that are the real source of social domination; and, consequently, this idealist theorizing does nothing to challenge the status quo (and may even reinforce it), regardless of the aims of the idealists themselves. In short, we have a case that fits the ideological schema we outlined in our introduction: idealist views are false (the epistemic component); they originate in the biases of those who theorize them (the genetic component); and they help to sustain (sometimes inadvertently) the prevailing social structures (the functional component).

2. The Extended Account: Ideology as the Expression of Class Interests

After *The German Ideology*, Marx is less interested in sociological idealism, and more interested in a different critique of ideology—namely, as the expression of powerful class interests, especially ruling-class interests.[3] In societies riven by class conflict, this means ideologies will typically work against the interest of the non-dominant classes. The form of the concept remains the same: the various critiques of ideology in the extended sense that Marx presents still involve highlighting false beliefs, which have been distorted by various biases affecting those who originally theorize them, and which serve to support or sustain the prevailing social structures. However, the content has expanded: in these extended cases the epistemic failings and genetic explanations of the latter are no longer attributed primarily to sociological idealism.

Marx's writings on politics, particularly his responses to the 1848 revolution in France and its aftermath, are a rich source of this extended reading. In *The Class Struggles in France* (1848–50), for example, Marx repeatedly describes the guiding ideals of the various class factions that he discusses as ideological. Whereas the restored Bourbon Monarchy in France (1814–1830) had represented the interests of the landowners, the subsequent Orléanist Monarchy (1830–1848) had represented the interests of the financiers. Orléanist King Louis-Philippe, however, was careful to appoint puppets to public positions rather than the financiers themselves, since effective governance required keeping up the appearance of neutrality, and this meant that "privileged interests had to bear ideologically disinterested names" (MECW 10: 114).

Mass uprisings of workers toppled the Orléanist Monarchy in February of 1848, and what is known as the Second Republic was established as an unsteady coalition of competing social classes. Within six months the moderate Republican faction of the Second Republic had driven working-class representatives out of the government. Briefly dominant, these Republicans valorized formal political rights (e.g., universal suffrage, press freedom, etc.) and inscribed these "ideal basic features in the constitution," although they actively worked at the same time to undo the social rights (most significantly, programs guaranteeing employment) that the working-class representatives in the government had briefly achieved (MECW 10: 85). Within another six months, however, the Republicans themselves were largely driven out by a coalition of Bourbon and Orléanist monarchists known as the "Party of Order" who set out to "strip the constitution of its ideological trimmings" and complete the renewed and undisguised "subjugation of the proletariat" (MECW 10: 86). Marx writes that the Republicans were so "steeped in [their own] ideology" as to be "stupefied" at this turn of events (MECW 10: 86). However, their commitment to their own ideals ultimately proved quite thin, as they too worked to alter the constitution (for example, repealing freedom of association protections) in an attempt to preserve what little power they had left: "the respectable republicans surrendered the exaltation of their ideology more cheaply than the worldly enjoyment of governmental power" (MECW 10: 90).

What is notable about this case study is that the ideologies of different powerful classes are in conflict. However, Marx is especially interested in the role of the ideology of the ruling class in mature capitalist societies, namely, the capitalist class—that is, those who own the main forces of production. In *Capital*, for instance, Marx claims that the capitalist seeks to conquer economic markets both at home and abroad. In foreign markets, the capitalist "has at his back the power of the mother country," and so is able to simply "clear out of his way by force" those who oppose him (this is how the British Empire mostly worked, and Marx would have been familiar with it). However, at home, the capitalist class is better served by winning people over with ideas; and it does so, according to Marx, by employing an ideologist—"the sycophant of capital, the political economist"—to proclaim the legitimacy of the capitalist's aims, which the economist does "with all the more anxious zeal and all the greater unction, the more loudly the facts cry out in the face of his ideology" (MECW 35: 752). Marx continues to highlight the symbiotic relationship between the "capitalist and his ideological representative, the political economist" throughout his later writings (MECW 35: 573). At the heart of his critique is the idea that the theorizing of the economists "corresponds to the interests of the ruling classes by proclaiming the physical necessity and eternal justification of their sources of revenue and elevating them to a dogma" (MECW 37: 817).

3. The Function (and Varieties) of Ideological Belief

In both the Narrow and Extended Accounts, ideology functions to support the interests of the dominant class, at the expense of the interests of other classes. We shall discuss four ways in which ideological beliefs promote ruling-class interests (three of which Marx identified, and a fourth that later Marxists have emphasized). All four impair the epistemic capacity of people—that is, their capacity to recognize what is actually happening in their social and economic environment and how it affects their "interests" (about which more, below). The first two share in common that they accomplish this by directly promulgating *false* claims about the social and economic environment (we will call these the *Core Cases of Ideologies* since these are the most familiar ones for the later Marxist tradition). The latter two share in common that they do this by *diverting attention* from social and economic reality and how it affects people's interests, often doing so inadvertently (we shall call these *Distraction Ideologies*).

A. Core Cases of Ideologies

In the "Core Cases," ideologies promote the interests of the ruling class, and harm the interests of other classes, by misrepresenting the nature of the social and economic world along one or both of the following dimensions: (1) they represent what is really in the interest of only a particular class (the ruling class) as though it is in everyone's interest (i.e., "the general interest"); and/or (2) they represent social and economic phenomena that are, in fact, contingent and local as being necessary and universal.

A nice example of the first Core Case is Marx's discussion of how, during the French Revolution, the ascendant bourgeoisie enlisted the other classes in common opposition against the monarchy. This required, in part, persuading the other classes—particularly the peasants and urban workers carrying out the actual fighting—that the formal political principles the bourgeois class was pressing for (personal freedoms, property rights, modest extensions of voting rights, etc.) were the true aims of the revolution and the conditions of general emancipation:

> No class of civil society can play this role without arousing a moment of enthusiasm in itself and in the masses, a moment in which it fraternises and merges with society in general ... only in the name of the general rights of society can a particular class lay claim to general domination.
>
> (MECW 3: 184)

Having consolidated power, however, Marx argues that bourgeois principles in fact proved to be emancipatory only for its own members, since formal political freedoms mean very little for those lacking the means to realize them. Marx thus concludes that the bourgeoisie "emancipates the whole of society but only provided the whole of society is in the same situation as this class, e.g., possesses money and education or can acquire them at will" (MECW 3: 184). The primary task of the ideologist in this context is to carry on promoting the belief that the new ruling class continues to represent everyone's interest, and to obscure the fact that life for most under the new regime is not so very different from how it was under the old one.

Marx offers many examples of the second kind of Core Case. The economist and clergyman Thomas Malthus (1766–1834), for instance, did not deny that some lived in opulence while most endured lives of miserable toil. However, he provided arguments that purported to explain why this unfortunate state of affairs was necessary. First, he argued that the demand for luxury items by the unproductive classes (landlords, financiers, etc.) was the real motor of the economy, and that therefore a society's economic health required protecting the standing of these privileged classes. Second, he argued that any relief offered to the poor only led to an increase in the population, which would in turn undermine any benefits this relief initially provided, and so there is ultimately nothing that anyone can do to help. Marx found Malthus especially contemptable, dismissing him as a "bought advocate" who provided "a new justification for the poverty of the producers of wealth, a new apology for the exploiters of labour ... a sycophantic service" for the ruling class (MECW 31: 350, 347).

Marx faults both Adam Smith and David Ricardo, two thinkers he otherwise respects tremendously (see Chapter 4), for having taken for granted that the capitalist system was simply the highest expression of the form of social organization that had always characterized human activity, rather than being a contingent form of social organization made possible by technological progress (MECW 35: 14; 32: 243–244). This was manifest in several ways in their work. At its foundation was a picture of natural man as engaged in self-interested free trade, which Marx considered a fantasy of the 18th-century imagination (MECW 28: 17–18). Similarly, they failed to recognize wage labor and commodity production as recent forms of economic organization distinct from prior forms of production and trade that they only superficially resembled (MECW 34. 406–407). This resulted in a failure to grasp the exploitation of labor distinctive of capitalism (see Chapter 4, Section 5) and to underestimate the significance of the class conflict emerging in response to it (MECW 35: 14). In short, Marx's charge is that the classical economists read capitalism into human nature itself. Their work aimed to understand capitalism, as well as to improve what it did best (efficient production); but they treated its harsher commitments (the inevitability of triumphant winners and immiserated losers) as inherent features characteristic of social life generally. Consequently, their "conception is, on the whole, in the interests of the industrial bourgeoisie" (MECW 31: 348).

B. Distraction Ideologies

Marx and later Marxists have identified three phenomena here: (1) ideologists who deflect intellectual attention away from what actually matters for changing society to ephemera; (2) ideologists who deflect attention away from the primary causes of people's suffering through scapegoating; and (3) ideologists who distract people through intellectual diversions or cultural amusements.

Marx's primary example of the first kind of ideologist, as we saw in Section 1 of this chapter, were the Left Young Hegelians who, by fixating on changing people's ideas instead of their material circumstances, left the status quo intact and deflected intellectual energy in a direction that was impotent to change anything. Marx's critique of contemporaneous "utopian socialist" theorists such as Henri de Saint-Simon (1760–1825), Charles Fourier (1772–1837), and Robert Owen (1771–1858) was similar. These progressive thinkers noted many of the same social ills that Marx himself highlighted, and similarly diagnosed class division as their cause. In contrast to Marx, however, their attempts at change consisted in making moral appeals to both the dominating and dominated classes alike, as well as creating little communities that might model in miniature the practicability and desirability of a fair society. Marx considered these attempts to be inefficacious distractions from meaningful political engagement:

> they reject all political, and especially all revolutionary, action; they wish to attain their ends by peaceful means, and endeavour, by small experiments, necessarily doomed to failure, and by the force of example, to pave the way for the new social Gospel.
>
> (MECW 6: 515)

Marx echoes this criticism of inefficacious moral appeals in general and of socialist utopianism specifically three decades later in *Critique of the Gotha Programme*, objecting that:

> [It is] a crime … to force on our Party … ideas which … have now become obsolete verbal rubbish, while again perverting, on the other, the realistic outlook, which it cost so much effort

to instil into the Party but which has now taken root in it, by means of ideological … trash so common among the … French Socialists.

(MECW 24: 87)[4]

The second sort of distraction ideology—in which the ideologist deflects attention away from the primary cause of people's suffering through scapegoating—is exemplified in the sort of xenophobia the British elites cultivated among the British working class against the Irish, as discussed in Chapter 3. British colonization of Ireland led to displaced Irish populations seeking work in England, which drove down the wages of the already exploited English working class. As a result, "[t]he ordinary English worker hates the Irish worker as a competitor who forces down the standard of life." This resentment, Marx writes, "is the secret of the English working class's impotence, despite its organisation. It is the secret of the maintenance of power by the capitalist class. And the latter is fully aware of this" (MECW 43: 474, 475). Since this antagonism keeps the British working class focused on the Irish working class as a threat, rather than as an ally whom it should join in solidarity against the capitalists, its resentments are encouraged by the capitalists, who ensure that "this antagonism is kept artificially alive and intensified by the press, the pulpit, the comic papers, in short by all the means at the disposal of the ruling class" (MECW 43: 475). Marx adds that this cultivated antagonism is roughly the same as that which characterizes the relationship between the poor white people and the former slaves in the United States.

The third kind of "distraction" was emphasized by later writers in the Marxist tradition, one in which intellectual or cultural activity that does not explicitly aim at the defense of capitalism can nonetheless serve to distract attention from its ill effects and those who profit from it. The most potent critique along these lines in the Marxist tradition was the Frankfurt School's attacks on the "culture industry"—the profit-driven system that produces and mass distributes cultural products (television shows and movies, popular music, magazines, etc.) that increasingly occupy most people's free time. These products promise their consumers some entertainment to ease the drudgery of the workweek. One can "turn off one's mind" and relax into the deeply familiar (because endlessly recycled) characters and plotlines, melodies and rhythms, and jokes and truisms it offers up.

At the same time that these products are aiming to entertain, they are also training their consumers in conformity. For example, a miserable young woman who is exploited and harassed at her workplace can unwind after hours by turning on a television "comedy" that features a heroine in a situation resembling her own. Overworked and underpaid, the charming and quick-witted heroine tries to navigate a series of "funny" escapades like securing enough food to eat. "The script," Adorno writes,

> is a shrewd method of promoting adjustment to humiliating conditions by presenting them as objectively comical and by giving a picture of a person who experiences even her own inadequate position as an object of fun apparently free of any resentment.
>
> (2001: 167)

He emphasizes that the cultural industry does not succeed in providing all that much satisfaction to the consumers who have become dependent on it: "without admitting it they sense that their lives would be completely intolerable as soon as they no longer clung to satisfactions which are none at all" (Adorno 2001: 112). Nevertheless, the culture industry is tremendously successful at preventing consumers from developing the attention and critical skills necessary to recognize and oppose the social and political forces primarily responsible for their suffering.

Notice that the latter Distraction Ideology, unlike the Core Cases, does not necessarily involve falsehoods or claims underdetermined by evidence. (The sociological idealists make an implicit mistake about causation, but the "culture industry" often does not have any representational content that could be false.) In the discussion that follows, we shall, accordingly, focus on the Core Cases of ideology that promote ruling-class interests by misrepresenting the interests of a particular class as in the general interest, and by presenting local or contingent phenomena as universal or necessary.

C. Interests

Ideologies promote the interests of the ruling class in the fairly simple sense that they help the ruling class remain in power by legitimizing its rule, and thus its control of wealth. But ideologies also have the striking characteristic that those not in the ruling class who accept an ideology are harming their own interests (their own well-being, we might say), even though they do not realize it. This is central to Marx's account, which means the concept of "interests" is crucial, and we need to say more than simply that the ideology allows the rulers to rule and prevents the subjugated from doing so.

How can people make a mistake about their "interests"? This depends on how one understands the idea of "interests" (we return to this topic in Chapter 6). Marx, early to late, clearly accepts an "objectivist" view of interests in the following precise sense: while a person's subjective mental states like desires, preferences, and attitudes (hereafter "desires" for short) may provide *evidence* about a person's interests, they play no constitutive role. Someone's true interests do not depend on what the person desires, even under ideal epistemic conditions (for example, when the person has all relevant information). Objectivist views of interests are compatible with the possibility of mistake, since what is in a person's interest does not depend on what the person desires (on the plausible assumption that people are typically not mistaken about what they consciously desire): people can be unaware of the objective facts about their interests, just as they can be unaware of the objective facts discovered by physics or biology.

Why accept an objectivist view of interests? Many objectivist views are what the English philosopher Derek Parfit dubbed "objective list" views (1984: 4) that identify a list of activities, accomplishments, and/or capacities that are constitutive of well-being or a "good life." What justifies belonging on the list is typically an appeal to intuition or what is purportedly "self-evident"—a methodology totally foreign to Marx, early or late, who recognized that judgments of this kind are always influenced by historical and economic context. Sometimes, however, the list is justified by appeal to a second objectivist strategy, which seems closer to Marx's view. The young Marx was clearly attracted to a kind of Aristotelian argument, according to which what is good for a person (what is in that person's interests) is the full realization of her essential (natural) capacities: flourishing according to one's nature is central to a person's interests. Marx never published his main arguments for this view, recognizing that they were irrelevant to political practice: the capitalist class was not going to abandon its economic system because it is wrong to interfere with human flourishing. The early Marx's developed views on this score (especially in The 1844 Manuscripts) are evocative but also not wholly plausible, for reasons we return to in Chapter 6.

Throughout his work, however, including his mature work, Marx presupposed something like an objectivist view, albeit in a much thinner sense than in his early writings of 1844.[5] First, Marx plainly believed that what would really precipitate revolutionary resistance to capitalism was the immiseration of most people—i.e., the failure of capitalism to meet their "basic needs": for adequate food, clothing, shelter, leisure, and the like. One might think, plausibly, that the latter are set by the basic biological and psychological nature of human beings. Second, and more ambitiously, Marx always presupposed that humans, by their nature, need to engage in productive activity unrelated to trying to meet basic needs. In his early work, Marx described this as "spontaneous activity" in which a person produced things "even when he is free from physical need."[6] Indeed, humans sometimes "also form objects in accordance with the laws of beauty" (MECW 3: 274, 276, 277)—that is, simply for aesthetic satisfaction.[7] (The contrast is with the non-human animals that produce "only under the dominion of immediate physical need" (MECW 3: 276). Human beings are, in Marx's view, sui generis not in their ability but in their need to work independently of meeting their basic needs: humans need to satisfy their aesthetic and expressive interests through productive activity (we will refer to these in what follows simply as "expressive" interests or needs). That is the most important legacy throughout Marx's corpus of his early attempts to develop an objectivist view about interests.

It might seem surprising, of course, that people could possibly fail to realize that they have an interest in meeting their basic needs! It is perhaps more plausible that people who have been ground down their whole lives by the need to earn wages to survive might not realize they have expressive needs; but then the plausibility of the claim turns on the objectivist assumption that people really have such needs, even if they do not recognize them.

In both cases, however, there is a further important point about Marx's critique of ideology at stake. Recall the first Core Case of ideology, involving confusing the general interest with what was really in the interest of a *particular* class. There are two ways to suffer such confusion: either by being confused about *intrinsic* or *extrinsic* interests. Intrinsic interests are objective goods that are either ends in themselves for the agent or interests that are essential to survival. Extrinsic interests are the agent's interests in the means towards realizing their intrinsic interests. *Confusion about extrinsic interests is actually the dominant modality of Marx's critique of ideology.* To put it rather too simply, Marx assumes that the immiserated want to satisfy their intrinsic interests; but, thanks to ideology, they mistakenly think their inability to do so under capitalism is due to something other than the economic system in which they live (a mistake about extrinsic interests). They mistakenly think that capitalism is in everyone's interest, when it is only in the extrinsic interest of the ruling class.

Recall Marx's French Revolution example. On his telling, the peasants and urban workers (those who did the actual fighting against the monarchy) certainly recognized that they were badly off under the monarchy. Their mistake was in thinking that the replacement of the monarchy with bourgeois political liberties would actually emancipate them. They correctly perceived that the monarchy was not in their (intrinsic) interest, but they were incorrect in thinking that a revolution *only* on behalf of political liberties was *actually* in their (extrinsic) interest.

The same is true of Marx's example of Malthus. Those who lived in conditions of poverty and toil clearly recognized their basic needs were not being met adequately, and neither Marx nor Malthus denies that. Malthus, however, purported to explain to them why that was necessary: the ideology he propagated did not try to convince the miserable that they were not miserable, only that it was *necessary* that they be miserable. It is the latter that Marx derides as mere "ideology": Malthus falsely represents as necessary a form of socio-economic organization that is not in the extrinsic interest of the vast majority.

Ideological mistakes attract Marx's attention precisely because they adversely affect the intrinsic or extrinsic interests of the majority. Marx was most often, but not exclusively, concerned with mistakes about extrinsic interests.[8] Mistakes about extrinsic interests, however, are only of concern if the underlying assumptions about intrinsic interests are correct (a mistake about the means towards ends not worth realizing is not a mistake anyone would care about): in that respect, Marx needs the idea of mistakes about *intrinsic* interests as well.

4. Explaining Ideological Mistakes

Jon Elster aptly observes (1985: 459) that:

> Marx was never content with stating his own views and criticizing those of others. In addition, he wanted to explain how others came to hold their erroneous views. The theories of others were not treated mainly as alternative views of the same social reality that he also studied ... Rather he considered them to be part of the reality to be explained.

This is central to Marx's treatment of ideology: he wants to explain how it is people believe false claims that are actually against their own interests. We have already remarked that in the Core Cases, an ideology is the product of ideologists who systematically make claims underdetermined by evidence, typically due to shared biases that undermine their theorizing. In this regard, what ideologists do is an instance of poor theorizing more generally. It is important to emphasize that Marx rarely imputes insincerity to the ideologists. For example, when critiquing the bourgeois ideologist's belief that their particular class interests represent the general interest, Marx cautions,

> one must not form the narrow-minded notion that the petty bourgeoisie, on principle, wishes to enforce an egoistic class interest. Rather, it believes that the special conditions of its emancipation are the general conditions within which alone modern society can be saved.
>
> (MECW 11: 130)

Ideology is typically born of error, not deception. This means that we do not need to imagine that all the economic, social, and political ideologists are part of a secret cabal working together producing propaganda in order to dominate the masses. It does mean, however, that we will want some plausible explanations for how typically sincere ideologists could be so prone to systematic error, and in a way that tends to favor the dominant interests. Marx sketches several and, strikingly, recent empirical results from the cognitive sciences help flesh out and support his claims.[9]

Many of Marx's explanations of the mistakes of ideologists are instances of what social psychologists now call "cognitive biases," which lead sincere theorists to respond too uncritically to the evidence before them. The tradition of cognitive bias research is most closely associated with the work of psychologists Daniel Kahneman and Amos Tversky, whose central claim (which has now become a central tenet of contemporary work on human judgment) is that our judgments are typically made using heuristics—automatic and simplifying mental shortcuts that focus our attention on certain features of a situation while ignoring others (Tversky & Kahneman 1974). While these heuristics can expedite cognitive processing, they also lead to significant and systematic errors in our judgments. Considered separately, these various biases reveal curious vices that undermine our ability to judge accurately; taken together, they demonstrate myopia that affects our theorizing more generally—a pronounced tendency to orient our thinking around the information that is directly before us, and in ways that confirm rather than challenges it, while resisting subsequent epistemic updating and revision. Moreover, these cognitive biases that favor ready-to-hand information will simultaneously favor the status quo, since status quo ideas and expectations constitute the majority of ready-to-hand information (see Eidelman & Crandall 2009).

Marx suggests at least three general ways that ideologists err in their theorizing along these lines. First, theorists overgeneralize based on how things presently appear to be—including, for example, a tendency to treat the currently existing state of affairs as reflecting deep facts about human nature and the nature of the world. As Marx puts it,

> [The theorist's] reflections on the forms of social life, and consequently, also, his scientific analysis of those forms, take a course

directly opposite to that of their actual historical development. He begins, *post festum* with the results of the process of development ready to hand before him [at which point things have] already acquired the stability of natural, self-understood forms of social life.

(MECW 35: 86)

So, for example, under capitalism, most individuals must compete in the marketplace to sell their labor power to survive, so self-preservation under capitalism demands constant competition and self-interested calculating. Ideologists interpret this as evidence that egoism and competition are characteristics of human nature, rather than a consequence of economic circumstances. Subsequent ideological theorizing works from these presumptions rather than disabusing us of them.

Second, theorists often take it for granted that the familiar problems are the most important ones, and that the received ways of approaching these problems are the most apt. Consequently, they inevitably fail to recognize new issues that emerge (e.g., David Ricardo's failure to grasp the significance of the class conflict emerging around him) and/or they lack the intellectual imagination to address them, "driven, theoretically, to the same problems and solutions" (MECW 11: 130), while also tending to close their minds off to those who would challenge status quo orthodoxy, "just like a man who believes in a particular religion and sees it as the religion, and everything outside of it only as false religions" (MECW 32: 158).

Third, theorists uncritically accept the testimony of others, and especially of other ideological theorists. Marx writes that they "take every epoch at its word and believe that everything it says and imagines about itself is true" (MECW 5: 62, amended slightly)—a point emphasized again a bit more forcefully by Engels in The Peasant War in Germany, writing "ideologists are gullible enough to accept unquestioningly all the illusions that an epoch makes about itself, or that ideologists of some epoch make about that epoch" (MECW 10: 411). This results in an ideological echo-chamber that increasingly amplifies and reinforces the apparent legitimacy of the prevailing social structures.

The sorts of cognitive errors described above are often the focus of Marx's critiques. However, he also notes cases where the *motivations* of the theorists are the source of error, even though the theorists are not aware of how these motivations are influencing them. As the English philosopher Francis Bacon (1561–1626), another great early expositor of bias, observed: "The human understanding is not composed of dry light, but is subject to influence from the will and emotions, a fact that creates fanciful knowledge; man prefers to believe what he wants to be true" (Bacon 2000: 44). "Motivated reasoning," as psychologists call it, is the process of evaluating evidence and argumentation in a way that enables one to reach a desired conclusion, though typically without realizing that this is what one is doing. The most obvious way in which motivation can affect judgment is by establishing the desired outcome as the hypothesis, and then working to confirm this hypothesis through asymmetrical testing of confirming and disconfirming evidence (Kunda 1990). This has helpfully been characterized as the difference between asking, "Can I believe this?" of evidence supporting the desired conclusion, and "Must I believe this?" of evidence contrary to it (Gilovich 1991). Consequently, we can work ourselves into sincerely believing all sorts of false or insufficiently supported things we wish to be true.

In this vein, Marx argues that when some bourgeois theorists confront a phenomenon that serves the capitalists while harming the working class, they experience a moment of cognitive dissonance. They chiefly desire preserving the capitalist system, but they are initially troubled at the suffering it produces. To resolve this tension, they are motivated to construct a theory that shows this phenomenon to be inevitable, and therefore something to be accepted rather than overcome a theory that

> silences his conscience, makes hard-heartedness into a moral duty and the consequences of society into the consequences of nature, and finally gives him the opportunity to watch the destruction of the proletariat by starvation as calmly as other natural events without bestirring himself.
>
> (MECW 6: 433–434)

Similarly, Marx observes that the political economist, motivated both by a desire to quiet his conscience and to resolve theoretical headaches, attempts to theorize away the tensions in the economic system that he promotes: "the desire to convince oneself of the nonexistence of contradictions, is at the same time the expression of a pious wish that the contradictions, which are really present, should not exist" (MECW 32: 149). Here the theorist is subject to the sorts of cognitive dissonance reduction strategies characteristic of much motivated bias and their theorizing aimed more at reaching a desired outcome than discovering the truth.

Unlike all the prior sources of ideology, a final one Marx sometimes invokes attributes to ideologists the *intent to deceive* and is best exemplified by the deliberate bad faith apologia offered by Malthus and his economic heirs. The source is again motivational, though in this case the theorist is perfectly cognizant of this fact. The aim is to provoke belief in others, whether or not the theorist shares this belief (or the grounds of it). Malthus's singular aim was to bolster the dominant classes, and he appealed to scientific principles when these seemed to serve this goal, and quickly abandoned them when they threatened to undermine it (MECW 31: 349–350). As the bourgeoisie "conquered political power," Malthus's economic heirs increasingly worked to bolster this new arrangement:

> It was thenceforth no longer a question, whether this theorem or that was true, but whether it was useful to capital or harmful, expedient or inexpedient, politically dangerous or not. In place of disinterested inquirers, there were hired prize fighters; in place of genuine scientific research, the bad conscience and the evil intent of apologetic.
>
> (MECW 35: 15)

It is important to remember that this is, by Marx's lights, an unusual case: most ideologists make mistakes, but they operate in good faith and genuinely believe the false claims their ideologies propound.

A common challenge to Marx's treatment of ideology is that it seems puzzling that ideologists should make these kinds of mistakes, and that those whose (intrinsic or extrinsic) interests are harmed by ideology should nonetheless accept these ideologies. In fact, research into cognitive biases in recent decades makes these phenomena far less mysterious, and helps support, elucidate, and extend those explanations Marx himself proposed. A cursory canvassing of some of the central findings of the social-psychological tradition shows that both experts and non-experts alike are subject to pervasive cognitive and motivated biases that undermine their judgments in quite profound ways. Moreover, these biases are not only pervasive but directional, tending to distort beliefs in ways that systematically favor the status quo, which in turn supports the underlying economic structures, as well as those who benefit most from these arrangements.

There are roughly two broad varieties of cognitive biases. The first are *order-of-information* biases. These are manifest in the variety of ways in which the information we receive first and/or our prior beliefs exert a disproportionate influence on our understanding of information we subsequently encounter. So, for example, our initial impressions of a stimulus significantly influence how we process new information about it, anchoring our initial judgments in a way that proves difficult to revise (Asch 1946; Jones et al. 1968). People maintain beliefs based on initial information, even after that early information has been totally discredited (Nisbett & Ross 1980); prior expectations, especially those based on stereotypes, lead people to imagine correlations between variables that do not actually exist (Hamilton & Rose 1980), as well as to overlook significant correlations that do (Sanbonmatsu et al. 1994); and, in predictive judgments, the initial consideration of a possible outcome substantially inhibits the subsequent generation of alternatives (Kahneman & Tversky 1982). These order-of-information biases will tend to support and sustain status quo beliefs because they bias the judgments we go on to make about the social and political world in a way that confirms our initial expectations, and these expectations are typically informed by the prevailing social and political discourse.

The second category of cognitive biases are *availability* biases which are manifest in the variety of ways that information at hand exerts too great an influence on judgments, while less readily accessible information is neglected altogether. For example, information that is salient and frequently encountered is more readily brought to mind, resulting in overestimations in likelihood and/or frequency judgments (Tversky & Kahneman 1973; Kuran & Sunstein 1999);

people are insensitive to the importance of missing information (e.g., unaware of the relevance of non-occurrences to estimations of covariation), and confident in judgments made on the basis of evidence known to be weak and one-sided (Ross 1977); people engage in counterfactual thinking only when confronted with surprising disruptions from their routines and expectations, and, even when provoked to do so, they almost exclusively consider only the most easily imagined alternatives (Hitchcock 2011; Kahneman & Tversky 1982); people overestimate the extent to which others share their beliefs and opinions, while often denigrating those who do not (Ross et al. 1977); finally, repeated exposure to something heightens one's positive evaluation of it (Bornstein 1989), as does simply being told that it is the status quo option (Eidelman & Crandall 2012).

As with order-of-information biases, these availability biases systematically favor the status quo, since the status quo is almost by definition that which will be most available. Readily available alternatives may go unnoticed and counterfactual possibilities unimagined. There will be a presumption that status quo norms are more widely held than is the case, while those holding alternative views will be dismissed in advance as unreasonable. The status quo will benefit from the favorability that frequent exposure brings, as well as from it merely being identified as the way things are or have been.

Compounding the influence of these cognitive biases, motivated biases often favor the status quo in pronounced ways. A rich body of research into status quo bias developed from Melvin Lerner's just world research. Just world theory posits that people are motivated to believe that the world is a fair place where people get what they deserve:

> We (humans) do not believe that things just happen in our world; there is a pattern to events which conveys not only a sense of orderliness or predictability, but also the compelling experience of appropriateness expressed in the typically implicit judgment, Yes, that is the way it should be.
>
> (Lerner 1980: vii)

Lerner found that people respond to injustice with a variety of strategies aimed at restoring a sense of order. In the best cases, they respond by trying to right the injustice (e.g., intervening, offering restitution, etc.). However, people also employ a number of alternative strategies: denying the injustice or withdrawing (psychologically and/or physically) from the scene of it; reinterpreting the cause, paradigmatically, by blaming the victim's behavior; denigrating the victim's character so that they seem deserving of the injustice; and reconstructing the injustice in order to minimize it, for example, by focusing on the good consequences of otherwise bad events. Lerner argued that this theory helped to explain the puzzling fact that people denigrate victims in concrete situations, as well as assent to norms, policies, and regimes that consistently inflict suffering on blameless people. These biases will, of course, work to the advantage of ideologists rationalizing the status quo, and will predispose people harmed by the status quo to find ideological rationalizations attractive.

Lerner's research has been supported and extended in the subsequent decades (Hafer & Bègue 2005; Jost 2020), confirming that most people appear to hold just world beliefs, at least implicitly: people avoid exposure to cases of injustice (Pancer 1988), and reinterpret injustice so as to minimize it (Jost & Banaji 1994), as Lerner suggested. And, of course, people denigrate the injustices they perceive: poverty is attributed to character and behavior (Campbell et al. 2001); the elderly are blamed for their poor health and finances (Bègue & Bastounis 2003); refugees are blamed for their plight (Montada 1998), as are victims of natural disasters (Napier et al. 2006); racial groups are denigrated (Neville et al. 2000), as are those suffering from chronic illness (Correia & Vala 2003), and victims of sexual harassment (De Judicibus & McCabe 2001), and so on. Conversely, belief in a just world also correlates with post-hoc rationalizations of unfair advantages enjoyed by oneself and by others (Ellard & Bates 1990; Smith 1985). Finally, research after Lerner has more thoroughly examined various stimuli that heighten expressions of support for the status quo, finding that threats to the system, perceived system inevitability, and system dependence do so in pronounced ways (Jost 2020).

In short, people are motivated to believe that the groups, institutions, and communities to which they belong (or are required to abide) are fair and legitimate. This holds for laypeople and social and political theorists alike, which of course disposes both to ideologies that rationalize inequity and suffering instead of acknowledging and addressing them. Of course, the motivation to support the status quo is neither omnipotent nor omnipresent: people do sometimes profess outrage and things do change over time.[10] What this bias demonstrates, however, is a pronounced tendency by the overwhelming majority of people to over-rationalize the status quo up until the moment that change appears inevitable, at which point attitudes can rapidly shift, as Marx notes happening during epochal transitions.

We have now seen several psychological mechanisms that would help explain why most people suffer, as later Marxists would put it, from "false consciousness"—that is, accepting as true claims that are both false and whose falsity is contrary to their own interests. Marx himself did not give extensive attention to psychological mechanisms, but the contours of his basic explanation seem clear: in addition to experiencing the world as filtered through the very same sorts of biases that affect the ideologists themselves, members of society are subject to a constant barrage of elite messaging:

> The ideas of the ruling class are in every epoch the ruling ideas
> ... The class which has the means of material production at its
> disposal, consequently also controls the means of mental pro-
> duction, so that the ideas of those who lack the means of mental
> production are on the whole subject to it ... [They rule] as
> thinkers, as producers of ideas, and regulate the production and
> distribution of the ideas of their age.
>
> (MECW 5: 59)

The ruling class exerts influence on all of the major institutions that formulate and promote ideas throughout the society (major media, political parties, advocacy groups, universities, the church, and so on), either through ownership, membership, patronage, or their power to sanction. This influences who is admitted into these institutions, the ideas that they consider, and the ideas that they circulate. Marx takes it for granted, plausibly, that even those in non-dominant positions will largely imbibe the messages that surround them from birth onwards.[11] Since all of these messages are filtered through the biases already canvassed, their ability to "stick" should hardly be surprising.

Moreover, it is not just that the vast majority accept the ideas that are constantly broadcast at them; but these ideas then influence how they subsequently process the world around them, which has the perverse consequence of reinforcing these beliefs. The story Marx tells in *Capital* of Mr. Moneybags is cautionary in this respect.[12] We meet Mr. Moneybags, our capitalist, and his new hire as they negotiate the terms of their agreement. This scene, says Marx, appears to be

> a very Eden of the innate rights of man. There alone rule Freedom, Equality, Property and Bentham. Freedom, because both buyer and seller of a commodity ... are constrained only by their own free will. They contract as free agents, and the agreement they come to, is but the form in which they give legal expression to their common will. Equality, because each enters into relation with the other, as with a simple owner of commodities, and they exchange equivalent for equivalent. Property, because each disposes only of what is his own. And Bentham, because each looks only to himself.
>
> (MECW 35: 186)

But, of course, all of this conceals what is in fact coercion on pain of starvation (sell your labor power at this wage, or else remain unemployed and have nothing), which only *appears* to be a mutually beneficial agreement among equals. This transaction, however, would never have appeared as such to anyone not already inundated with capitalist messaging that the labor market is "free," and that anyone is "free" to accept or decline a job.[13] It is only against this background that the economic exchanges embodying them can appear in the manner Marx parodies. This is true for bourgeois observers of such transactions; but it is equally true for the workers, who, thanks to the prevailing ideology, will be deluded into idealizing their own subjection instead of recognizing it as such.

A common objection to the claim that massive ideological indoctrination—due to ruling-class control of the major means of communication—explains the rule of the "few" over the "many" is that there is another reason the "many" may not revolt: namely, a coordination problem (Rosen 1996: 260–262). Coordination problems arise when a large number of people must coordinate their actions in pursuit of a common goal, but it would be in the "interest" of any particular individual to "free ride" on others taking the risks of action. Even putting to one side the doubts raised in Chapter 4 about the claims of rational choice theory that undergird the analysis of coordination problems,[14] the existence of a coordination problem is simply irrelevant to Marx's theory of ideology. Even if the many cannot coordinate their behavior to overthrow the few, the *actual* phenomenon the Marxist theory explains is that the many typically do not *see the need* to overthrow the few—indeed, do not even see that the few rule the many: they accept an ideology that renders the status quo acceptable (because it is supposedly in their interest or because there is no alternative). This is the *actual* explanandum of Marx's theory of ideology.

On the actual point, skeptics retort that the Marxist theory of ideological indoctrination purportedly presupposes

> a view of those who live under the domination of the ruling class as passive victims, taking their ideas from those who control the 'means of mental production' like obedient chicks, with no critical reflection on their part as to whether the ideas are either true or in their own rational interests. This, it seems, is an almost paranoid view. Why should one suppose that the ruling class is capable of promoting its own interests effectively, forming its ideas in response to those interests, whereas the dominated class simply accept whatever is served up to them?
>
> (Rosen 1996: 182–183)

Putting to one side the rhetorical abuse (Marx is "paranoid"), we have already seen the empirical evidence that common psychological mechanisms are conducive to leading people to accept ruling-class ideologies. That helps answer the question why "the dominated class simply accept whatever is served up to them."[15] The more interesting question is why the ruling class "is capable of promoting its own interest." Let us consider a concrete example.

In the United States, a majority of the population favors abolition of the estate tax—what the ideologues of the ruling class now call a "death tax"—believing that it affects them and that it results in the loss of family businesses and farms (Johnston 2001).[16] In fact, only

2 percent of the population pays the estate tax, and there is no docu-
mented case of families losing their farms or businesses as a result
of the tax's operation. Examples like this—in which the majority
have factually inaccurate beliefs that are in the interests of those with
money and power—could, of course, be multiplied. Skeptics about
ideology ask: Why is the ruling class so good at identifying and promoting its interests, while the majority is not? Note, to start, that it is
quite easy to identify one's short-term interests when the status quo
operates to one's material benefit. If the status quo provides tangible
benefits to the few—lots of money, prestige, and power—is it any
surprise that the few are well-disposed to the status quo, and are
particularly good at thinking of ways to tinker with the status quo
(e.g., repeal the already minimal estate tax) to increase their money,
prestige, and power? (The few can then promote their interests for
exactly the reasons Marx identifies and that we noted earlier: they
own the means of mental production.[17])

By contrast, it is far more complex for the vast majority to assess
what actions might be in their interest, precisely because it requires
a counterfactual thought experiment, in addition to evaluating complex questions of socio-economic causation. More precisely, the
"many" have to ascertain that: (1) the status quo—the whole complex socio-economic order in which they find themselves—is not
in their interests (this may be easy if the "many" are immiserated);
(2) there are alternatives to the status quo which would be in their
interest (this is what Marx's theory seeks to explain); and (3) it is
worth the costs to make the transition to the alternatives—to give
up on the bad situation one knows in order to make the leap in to
a (theoretically) better unknown. Obstacles to the already difficult
task of making determinations (1) and (2)—let alone (3)—will
be especially plentiful, precisely because the few are strongly, and
effectively (given their control of the means of mental production),
committed to the denial of (1) and (2). Equally important, the psychological biases discussed earlier will pose a further obstacle. Given
all this, it is hardly surprising that the ruling class, which benefits
from the status quo, has an easier time seeing the merits of the status
quo, while the vast majority are both psychologically predisposed to
accept ruling-class ideologies and face both psychological and intellectual obstacles to assessing the counterfactual alternatives.

5. Marxist Accounts of the Concept of Ideology after Marx

Marx's account of ideology has been variously interpreted and extended by those writing after him. We will devote Chapter 7 to a critical examination of Marx's legacy and influence more broadly; but we should mention here the most prominent post-Marx developments of the concept of ideology, which, while extending Marx's account in (sometimes) illuminating ways, are also often misleadingly equated with it. We discuss them here because they have had a significant impact on the concept of "ideology" that is often associated with Marx and Marxism.

We can distinguish two broad families of post-Marxian uses of ideology: first, those that abandon the pejorative connotation altogether and treat ideology as a neutral term that refers to ideas generally and/or to ideas reflecting specific class interests; and second, accounts that retain the pejorative connotation we found throughout Marx's discussions while also reaching the deeply pessimistic conclusion that capitalism so thoroughly influences our beliefs and values that it is practically impossible to think our way out of the ideological illusion that grips us all.

Ideology as a neutral (or non-pejorative) term is a usage that can plausibly be traced back to Marx himself, particularly to his summary statement of historical materialism in the Preface of *Contribution to the Critique of Political Economy*, where he writes:

> Changes in the economic foundation lead sooner or later to the transformation of the whole immense superstructure. In studying such transformations it is always necessary to distinguish between the material transformation of the economic conditions of production ... and the legal, political, religious, artistic or philosophic—in short, ideological forms in which men become conscious of this conflict and fight it out.
>
> (MECW 29: 263)

As a general description of social-political consciousness and historical transformation, this passage would seem to include the emerging proletariat's own consciousness of class conflict among the forms ideology can take. Insofar as Marx does not treat proletariat consciousness pejoratively, this would indicate that there is nothing inherently wrong with ideological belief. For the first generation of Marxist writers, who lacked access to Marx's most sustained and critical application of the concept in the then-unpublished *German Ideology*, this non-pejorative, inclusive reading may have seemed natural—although it was still in tension with Marx's sustained emphasis throughout his writing on the way in which religious, philosophical, and economic beliefs were false and skewed in favor of the interests of dominant economic groups.

The writings of Vladimir Lenin (1870–1924)—who led the Russian Revolution in 1917 that established the Soviet Union—are a key source for the mainstreaming of the wholly neutral use of ideology within the Marxist tradition, particularly his *What Is To Be Done?* (1902), which foregrounds the development and promotion of "socialist ideology." Here Lenin argues that the proletariat will not "spontaneously" develop the degree of class consciousness requisite to carry out a workers' revolution, as many orthodox Marxists were suggesting at the time. Such a consciousness requires a comprehensive education in economics, politics, and history. While the spontaneous consciousness of the worker mired in their daily grind will register their conflict with the bourgeoisie to a degree, this will remain a myopic "trade unionist" consciousness fixated on receiving small concessions (increased wages, reduced working hours, etc.) instead of recognizing that it is their historical mission to topple bourgeois rule altogether and that now is the time.[18] Consequently, this spontaneous trade unionist consciousness exemplifies rather than combats "the ideological enslavement of the workers by the bourgeoisie" (Lenin, MECW 5: 384). What prevents the typical workers themselves from ever spontaneously transcending this trade union consciousness altogether?

Echoing Marx's thesis that the ruling ideas in a society are those of its ruling class, Lenin claims that this is because of "the simple reason that bourgeois ideology is far older in origin than socialist ideology … it is more fully developed … it has at its disposal immeasurably more means of dissemination" (Lenin, MECW 5: 386). Lenin concludes that, since the proletariat cannot develop a revolutionary class consciousness spontaneously, "class political consciousness can be brought to the workers only from without" (MECW 5: 422)—which is the chief task of the party's intelligentsia, and one that Lenin equates with the promotion of socialist ideology.[19]

Georg Lukács (1885–1971), the Hungarian philosopher and political exile whose 1923 *History and Class Consciousness* is widely regarded as the founding text of "Western Marxism," adopts Lenin's neutral use of ideology. "Marxism," he writes, is the "ideological expression of the proletariat in its efforts to liberate itself" (Lukács 1972: 258–259). The problem he aims to address is why the proletariat has been hampered on its path to achieving "ideological maturity ... a true understanding of its class situation and a true class consciousness," a maturity upon which "the fate of the revolution ... and with it the fate of mankind" (1972: 76, 70) depends. Lukács identifies "reification" as the central obstacle. Recall that in the "commodity fetishism" section of *Capital* I, Marx argues that in the marketplace people's social relations (who makes what, under which conditions, while working for whom) appear merely as relations between things (this object is worth such-and-such compared to that one).[20]

Lukács argues that as the market has increasingly come to dominate all aspects of social life under capitalism, so too does commodity fetishism. Consequently, this process

> stamps its imprint upon the whole consciousness of man; his qualities and abilities are no longer an organic part of his personality, they are things which he can 'own' or 'dispose of' like the various objects of the external world. And there is no natural form in which human relations can be cast, no way in which man can bring his physical and psychic 'qualities' into play without their being subjected increasingly to this reifying process.
>
> (Lukács 1972: 100)

Under capitalism we come to see ourselves and others as we do any other commodity, as instrumentally valuable things of calculable worth; and this appearance in turn reinforces the seeming naturalness of the capitalist system itself. Whereas Lenin explains bourgeois ideological domination in terms of its monopolization of the channels through which ideas are communicated, Lukács explains this ideological domination through the ideas that spontaneously occur to people based on the way that things appear to them as they go about their daily lives in the capitalist system, even apart from any ruling-class messaging. As with Lenin, however, it is bourgeois ideology, not ideology as such, that is the problem. Lukács claims that developing a proletariat "ideology ... [is] the objective and the weapon itself" (1972: 258–259), and his project is an attempt to show how the working class's distinct position vis-à-vis the means of production will enable them to do so, and thereby overcome the reification gripping society.

Antonio Gramsci (1891–1937) was an Italian philosopher, politician, and eventual political prisoner whose *Prison Notebooks* of the 1930s similarly influenced the trajectory of Western Marxism. Like Lukács, Gramsci adopts the non-pejorative use of ideology; and, also like Lukács, he concentrates his theorizing on the ideological forces he identifies as the primary cause of the failure of workers in advanced European countries to revolt as orthodox Marxists had predicted.[21] Gramsci explores the ways in which the ruling class is able to achieve "hegemony"—cultural control through which the other classes come to endorse their own economic and political domination. He endorses Marx and Lenin's general claim that the ruling class monopolizes the institutions responsible for cultivating and disseminating ruling-class ideas, while doing more to detail the particular institutions involved (religious, educational, media, etc.) and the ways in which they carry out their ideological function— emphasizing, in particular, that ideological ideas are cultivated and communicated across a range of domains of varying intellectual rigor (philosophy, religion, common sense, and folklore). Moreover, and most distinctively, Gramsci's account treats ideology not only as the indoctrination of ideas but also as the cultivation of attitudes and orientations: "[ideologies] organise human masses, and create a terrain on which men move, acquire consciousness of their position, struggle etc." (Gramsci 1971: 377). Religion is a paradigmatic instance of ideology in this sense, according to Gramsci, insofar as it results in "a unity of faith between a conception of the world and a corresponding norm of conduct" (1971: 326).

Gramsci's emphasis on attitudes and orientations extends the scope of ideology beyond Marx (among other things, it is not clear how "orientations" can be false as Marx's Core Cases of ideology are), while perhaps helping to explain its recalcitrance in the face of rational critique. As with Lenin and Lukács, however, the problem is not ideology as such, but bourgeois ideology in particular, and Gramsci's project is similarly one of encouraging the development of a proletariat ideology capable of combating it.

The French philosopher Louis Althusser (1918–1990), most notably in his 1970 essay "Ideology and Ideological State Apparatuses," largely restores the pejorative sense of ideology familiar from Marx, while claiming that ideology is not simply a complex of false beliefs that one might unfortunately adopt. It is rather a power that shapes people into the sorts of subjects suitable to the needs of the prevailing economic structure and ensuring that they maintain their usefulness to it. The ruling class controls the "repressive state apparatuses" (the government, military, police, etc.), and is therefore able to control the dominated classes through the threat and/or use of violence. Just as important, however, the ruling class also controls the "ideological state apparatuses" (educational institutions, media, religious and civic organizations, etc.), which it employs to secure social cohesion and sustain prevailing socio-economic relations (Althusser 2014: 256).

Like Gramsci, Althusser understands ideology as the entire complex of ideas, attitudes, and orientations that sustain ruling-class domination. Althusser, however, attempts to go even further in presenting ideological inculcation as a force so pervasive and thorough that individuals are essentially constituted through it: "ideology 'acts' or 'functions' in such a way that it 'recruits' subjects among the individuals ... or 'transforms' the individuals into subjects" (Althusser 2014: 190). Society presents the nascent subject with a delimited set of socially useful roles, which the subject adopts and performs accordingly, thereby completing the process of "interpellation" that simultaneously creates and subjugates the person. Althusser does attempt to distinguish "science" from "ideology," and asserts that the former opens up the possibility of escaping the thoroughgoing subjugation of the latter—though few (including eventually Althusser himself) saw how this was actually possible on the basis of the account he presented.

Finally, with the Frankfurt School—the collaboration of "critical theorists" founded in 1929 in Germany—the conception of ideology as both pejorative and thoroughgoing reaches its high-water mark. The School's members (such as Theodor Adorno and Max Horkheimer) observe that the workers not only fail to revolt, but actively embrace and identify with the capitalist states—even the fascist ones (like those in Germany and Italy in the 1930s)—that increasingly dominate every aspect of their lives. Not only has the ruling class monopolized the state and the ideological institutions, but reason itself has been thoroughly enlisted in its service. The evaluative capacity of reason requisite for social critique and emancipation has now been dismissed as a pre-scientific fiction, reducing reason to an instrumental rationality that treats everything merely as objects to be manipulated in whatever manner one is inclined.[22] Consequently, the role of theorizing itself is now essentially that of futile protest:

> [Philosophy is] thought's powerless attempt to remain its own master and to convict of untruth, by their own criteria, both a fabricated mythology and a conniving, resigned acquiescence … Not that there is any hope that it could break the political tendencies that are throttling freedom throughout the world both from within and without and whose violence permeates the very fabric of philosophical argumentation … In a world that has been thoroughly permeated by the structures of the social order, a world that so overpowers every individual that scarcely any option remains but to accept it on its own terms, such naiveté reproduces itself incessantly and disastrously.
>
> (Adorno 2005: 10–12)

Ideology, on this most pessimistic of accounts, is terrible and very little hope of emancipation remains.

As we noted earlier, although the non-pejorative use of ideology can plausibly be traced back to some things Marx said, it is important to emphasize that this was not his standard usage. We have already seen that in the particular cases of ideological belief that Marx discusses, he employs the term in a critical fashion—ideological beliefs are illusions, inversions, semblances, hypocrisies, and so on. Moreover, Marx frequently characterizes ideological beliefs as illusory, not just in particular cases but generally: "the illusion of ideologists in general [*überhaupt*]" (MECW 5: 62), "as in general with ideologists ... they inevitably put the thing upside-down" (5: 420), "a [false] belief he shares with all ideologists" (5: 468), and so on.[23] Finally, Marx, unlike Lenin, Lukács, and Gramsci, nowhere refers to his own thoughts as ideological; nor does he ever speak of the proletariat ideology; and he certainly never treats the development of a proletariat ideology as the last hope of humanity. He emphasizes that the Communist Party will help the proletariat in seeing through ideology, not by developing its own substitute ideology but by giving it a factually correct understanding of its historical situation.

Nevertheless, there are a few passages where Marx's precise meaning is ambiguous; whether he used the term inconsistently at various points is a controversial point we will not attempt to settle here. What is most important is the distinctive features of Marx's actual critiques of the Core Cases of ideology that we have discussed above, namely: (1) religious, philosophical and economic thought incorporates many false beliefs, which (2) have been systematically distorted by psychological facts and social circumstances affecting the theorizing of the ideologists who originally formulated them; and (3) these beliefs function to support the interests of the ruling class while undermining the interests of the vast majority in capitalist society.

With respect to the second extension of the concept of ideology (which retains Marx's pejorative use of the term while amplifying its pessimistic and totalizing dimensions), whatever its merits may be, here we can safely say that it does not represent Marx's own view. The world is saturated with ideological beliefs on Marx's account; but his project is one of disabusing his readers of these false, system-justifying beliefs born out of various kinds of bias. This is hard work: Marx writes,

> The history of mankind is like paleontology. Owing to a certain judicial blindness, even the best minds fail to see, on principle, what lies in front of their noses. Later, when the time has come, we are surprised that there are traces everywhere of what we failed to see.
>
> (MECW 42: 557)

Moreover, this difficulty increases the more that theorists have a personal stake in the outcomes of their investigations: in economics, for instance, free scientific inquiry meets not merely the same enemies as in all other domains. The peculiar nature of the material it deals with, summons as foes into the field of battle the most violent, mean and malignant passions of the human breast, the Furies of private interest.

(MECW 35: 10)

Yet, Marx never once expresses doubt that these obstacles to truth can eventually be overcome; quite the opposite. As frequently as Marx points out new illusions, he also notes the way in which previous illusions dissipate, giving way to a "truth demonstrable to every unprejudiced mind, and only denied by those, whose interest it is to hedge other people in a fool's paradise" (MECW 20: 9). Early in his career, Marx wrote about the purpose of philosophy as follows:

The task of history ... is to establish the truth of this world. The immediate task of philosophy, which is at the service of history, once the holy form of human self-estrangement has been unmasked, is to unmask self-estrangement in its unholy forms.

(MECW 3: 176)

This is a long way from the futile protest that Adorno sees as philosophy's purpose; and all of Marx's work in the decades that followed this statement were clearly attempts to carry out this task.

6. Conclusion

Marx frequently claims that moral, religious, philosophical, and economic ideas are "ideological." Though he never precisely defines "ideology," and his application of the term (and its cognates) evolves, core features unite his various discussions. An ideology is a cluster of inferentially related *beliefs* (and also *causally* related *attitudes*) that have three characteristics: (1) at least some of the ideology's central beliefs are false; (2) the ideology is the product of ideologists (economic, religious, and philosophical "theorists") who systematically make claims underdetermined (or even contradicted) by evidence (typically due to shared biases that undermine their theorizing); and (3) the ideology supports the interests of the ruling class and harms the interest of the vast majority, most often by misrepresenting how the existing state of affairs affects their interests. Thus, an ideological critique aims to unmask false beliefs that harm the interests of those who hold them, while also explaining their genesis in a way that simultaneously explains their prevalence and intractability.

In his earlier writings, Marx uses ideology in what we called his Narrow Account. This is a critique of all Hegelian-like idealism that treats ideas rather than material conditions as the motor of history. This variety of ideological critique is most prominent in Marx's criticism of the Young Hegelians in *The German Ideology*, whom he accused of futilely attempting to change the world by changing one's thinking, yet without addressing the material conditions that give rise to this thinking in the first place. Though Marx maintains his skepticism about this sort of idealism throughout his career, his later writings shift to what we called an Extended Account. This is a critique of ideology as the expression of ruling-class interests more generally, whether idealist in the narrower sense or (mostly) not, which is found throughout his political and economic writings.

In both the Narrow and Extended Account, Marx highlights the functional role ideology plays—namely, to support the interests of the dominant class at the expense of the interests of other classes. There are two sorts of ways in which ideological beliefs do so, both of which impair the epistemic capacity of people to recognize what is actually happening in their social and economic environment and how it affects their interests. The first sort (the Core Cases) accomplishes this by directly promulgating false claims about the social and economic environment. The second sort (Distraction Ideologies) does this by diverting attention from social and economic reality and how it affects people's interests. Ideologies promote the interests of the ruling class in the sense that they help the ruling class remain in power by legitimizing its rule. Most of those who accept an ideology are harming their own interests even though they do not realize it.

Throughout his work, Marx presupposed an objectivist view of intrinsic interests, albeit a thinner one than philosophers typically proffer, and one which he thought required no systematic defense. He believed people had "basic needs" (for adequate food, clothing, shelter, leisure, and the like) but also for the opportunity to work independent of the need to survive ("spontaneous activity"). While most people are conscious of these basic needs, because of ideology, they mistakenly think their inability to satisfy these under capitalism is due to something other than the economic system in which they live (a mistake about extrinsic interests). They mistakenly think that capitalism is in everyone's extrinsic interest, when it is only in the extrinsic interest of the ruling class.

In addition to highlighting the functional role ideology plays, Marx wants to explain the origin of these beliefs and, in doing so, to explain their prevalence and intractability. This means explaining why the ideologists themselves (typically sincere theorists) are so prone to systematically making claims underdetermined by evidence and in a way that favors the interests of the ruling class. It also means explaining why those in non-dominant positions whose interests are frustrated by accepting these beliefs would ever come to do so. Towards this end, Marx's various discussions of ideological beliefs are replete with proto-social-psychological explanations of their origins. Some of these explanations attribute the errors to what contemporary social psychologists call "cognitive biases," by which theorists respond too uncritically to the evidence before them; and others of these are attributed to what are called "motivated biases," by which theorists evaluate evidence and argumentation in a way that enables them to reach a desired conclusion. In addition to being subject to these same biases, those in non-dominant positions are subject throughout their lives to elite messaging that aims to justify the status quo to them.

Contemporary empirical work has been favorable to Marx. Social psychological research has extensively explored and cataloged numerous cognitive and motivational biases, demonstrating these biases to be both pervasive and tending to systematically distort belief formation in ways that favor the status quo and, thereby, the dominant class that benefits from it; and contemporary political science has demonstrated the population's susceptibility to elite messaging.

Marx's account of ideology has been interpreted and extended in various ways by subsequent Marxist writers. While sometimes developing Marx's account in illuminating ways, they are often misleadingly equated with it. In contrast to Marx's primarily pejorative use of the term ideology, Lenin popularizes a non-pejorative use of the term. In contrast to Marx's epistemic focus on false beliefs, Western Marxist thinkers (most prominently Lukács, Gramsci, and the Frankfurt School) develop accounts that focus on attitudes and orientations. Finally, in contrast to Marx's optimism that ideological beliefs can be debunked, later Marxists (most influentially, Adorno and Althusser) often portray ideology as thoroughly dominating and inescapable.

Notes

1 Beliefs can be true or false, and can stand in logical relations with other beliefs, while attitudes (which are neither true nor false) can stand in causal relations with beliefs and other attitudes. So, for example, the belief that Kings have a divine right to rule may cause attitudes of approbation and respect in some, and attitudes of dismay and anger in others. The belief itself is false (Kings do not have a divine right to rule); and, while the attitudes may be caused by the belief that it is false, the attitudes themselves are neither true nor false.

2 For a highly revisionary, and provocative, account of the origin of "ideology" in Marx, see Dallman (2021), who argues that the crucial source was remarks by Hegel in his *Lectures on the History of Philosophy* about Kant's idea of "effective illusions."

3 Forster (2015) takes a different view of the evolution of Marx's ideas about ideology. Forster argues that the roots of Marx's critique of ideology can be traced back to the critique of religion developed by Hegel, Feuerbach, and Bauer. However, beginning in the Preface to the *Critique of the Philosophy of Right*, Marx's concept of ideology evolved as a more adaptable expansion of this critical framework that allowed Marx to offer a compelling critique of a broader set of erroneous beliefs, which he argued function to advance specific class agendas at the expense of others and exist precisely because they fulfill those roles.

4 Anglophone analytical Marxism eventually collapsed into what Marx would have viewed as a Distraction Ideology. So, for example, Cohen (2000) argued that what was needed was a transformation in moral consciousness.

5 The "thicker" account of the early Marx is usefully surveyed by Leopold (2007: 227–241), and includes fourteen items, ranging from "interests" in meeting what we call in the text "basic [biological] needs" to interests in recreation, education, intellectual activity, culture, and "fulfilling work." Our claim is that, for the mature Marx, the crucial "interests" are the "basic needs" and the interest in spontaneous activity (which is something like Leopold's notion of "fulfilling work").

6 Cf. the discussion of "freedom from necessity" in Chapter 3, Section 4C.

7 The anthropological/archaeological record is replete with examples of how human beings, under multivarious and often adverse circumstances, have

produced things purely for aesthetic reasons: think of the cave paintings of Lascaux (France) or the desert paintings in the Sahara and in Australia (see Curtis 2008). (Thanks to Janet Roitman for guidance on this topic.) Independent of the status of the claim as one about fundamental human needs, it certainly articulates an attractive normative ideal. Consider the role that education assigns to opportunities for young people to engage in expressive and aesthetic activity, from painting to make-believe games and so on—activities that children take to quite naturally. It is not clear why adults should be supposed to have no interest in or need for similar activities.

8 The Frankfurt School is different on this score, since its members tend to assume people have a plethora of "interests" that the capitalist marketplace obscures, and beyond what we called earlier the expressive interests. A classic example is Marcuse (2007 [1964]). In so-called "Western Marxism" (i.e., Marxism after Lukács and The 1844 Manuscripts), Heller (1976) is an example, but, in our view, a misreading of the mature Marx (she relies heavily on the unpublished materials of 1844). See Chapter 7.

9 The discussion that follows draws on a systematic and extended development of these ideas in Edwards (2018).

10 According to Marx, of course, such changes only occur in the presence of changes in the material circumstances, as we saw in Chapter 2.

11 Consider, as just one example, the school textbooks in use in Britain and Germany in the first half of the 19th century, which inculcated "a view of the world in which moral and economic matters were intrinsically linked" with an eye to "the inculcation of a work ethic into the lower orders" (Maß 2019: 35). One popular 1828 German textbook on "political economy" "assumed close links between the household, the family, and the state," thus providing a "basis for an overarching social moral compass" (ibid.: 36). Orphans and pauper children, in particular, needed "training in frugality, the inculcation of a work ethic" as well as training in manual labor: "The good education of such children will thus win for society a number of assiduous and morally upstanding citizens in place of the same number of feral idlers" (ibid.: 36–37). (Thanks to Eileen Brennan for guidance on this topic.)

12 See the discussion in Chapter 4, Section 4.

13 Sometimes people are free to decline a job, but the logic of capitalism discussed in Chapter 4 makes clear why at the limit this will not be an option.

14 See Chapter 4, Section 7B.

15 To be clear, the hypothesis is not that they accept "whatever is served up to them," but that they accept whatever renders the world intelligibly "just."

16 As the economist Paul Krugman notes (2003: 59), a successful propaganda campaign resulted in the following bit of false consciousness by early 2003: "49 percent of Americans believed that most families had to pay the estate tax, while only 33 percent gave the right answer that only a few families had to pay."

17 See, e.g., Herman and Chomsky (1988), Chomsky (1989), Bagdikian (1997), McChesney (1997), and Alterman (2003).

18 The latter was a mistaken and un-Marxian assumption, as we saw in Chapter 4: communism presupposes a far greater development of productive power than the largely agrarian Russia of 1902 and 1917 had achieved.

19 In a later Preface to History and Class Consciousness, Lukács (1972) rejects the conflation of "reification" with fetishism in the original edition.

20 See the discussion in Chapter 4, Section 6.

21 Once again, and as we saw in Chapter 4, "orthodox Marxists" often did not take Marx seriously enough regarding the preconditions for successful communist revolution (e.g., global capitalism, widespread immiseration). That their predictions of imminent revolt were not borne out is hardly surprising, even if Marx himself was guilty of being overly optimistic about the rate of development of productive power.

22 Horkheimer and Adorno share with Kant and Hegel the idea of reason as a faculty capable of evaluating the ends that are worth pursuing. By contrast, as we saw in Chapter 4, Marx's critique of capitalism requires only instrumental rationality.

23 Marx's metaphor of "inversion," which he adopts from Hegel, recurs throughout his writings to describe how real-life "contradictions"—conflicts within the economic and social structures—distort understanding of the economic and social world. Initially, following Feuerbach, Marx uses "inversion" to illustrate how, in religion, human qualities are ascribed to deities, reversing our understanding of the human essence, and he adds that this ascription is owing to the fact that the world itself is "inverted": "This state, this society, produce religion, an inverted world-consciousness, because they are an inverted world" (MECW 3: 175). The use of the inversion metaphor here is not meant to suggest that the world is literally upside-down or somehow itself reversed (whatever that could mean), but rather indicates a social and economic structure that generates misunderstanding. Marx subsequently applies the metaphor to capitalist economics, where he sees contradictions, such as those between the interests of labor and capital, leading to a reality that appears "inverted" (MECW 35: 537). Economic phenomena like the value of commodities or the supposed freedom of workers to contract with capitalists as equals are interpreted as they appear at the most superficial level by theorists who fail to see beyond the capitalist veneer. Marx contends that this misrecognition is not accidental, but arises from the very nature of capitalist society, which is rife with contradictions that obfuscate true social relations. Inversion, however, is not a distinct sort of ideological critique; rather, it is a metaphor Marx uses as shorthand for the numerous ways ideologists are prone to misunderstand social phenomena that we have detailed throughout this chapter.

Further Reading

Edwards (2018) explores in detail the evidence from the social sciences (psychology, political science, sociology) in support of Marx's theory of ideology.

Elster (1986), Chapter 9, presents a useful overview of Marx's account of ideology, and outlines several challenges that a plausible account of ideology would need to answer (and which we try to answer here).

Jost (2020) details decades of empirical work on "system justification" theory and related social psychological research.

Larraín (1979) provides an excellent overview of the concept of ideology in Marx and the Marxist tradition.

Leiter (2024) offers a systematic account of the kinds of mistakes about interests involved in Marx's theory of ideology.

Rosen (1996) offers an illuminating account of ideology in the Marxist tradition, but the later parts of his book are marred by some implausible criticisms of Marx's theory (discussed in the text).

6

Human Nature and the Good Life

The Public/Private Distinction and Alienation in Marx's Early Writings

As we saw in Chapter 4, moral criticism and advocacy played no role in Marx's picture of the transition from capitalism to communism: communism was presented as in the self-interest of the vast majority. Marx undoubtedly thought this majority would be better off under communism; but he did not think a *philosophical theory* in the manner of Kant or Hegel about the nature of right or moral goodness would make any contribution to bringing about that change. As one commentator aptly put it: "The moralist [or moral philosopher] turns out to be little help to a revolution and to be positively pernicious if many people take up her useless activity" (Brudney 1998: 324).[1]

As we saw in Chapter 5, Marx also views a society's dominant moral ideas as ideological in the pejorative sense that we discussed: they serve mainly to legitimate the domination of the existing ruling class and its continued exploitation of the forces of production. It should be unsurprising, then, that Marx never published a normative moral and political philosophy of his own, one that would try to offer a systematic account of his normative ideas, and aim to justify or vindicate his own plentiful normative judgments: that capitalism is bad; that it hinders freedom and human well-being; that people would be better off without capitalism at a certain historical point. These normative judgments do seem to be informed by an implicit and inchoate conception of human well-being and flourishing, even though Marx thinks a successful critique of capitalism does not depend on making such a conception theoretically explicit or trying to defend it.[2]

DOI: 10.4324/9781315658902-6

Early in his life, however, when he was still much more under the influence of Hegel, Marx did venture into explicit theorizing about the good life and human flourishing, although he only published one essay on the subject—"On the Jewish Question," in 1843 in an obscure venue (Leopold 2007: 1). In 1844, he continued to pursue those themes in what have become known as the *Economic and Philosophic Manuscripts of 1844* (the *1844 Manuscripts*), which Marx himself never published (they were not published until 1932). During the period 1843–45, Marx was breaking from Hegel and other "Left" Young Hegelians, and was also very much under the influence of Feuerbach, as we discussed in Chapter 1. That Marx left the *1844 Manuscripts* unpublished during his lifetime while concentrating on other theoretical questions is one indication that he, indeed, felt this kind of normative moral and political theorizing was an idle pastime, of no relevance to political goals or *wissenschaftlich* understanding.[3] These writings of Marx's youth have, however, exercised a strong attraction on academic moral and political philosophers since.[4] In inchoate form, some of their ideas lie in the background of Marx's mature work as well, even if he no longer considered them theoretically important.

For all these reasons, we try to set out Marx's theory of human well-being (his theory of "the good") in this chapter. In this early work, it seems clear that Marx believes that: (1) human beings have an *essential* nature, which determines what would constitute their flourishing; and (2) human beings are essentially creatures who cannot flourish if alienated from the world they inhabit—*reconciliation* (*Versöhnung*) to the world, and especially other human beings, is a condition of flourishing (an idea clearly taken over from Hegel [cf. Hardimon 1994]).[5] Marx's view of what is good for human beings is, then, an "objectivist" view in ethics[6]—that is, a view according to which what is good for someone does not depend at all on their subjective desires or attitudes, even the desires or attitudes they might have under different, for example "ideal," conditions (such as when they have full information and are perfectly rational). This aligns the early Marx with ancient philosophers like Aristotle, who also believed that the good life for a human being depended on what human beings are really like (and what would constitute realization of their essential nature), not on what people desire or might desire.[7]

We start with "On the Jewish Question" and then turn to the 1844 *Manuscripts*.

1. "On the Jewish Question" (1843) and the Public/Private Distinction

The "Jewish Question" in 19th-century Europe concerned which civil and political rights to grant to the Jewish populations of the different countries, and was widely debated. The rights at issue included not just familiar civil and political rights (such as freedom to practice one's religion and the right to vote), but also the right to enter various professions, such as law. Marx's own father, who was Jewish, had been forced to convert to Christianity prior to Marx's birth in order to continue practicing law after the Prussian government reversed the more liberal policies of the prior French (Napoleonic) rulers of Trier (Seigel 1978: 42).

The specific form of the "Jewish Question" that Marx addressed is framed by writings on the subject by his former friend and teacher from his university days, the Left Young Hegelian Bruno Bauer (see Chapter 1, Section 3). Bauer shared with Marx the hope that humanity would eventually be liberated from religion altogether; but, unlike Marx, he opposed extending full civil and political rights to Jews because of their commitment to their religious identity. For Bauer, as Marx puts it, "we must emancipate ourselves [from religion] before we can emancipate others [i.e., the Jews]" (MECW 3: 147). Thus Bauer, says Marx, transforms the "Jewish Question" into "a purely religious question," namely, "which makes man freer—the negation of Judaism, or the negation of Christianity" (MECW 3: 168). (Indeed, Bauer had even argued that Jews should first become Christians, since Christian consciousness was a bit closer to full emancipation than Judaism![8]) Anticipating his later historical materialism (discussed in Chapter 2), Marx says it is a mistake to regard religion as the "essence of the Jew" (MECW 3: 169), and suggests we should not consider the "*Sabbath Jew*" but the "*everyday Jew*" (MECW 3: 169)—that is, the actual economic lives Jews lead in most of Europe. Marx writes:

> What is the worldly basis of Judaism? *Practical need, self-interest.* What is the worldly cult of the Jew? *Huckstering.* What is his worldly god? *Money.*

Very well then! Emancipation from huckstering and money, consequently from practical, real Judaism, would be the self-emancipation of our time...

In the final analysis, the [human] emancipation of the Jews is the emancipation of mankind from Judaism.

(MECW 3: 170)

This inflammatory formulation can be misleading as to Marx's real point. Jews had, of course, been legally restricted for hundreds of years from entering most professions, other than money-lending (banking) and selling various goods. Actual Jews, in their economic lives, thus represent the condition in which most people live under capitalism: they pursue their self-interest, i.e., the acquisition of money, through business transactions. In this regard, the stereotypical or "everyday" Jew is much like the typical person under capitalism.[9]

Of course, Marx and Bauer both agree that liberation from religion is essential to true human emancipation. Unlike Bauer, however, Marx recognizes that "[p]olitical emancipation certainly represents a great progress"[10] (MECW 3: 155), referring to events like the French Declaration of the Rights of Man and of the Citizen in 1789 and the American Constitution's Bill of Rights of 1791. Political emancipation, however, is not a complete "human" emancipation for Marx—although not because Jews fail to convert to Christianity, as Bauer thought. Rather the problem is that political emancipation leaves intact "the conflict between the general interest and private interest" which is reflected in the legacy of political emancipation: "the schism between the political state [representing, in theory, the "general interest"] and civil society [the realm for expression of "private interest"]" (MECW 3: 155). The conflict between the "general interest" and the "private interest" (or the public and the private realm) is the crucial theme of the remainder of the essay, and the one that accounts for its interest today.

"Political" emancipation falls short, according to Marx, because while it frees the state from the influence of religion (e.g., by removing religious restrictions on the vote and on public service), it still protects the dominance of religion in the "private" sphere, i.e., civil society, and treats that realm as wholly other from the public domain. Indeed, it is not just religion that is permitted to exercise its tyranny by the existing doctrine of political emancipation:

The state abolishes, in its own way, the distinctions of birth, *social rank*, *education*, *occupation*, when it declares that birth, social rank, education, occupation are *non-political* distinctions, when it proclaims, without regard to these distinctions, that every member of the nation is an *equal* partner in national sovereignty, when it treats all elements of the real life of the nation from the standpoint of the state. Nonetheless, the state allows private property, education, occupation, to *act in their* way, i.e., as private property, as education, as occupation, and to exert the influence of their *particular* nature. Far from abolishing these *real* [*faktischen*] differences, the state only exists on the presupposition of their existence.

(MECW 3: 153)

The real problem with the "political emancipation" of the Jews is not, then, that it grants them the rights that are enjoyed by others (despite their continued affirmation of their Jewish identity, as Bauer objected), but rather that it only eliminates the relevance of badges of identity (such as religion, property ownership, occupation, etc.) in the public or political sphere, *but leaves these entirely intact and influential in the "private" sphere of so-called "civil society" where everyone pursues their self-interest.* "*The so-called rights of man* [e.g., to worship, to liberty, to security, to property] ... are nothing but the rights of a *member of civil society*, i.e., the rights of egoistic man, of man separated from other men and from the community," as Marx puts it (MECW 3: 162).[11] A truly "human" emancipation requires eliminating this distinction between the "private" realm of self-interest—in which the badges of identity are given free rein—and the "public" realm of politics occupied by "citizens."

This general observation—which still describes the current situation in most liberal democratic societies, perhaps most obviously in the United States—does not yet settle, however, what should be done to remedy the problem. One view (also the dominant one in liberal democracies) would be that what is needed for human emancipation are further restrictions on the influence of wealth and religion (and other badges of privilege in the private realm) on the political sphere. This is not, however, Marx's view, which is more radical. At least in this 1843 essay, Marx thinks that the very idea of a separation between people as they are in civil society and then as they are in their political or public life is pernicious and incompatible with their flourishing (in a sense we will clarify shortly). Marx writes that the "liberty" that political emancipation protects is "the right to do everything which harms no one else … It is a question of the liberty of man as an isolated monad, withdrawn into himself" (MECW 3: 162).[12] Marx expounds on this idea using the example of the right to property:

> The right of man to private property is, therefore, the right to enjoy one's fortune and to dispose of it at one's discretion … without regard to other men, independently of society. It is the right of self-interest. This individual liberty and its application form the basis of civil society. It makes every man see in other men not the *realization* of his own freedom, but the *barrier* to it.
>
> (MECW 3: 163)

In what sense, though, could other people be the "realization" of an individual's freedom rather than a potential "limitation" on that freedom? This gets us to the key issue, namely, what "freedom" means for Marx in 1843.

A. Freedom

On this topic, Marx still follows Hegel fairly closely in this early work.[13] Hegel, like Kant, thought that to act freely is not simply to "do what you want," but to act "rationally"—in particular, to act in accordance with laws: rational self-governance by law is the essence of freedom.[14] Civil society, as the safe haven for egoistic decisions, protects only "do what you want" freedom (the freedom of caprice, as it were), but not actual freedom on the Kant/Hegel view. How can one act rationally, however, if everyone else is acting capriciously, according to their own egoistic desires? What would emerge would be chaos: I may have a desire to spend my days reading books of philosophy; but, unless others are spending their days producing food, electricity, public health and safety, etc., my desires will be frustrated. But the same goes for the desires of all these others who might want to produce these things I need. The farmer, for example, can only harvest crops if others are acting so as to provide the preconditions for that activity, and so on. Thus, genuinely free or rational action requires a kind of planned coordination of all our activities, not a state of affairs in which everyone acts on capricious desires.

It seems correct that unless we take account of what everyone else wants, and how to go about making it possible for those wants to be satisfied, we will have either chaos or what we currently have in most societies: namely, the sacrifice of most people's desires for the egoism of those with money and power. But perhaps those with money and power can realize their freedom and flourish, even if others could not. Marx's claim in these early writings seems to be stronger: namely, even those who are able to act on caprice (because of their wealth and power) are not really leading a good life. A further assumption is needed to motivate this thought, and the early Marx (following Hegel) is explicit about it: a good human life requires overcoming the divide (or "dualism") between "egoistic man … separated from other men and from the community" and healing "the schism between the *political state* [representing the community] and *civil society* [representing egoistic man]" (MECW 3: 162, 155). In other words, the interests of the "individual monad" are not independent of the interest of the community: the individual must identify with the interest of the community in order to flourish. As one commentator puts it: "Freedom as 'being at home with oneself in another' expresses … Hegel's recognition of … the problem of freedom [first] formulated by Rousseau: namely, how is it that a person can be autonomous [free] despite his dependence on others?" (Baynes 2007: 562). The Hegelian answer, simply put, is by seeing oneself in others, by seeing that their actions and well-being are not separable from one's own.[15]

These broadly Hegelian ideas are in the background of these kinds of remarks by Marx in "On the Jewish Question," although he will give them a new gloss with the idea of "species-being":

> None of the so-called rights of man, therefore, go beyond egoistic man, beyond man as a member of civil society, that is, an individual withdrawn into himself, into the confines of his private interests and private caprice, and separated from the community.

In the rights of man, he is far from being conceived as a species-being; on the contrary, species-life itself, society, appears as a framework external to the individuals, as a restriction of their original independence. The sole bond holding them together is natural necessity, need and private interest, the preservation of their property and their egoistic selves.

(MECW 3: 164)

Only when the real, individual man withdraws into himself [*in sich zurücknimmt*] the abstract citizen [i.e., the man who has the rights accorded by merely political emancipation], and as an individual human being has become a *species-being* in his everyday life, in his particular work, and in his particular situation, only when man has recognised and organised his [own powers] as *social* forces, and consequently no longer separates social power from himself in the shape of *political* power, only then will human emancipation have been accomplished.

(MECW 3: 168)

So human beings have an essential nature, and their "emancipation" consists in the realization of this nature, and thus in overcoming the dualism between the merely "private" realm of egoism and that of the "public" citizen. In particular, man is not essentially egoistic (the man of "civil society"), but, instead is essentially a species-being (*Gattungswesen*), a term that comes directly from Feuerbach, himself a Left Young Hegelian. One philosophical commentator offers this helpful explanation of the idea of "species-being".

The stress in Marx is on the idea that human beings are essentially connected to their species because man is by nature a "herd animal" or "social animal," an animal who dwells with others of the same kind and survives by living and working in some sort of co-operative relationship with them ... [There is also] an emphasis ... on the *consciousness* which men and women have of their interdependence, or of conduct that is consciously oriented to this interdependence ... It is essential to being human at all that we do have some conception of the human species,

that we "we make our species our object," and have an awareness of ourselves as members of this species.
(Wood 1981: 18–19; cf. Brudney 1998: 147–148)

The curious notion of "species-being" mostly drops out of Marx's later
work.[16] Perhaps to realize our essential nature and lead a good life we
need to recognize our membership in a species in which we depend on
others (and vice versa); but the history of the world, as Marx certainly
knew, is the history of a world in which people do not acknowledge
these things. Should we conclude that no one has ever led a good and
flourishing life? Neither Goethe nor Beethoven? Neither Shakespeare
nor Einstein? Perhaps in the post-capitalist future, as Marx writes late
in his life (in *Capital*, volume III), when "the realm of freedom actually begins" because "labour which is determined by necessity [i.e.,
the need to survive] and mundane considerations ceases" (MECW 37:
807) individuals would achieve Hegelian recognition of their mutual
interdependence and their identity of interests. It is striking, however,
that the mature Marx makes no reference to "species-being" in this
context. Indeed, as we saw in Chapters 3 and 4, in Marx's own account
of the transition from capitalism to communism the idea of "species-
being" and the Hegelian idea of freedom play no role. The freedom
the "wage-slave" is denied is far more basic and familiar: he cannot do
what he wants to do because he must spend his time doing whatever
will produce a wage to survive—he lacks "freedom from necessity"
(see Chapter 3, Section 4C). In 1843, however, these Feuerbachian and
Hegelian ideas still loomed large for Marx.

B. Money and Value

There is another feature of political emancipation's entrenching of
civil society and egoism that concerns Marx and deserves notice
here: namely, the role of money (and the fetishism of money).[17]
Marx writes:

> Practical need, egoism, is the principle of civil society ... The god of
> practical need and self-interest is money.
>   Money degrades all the gods of man—and changes them
> into commodities. Money is the universal self-established *value*

of all things. It has, therefore, robbed the whole world—both the human world of men and nature—of its unique [*eigentüm-lichen*] value. Money is the alienated essence of man's work and man's existence, and this alien essence dominates him, and he worships it.

(MECW 3: 172)

Here Marx seems committed to a very particular view about the nature of *value*, one now associated with a philosophical doctrine often called the "plurality" or "incommensurability" of values. The idea is that different kinds of things and activities should be *valued* and have their value assessed in different ways, depending on the kind of thing or activity they are. On this view, for example, *price* may be the appropriate way of valuing a toaster or a car, but not a child or a friend. Civil society, by protecting egoism (whose primary aim is the acquisition of money), has the (unintended) consequence of making it appear that all value is reducible to *monetary* value since, in civil society, at least under capitalism, *price* is the primary marker of value. Thus, the media regularly reports on the *price* for which great works of art sell at auction, and salary (the price for wage labor) becomes a metric of the worth of jobs.

Marx returns to this idea during the 1840s. The year after "On the Jewish Question," in one of the most famous passages from his 1844 *Manuscripts*, he writes:

That which is for me through the medium of *money*—that for which I can pay (i.e., which money can buy)—that am I myself, the possessor of money ... Money's properties are my—the possessor's—properties and essential powers. Thus, what I *am* and *am capable of* is by no means determined by my individuality. I *am* ugly, but I can buy for myself the *most beautiful of* women. Therefore I am not *ugly*, for the effective of *ugliness*—its deterrent power—is nullified by money ... I am *brainless*, but money is the *real brain* of all things and how then should its possessor be brainless? Besides, he can buy clever people for himself, and is he who has power over the clever not more clever than the clever? Do not I, who thanks to money am capable of *all* that the human heart longs for, possess all human capacities? Does not my money, therefore, transform all my incapacities into their contrary?

(MECW 3: 324)

Against this capacity of money under capitalism to overwhelm all other ways of assessing the value of some person, Marx concludes this discussion in the 1844 *Manuscripts* by affirming again something like the plurality of value:

> Assume *man* to be *man* and his relationship to the world to be a human one: then you can exchange love only for love, trust for trust, etc. If you want to enjoy art, you must be an artistically cultivated person; if you want to exercise influence over other people, you must be a person with a stimulating and encouraging effect on other people. Every one of your relations to man and to nature must be a *specific expression*, corresponding to the object of your will, of your *real individual* life.

(MECW 3: 326)

In the *Communist Manifesto* a few years later, he and Engels echo this last idea when they observe that the "bourgeoisie, wherever it has got the upper hand ... has left remaining no other nexus between man and man than naked self-interest, than callous 'cash payment'. ... It has resolved personal worth into exchange value" (MECW 6: 486–487). These ideas, like most of the ideas in the 1843 essay "On the Jewish Question," mostly disappear from Marx's later writings, but they do receive a further, systematic elaboration in the unpublished writings of 1844.

2. The 1844 *Manuscripts* and the Idea of Alienation

The unpublished 1844 *Manuscripts* are most famous for their treatment of the phenomenon of "alienation" (or estrangement) (*Entfremdung*).[18] One can, of course, be alienated or estranged, in the colloquial sense of those terms, from many things, some transitory and some important. One can be alienated from one's job this week because the boss is acting like an unpleasant jerk, but, once the boss behaves better, the sense of alienation passes. In that case, the "jerkiness" of the boss is unpleasant and annoying, but those disagreeable feelings can be alleviated rather quickly once the boss changes his manner. This is *not* what Marx in his early writings has in mind by alienation. According to Marx, capitalism produces an estrangement from who one really is, from one's fundamental nature. To be alienated or estranged is to be something like a "fish out of water"—that is, to be asked to live a life alien to one's essential character. All of the following are true of the early Marx's idea of alienation:

1. Alienation obtains when a person's essential nature is thwarted from expression or realization. At bottom, alienation is alienation from one's essence or essential being.
2. Alienation is *not* essentially a psychological condition—i.e., one constituted by a distinctive phenomenology (or set of conscious experiences) for the agent.[19]
3. Typical psychological/phenomenological consequences usually flow from (1) obtaining, but they are not criterial of alienation: someone could be alienated without having the conscious experience of feeling alienated.

As we learned in "On the Jewish Question," part of our essential nature has to do with (a) our being dependent on cooperative work with others, and (b) being conscious of the truth of (a). But the picture is now filled out in the 1844 *Manuscripts* in important ways. In a nutshell—and somewhat crudely—we might say that it is part of our essential nature that we achieve self-affirmation through productive activity ("free, conscious activity is man's species character" [MECW 3: 276]). "Private property"—more precisely, "capital," the money that the bourgeoisie acquires through the labor power of others—is incompatible with the expression of this part of our nature. It is the core task of the 1844 *Manuscripts* to explain these points.

A. Four Kinds of Alienation

Marx famously distinguishes *four kinds* of alienation that occur under modern capitalism, where the capitalist purchases the worker's labor power but owns all the products of his labor.[20] We discuss each in turn, although the first three—alienation from the product of work, from work itself, and from "species-being"—are the most important, the fourth being, arguably, redundant on the third.

First, there is *alienation from the product of labor*.[21] Consider the worker in a factory producing automobiles. Suppose the worker in question is responsible for installing the headlights on a vehicle, say the Mercedes-Benz sedan. In the end, a new Mercedes-Benz sedan rolls off the production line; but, for the worker who installed the lights, the product appears "as a *power independent* of the producer" (MECW 3: 272) in several senses: the worker does not own it (he owns only the wage he receives for the hours worked); the car has a price which he would have to pay in order to get the product of his own labor; and the worker's wages are, often enough, inadequate to purchase the product. As Marx famously concludes this part of the discussion (clearly thinking of the mind-numbing and often body-crushing labor of the English working classes famously described by Engels[22]):

> It is true that labor produces for the rich wonderful things—but for the worker it produces privation. It produces palaces—but for the worker, hovels. It produces beauty—but for the worker, deformity. It replaces labour by machines, but it throws one section of the workers back to a barbarous type of labour, and it turns the other section into machines. It produces intelligence—but for the worker, stupidity, cretinism.
>
> (MECW 3: 273)

The second type of alienation Marx identifies is *alienation from productive activity* (MECW 3: 274). This has several related components. First is

> the fact that labor is *external* to the worker, i.e., it does not belong to his intrinsic nature; that in his work ... he does not affirm himself but denies himself, does not feel content but unhappy, does not develop freely his physical and mental energy but mortifies his body and ruins his mind. The worker therefore only feels himself outside his work, and in his work feels outside himself. He is at home when he is not working, and when he is working he is not at home.
>
> (MECW 3: 274)

This sense of alienation is probably closest to the colloquial sense of the term in ordinary language. Even in countries with a five-day working week (itself an achievement of labor movements, after Marx's time), it would be typical for workers to feel "at home" when they are done with their compensated labor (when they are done with "punching the clock" as the idiomatic expression has it) and can go home, or to a bar, or engage in recreation. (Think of the intense cultural emphasis in a capitalist society like the United States on the difficulty of "Mondays" and the welcome relief of "Fridays," marking the beginning and end of the typical workweek.) While in the factory, laboring for a wage on an assembly line, it is, indeed, common for human beings to "not feel content but unhappy" (MECW 3: 274).[23] (Recall that alienation produces typical experiences and feelings, but these are not criterial of alienation, just characteristic of it.)

Labor does not belong to the worker's "essential being" under capitalism because it is "not the satisfaction of a need; it is merely a *means* to satisfy needs external to it. Its alien character emerges clearly in the fact that as soon as no physical or other compulsion exists, labour is shunned like the plague" (MECW 3: 274). This bears emphasizing, since it is crucial to the kind of freedom that is of special concern to Marx even in his mature work: namely, that wage slaves only work to earn a wage (to "satisfy needs external" to their work, such as their need for food, shelter, etc.), not because they want to do that work.[24] The wage slave's "labour is … not voluntary, but coerced; it is *forced labour*" (MECW 3: 274).

In the 1844 *Manuscripts* this is coupled with the thought that human beings have a fundamental need to engage in productive labor; but, even without that assumption, there is a quite ordinary sense in which workers under capitalism are not free: they would not freely choose to do their work *if they did not need the money*. Would the typical sanitation worker or janitor freely *choose* to haul garbage or clean toilets? What about the labor of the secretary or the worker on the assembly line? Rather than realizing or affirming herself, the worker under capitalism labors only to meet her other needs.

This is not to deny, of course, that many workers in modern capitalism grow accustomed to and content with their work; this may be particularly true of what are often called "white-collar" workers, such as lawyers or managers: those workers may not "feel" alienated. But their labor would still be unfree because it would fail a kind of counterfactual test of the form: would you have entered this line of work and continued doing it if you did not need the wage or salary you get for doing it? The evidence that the labor is unfree, merely a "means" (rather than a freely chosen end-in-itself), is that people would give it up if it were not necessary to sustain themselves.

Finally, the worker is alienated from his labor because it "is not his own, but someone else's" (MECW 3: 274)—that is, it belongs to the capitalist who dictates its terms and conditions (as well as owning its output). Notice that only if labor is essential to our nature could the fact that it belongs to someone else constitute alienation: because labor belongs to us essentially qua human beings, we are alienated from it when it belongs to someone else.

The third feature of alienation under capitalism is alienation from species-being (MECW 3: 275)—the notion we first encountered in "On the Jewish Question," but which receives more elaboration here. According to Marx,

> Man is a species-being, not only because in practice and in theory he adopts the species (his own as well as those of other things) as his object, but—and this is only another way of expressing it—also because he treats himself as the actual, living species; because he treats himself as a universal and therefore a free being.
> (MECW 3: 275)

There are three key ideas here, namely: (1) taking the species "as [one's] object"; (2) treating oneself as "universal"; and (3) being "free." Let us take these up in turn.

Regarding (1), what is it to take one's species as an object? At a minimum, it would seem to require being conscious of oneself as a member of a species with certain attributes. The contrast with non-human animals, which Marx himself invokes, is helpful here. Ants, for example, are social creatures, like humans: they do not live alone, but in colonies. Ants, however, are not conscious of themselves as members of a species, or even as actors that have goals, aspirations, desires, and so on; and they are certainly not aware of themselves as part of a species whose essential nature is productive activity ("the productive life is the life of the species" [MECW 3: 276]). Under capitalism, this essential aspect of who a person is appears simply as "a means of individual life"—that is, to his own subsistence: "*life-activity, productive life* itself, appears to man in the first place merely as a *means* of satisfying a need" (MECW 3: 276). As Marx sums up this first aspect of species-being: "Conscious life-activity directly distinguishes man from animal life-activity ... [I]t is only because he is a species being that he is a conscious being, i.e., that his own life is an object for him" (MECW 3: 276).

Regarding (2), man's "universality" consists in the way man

> makes all nature his *inorganic* body—both inasmuch as nature is
> (1) his direct means of life, and (2) the material, the objective,
> and the instrument of his life-activity. Nature is man's *inorganic
> body*—nature, that is, in so far as it is not itself the human body.
> Man *lives* on nature—means that nature is his *body*, with which
> he must remain in continuous interchange if he is not to die.
> That man's physical and spiritual life is linked to nature means
> simply that nature is linked to itself, for man is a part of nature.
> (MECW 3: 275–276)

This second aspect of species-being is more obscure than the first.[25] The idea seems to be that one characteristic of the human species is that it treats all parts of nature as a means to support its own life: humans will farm the land, chop the trees, fish the oceans, and so on. Other animals do nothing of the kind: each has its own typical habitat, where it finds its sustenance—whether the forest or the ocean or the plains or the mountains, but rarely more than one of these. Under capitalism, wage slaves are alienated from this aspect of their species-being presumably because they are paid to labor only on one small part of nature, thus obscuring their awareness of the way in which the species, unlike all others, can utilize all parts of nature for its survival. (Why it is a bad thing not to be aware of this aspect of one's supposed species-being is a question we return to below.)

Regarding (3), a member of our species is "free" insofar as he engages in productive labor "even when he is free from physical need" (MECW 3: 276), which Marx calls "spontaneous activity" (MECW 3: 277). Indeed, humans sometimes also form things "in accordance with the laws of beauty" (MECW 3: 277), that is, simply for aesthetic satisfactions. The contrast, according to Marx, is with the non-human animals which produce "only under the dominion of immediate physical need" (MECW 3: 276). This is a crucial aspect of Marx's view of human beings: we are creatures who want to labor, to work and produce things; but not simply to survive but as a kind of self-expression, including artistic expression. This conception of human nature survives into Marx's maturity and informs his view about the interests that are frustrated for the vast majority under capitalism. Wage slaves do not engage in such work; and nor do other non-human animals. Wage slaves work only to earn money to meet their physical needs, while non-human animals work only to meet their physical needs directly. Human beings are, in Marx's view, *sui generis* not simply in their ability but also in their need to work independently of meeting physical needs, including to satisfy their aesthetic and expressive interests.

The fourth and final kind of alienation Marx discusses, *alienation from other men*, is initially claimed to follow from the preceding three (MECW 3: 277). In fact, however, this kind of alienation is, arguably, just a variation on the alienation from species-being, as Marx soon admits: "the proposition that man's species nature is estranged from him means that one man is estranged from the other, as each of them is from man's essential nature" (MECW 3: 277). In other words, if each man is alienated from the fact of his being part of a species (with the attributes noted above), then necessarily one is alienated from the other members of that species since one fails to recognize their essential traits as members of a shared species.

We should emphasize, again, that Marx, in his later work, drops the idea of "species-being" and the worry about our being "alienated" from it (even if the idea of "free" work remains important to him as late as *Capital*, as we first discussed in Chapter 3, Section 4C). Part of the reason may be the extremely idealist character of the early description of the problem: to be alienated from species-being is to fail to have certain beliefs about the species-specific attributes that one exemplifies. As we saw in Chapter 2, to change society it is not enough to simply have the correct ideas; and, as we saw in Chapter 5, the ideas that dominate in class-based societies are those that serve to legitimize the existing relations of production and promote the interests of the ruling class. While it could be that under non-capitalist economic conditions people might come to have some appreciation for what the early Marx calls their "species-being," simply instructing them as to the "truth" about their species-being will not have any lasting effect on people or their material conditions.

Notwithstanding that some of these ideas are abandoned, Marx retains allegiance throughout his career to the ideal of freedom from necessity (as expressed by the counterfactual test) and to the objectivist assumption that human beings are the kinds of creatures who need, by nature, to engage in "spontaneous" work, work that serves expressive and aesthetic functions.[26]

B. Private Property, Alienation, and Communism

"*Private property is* ... the product, the result, the necessary consequence of *alienated labour*, of the external relation of the worker to nature and to himself," says Marx. "*Private property* thus results by analysis from the concept of *alienated labor*—i.e., of *alienated man*, of estranged labor, of estranged life, of *estranged* man" (MECW 3: 279). By "private property" Marx means, of course, only the kind of property that capitalists have: in the labor power of others, in technology, and in the products of labor power together with technology. But this kind of property is only possible if work and workers are alienated in the ways described in the previous section: the worker is alienated from the product of his labor because the capitalist owns it, not the worker; the worker is alienated from his labor because the capitalist owns it and dictates its terms; the worker's labor is not free because he works only for a wage to survive, not spontaneously, as a form of self-realization.

Of course, it might seem, when put as we just did, that private property *causes* the alienation of labor, but this is what Marx is at pains to deny here:

> [T]hough private property appears to be the reason, the cause of alienated labour, it is rather its consequence, just as the gods are *originally* not the cause but the effect of man's intellectual confusion. Later this relationship becomes reciprocal. [...] Only at the culmination of the development of private property does this, its secret, appear again, namely, that on the one hand it is the

product of alienated labour, and that on the other it is the *means* by which labour alienates itself, the *realization of this alienation*.

(MECW 3: 279–280)

The allusion at the start of this passage is to an idea Marx found in Feuerbach, according to which gods or God represent a projection of human attributes on to non-existent entities, which are then treated as having independent powers over humans—e.g., in the case of the Christian God, demanding obedience to various rules (cf. the discussion of fetishism in Chapter 4, Section 6). The idea of God *arises* from a kind of mistake, "an intellectual confusion," as Marx puts it; but then once the mistake is entrenched, and God is viewed as a real being whose demands must be satisfied, this idea of God contributes to further intellectual confusions and mistakes.

How does the analogy work in the case of private property and alienation? The thought seems to be that private property can only arise if first humans are alienated from their work, the product of their work, and from their true species-being nature. With institutions of private property now in place, however, thanks to law and force and ideology, the alienation of the worker is sustained and exacerbated.

Given the constitutive relationship between private property and alienation, it should be unsurprising that, even in these early writings, Marx announces that, since communism "annuls" private property, only under communism is non-alienated labor possible (MECW 3: 294). As he writes in the 1844 *Manuscripts*:

[C]ommunism ... is the *genuine* resolution of the conflict between man and nature and between man and man—the true resolution of the strife between existence and essence, between objectification and self-confirmation, between freedom and necessity, between the individual and the species. Communism is the riddle of history solved, and it knows itself to be this solution.

(MECW 3: 296–297)

Marx here echoes Hegel's project of "reconciliation," except of course that reconciliation for Marx is to be achieved only by changing the economic structure of society from a capitalist to a communist one.[27]

C. What Is So Bad about Alienation?

Is alienation a bad thing? The term, of course, has a negative con-notation, especially the way Marx uses it. Some critics have objected that unalienated labor will only be possible if, in fact, there is pro-ductive abundance, an issue we touched on in Chapters 3 and 4.[28] But we are raising here a separate question: What is so bad about alienation in Marx's sense? It is very far from obvious what is bad or harmful about failing to recognize the attributes of the species to which one belongs, which is central to the idea of alienation from species-being. Alienation from one's work is more obviously bad, even if one rejects Marx's idea that it is part of our essential nature qua humans to engage in productive activity.[29] It fits, for example, with an idea Marx emphasizes throughout his work: namely, that "wage slaves" only work because they need to work to survive—i.e., their labor is unfree, rather than "spontaneous." But notice that this kind of worry is compatible with a non-objectivist view of well-being: the problem with wage slavery is that its victims would, at least under the right conditions, *prefer not to do this work.*

Alienation from the product of one's labor presents a different issue. If a person labors *freely*—i.e., not as a wage slave but "spontaneously"—to produce something, what difference does it make who owns it? Of course, it matters to a wage slave if she does not own the product she produces, since she could, in principle, earn more money by selling her work product rather than letting the capitalist expropriate some of the value (cf. Chapter 4). But for someone who works spontane-ously, why would it matter that someone else owns what is produced? Perhaps it matters if the product of their labor is taken away from them involuntarily, rather than given away? Yet *Das Kapital* was presumably a profound labor of self-expression for Marx;[30] would it matter that he and his descendants did not get the royalties in a society if their needs were already met?

Marx has no clear answers to these questions, but we do not offer that as a criticism. The mature Marx realized that these kinds of questions do not matter for the issues he was really interested in: understanding how the world works *and* how revolutionary change is possible. Marx wanted to "change" the world, not simply "inter-pret" it, as he famously put it in his *Theses on Feuerbach* (MECW 5: 8).

Most academic moral and political philosophy remains in the "interpretive" mode, more often interpreting what Marx would regard as the ideological illusions of its era.

3. Conclusion

In the early 1840s, Marx did articulate—although largely in work he never published—something like a normative theory about what a good human life requires and the ways in which life under modern capitalism falls short. This early normative theory involves the following claims and commitments:

1. Human beings have an *essential* nature, which determines the conditions under which they could flourish (i.e., lead good lives).
2. It involves an *objectivist* theory of the good—i.e., it does not make what is good depend on a person's desires, actual or idealized.
3. Human beings are essentially creatures who need to engage in free productive activity—i.e., to produce things (to labor)—not simply to survive but to satisfy their expressive and aesthetic interests.
4. Human beings are also essentially creatures who need *reconciliation* (*Versöhnung*) with the world in which they live, including with their fellow human beings on whose productive labor they depend.

As we saw in earlier chapters, Marx objects to capitalism because he thinks it is harmful to the well-being of the vast majority: it not only immiserates them but deprives them of their freedom to engage in productive and expressive work (since all their work is driven by the necessity of survival). Marx's early writings offer an ambitious theoretical sketch of human well-being and the kind of damage capitalism does to it. Very little in Marx's later critique depends on the adequacy of this sketch. It suffices for the later Marx that the logic of capitalism gradually reduces most people to poverty (absolute or relative)—since their labor is increasingly useless in a world dominated by technology-driven production—and that such people are motivated to change things in order to survive.[31]

Of course, people who cannot meet their physical needs are, on all philosophical accounts of well-being, badly off, so nothing turns on whether their suffering is a matter of being alienated from their species-being or something else. As Marx writes in his second thesis about Feuerbach, criticizing metaphysical debates about idealism (that is, about whether the existence and character of the world is independent of how human beings think about it): "The dispute over the reality or non-reality of thinking which is isolated from practice is a purely *scholastic* question" (MECW 5: 6). This remains true, we suggest, with the kind of moral theory Marx flirted with in his youth and that now dominates academic discussion. It is a purely scholastic question whether the harm of capitalism is that it alienated people from their species-being, or reduces their net pleasure, or frustrates their desire-satisfaction under ideal conditions, or fails to respect their dignity. It is scholastic because if capitalism runs its course and produces mass immiseration, then none of this matters: those who are immiserated do not need a theory of why they are badly off. They need to understand what is happening and what could be done to change it: that is Marx's core ambition in his mature work.

Notes

1 Brudney, influenced by John Rawls, tries to resist that conclusion elsewhere in his book. For the contrary view, see Leiter (2015b). Ours is an instance of the "amoralist" reading of Marx usefully discussed by Raekstad (2022: 227–238, including a criticism of Leiter [2015b]). The core idea of the amoralist reading is that Marx grounds the normative appeal of his view entirely on "the desires, needs, and interests of the working class" (Raekstad 2022: 227), and thus only in an appeal to the interests of a class, not to any moral considerations that supposedly transcend class. "Freedom," however, can be in the interest of a class deprived of it, thus eliding the distinction between "simple" and "sophisticated" amoralism proposed by Raekstad (2022: 229). The crucial distinction is between what is in the interests of an individual (or class of individuals) (call this non-moral goodness) and what is not. When Raekstad suggests that a capitalist "could have good ethical reasons to care about the non-ethical goods of proletarians" (2022: 234–235), he is moving from an amoralist to a moralist interpretation of Marx. Of course, Marx does not deny that individual capitalists might care about this; but he claims, correctly, that (1) such capitalists will not survive in the marketplace, and (2) the charitable concern of some capitalists provides no reason for the vast majority not to resist capitalism.

2 The implicit and inchoate conception of human well-being and flourishing is visible at points in Marx's later works; but what is striking is that Marx abandons, after 1844, an attempt to elaborate and defend this account. The efforts of those whom Marx would have viewed as "bourgeois" moral philosophers to recover and defend such an account in recent decades itself invites a Marxist analysis of the modern academy.

3 His collaborator, frequent co-author, and financial supporter Engels was of the same view: see Leopold (2007: 3). Raekstad (2022: 228) thinks that "simple amoralist [interpretations of Marx] were … challenged by the discovery of … Marx's early writings of 1844," but it is hard to see why that follows unless one assumes that Marx never changed his views. The fact that he thought this material unworthy of publication, and that it has such an obvious discontinuity with the focus of Marx's later work, counts in favor of the amoralist interpretation. For a powerful account of the philosophical motivations for Marx's "break" with his earlier work in 1845–46 and the adoption of his mature "naturalistic" outlook, see especially Dallman (2021), who also shows that the continuity between the unpublished *German Ideology* and Marx's later work is much clearer.

4 Even Herbert Marcuse, who became a leading figure in the Frankfurt School, greeted them with enthusiasm, though for Marcuse (1932), as for other "Western Marxists" influenced by Hegel, they offered an antidote to the appropriation of Marx by the Soviet Union and an easier way to link Marx to his Hegelian background. As one commentator has aptly put it: "many welcomed the early writings because they appeared to cast doubt on the authority of the orthodox Soviet account of Marx's work" (Leopold 2007: 7). The Soviet orthodoxy was philosophically crude (and motivated by non-epistemic considerations), of course; but it was not wrong in seeing that Marx's ambition was a scientific account of historical and economic change.

5 "Reconciliation" for Hegel had conservative implications that are foreign to Marx: reconciliation for Marx is only possible when the actual world is changed, so that individual and communal interests *really* coincide.

6 For the standard demarcation, see Derek Parfit's "Two Kinds of Theory" (2011: 43–47); see also Brink (1989: 5–7).

7 The contrast is with views that claim what is "good" for someone depends on their subjective psychological states: e.g., whether they experience pleasure (Jeremy Bentham), happiness (John Stuart Mill), preference-satisfaction (neoclassical economics), or satisfaction of the desires they would have if informed about all relevant facts (Richard Brandt). Cf. the earlier discussion in Chapter 5, Section 3.

8 See the discussion in Seigel (1978: 115–116). See also, Brudney (1998: 124), who aptly observes that, "For Bauer, the Jewish problem is an instance of the general antagonism between religion and a rational state … To solve that problem, Jews, like Christians, must give up their religious identity, not seek its state sanction."

9 To be sure, Marx here utilizes anti-Semitic stereotypes to make his point. However, as one intellectual historian has noted: "Everyone acknowledges that anti-Semitism played no role in Marx's most influential writings, neither in the rhetorical declamations of the *Communist Manifesto* nor in the deeply theoretical analysis of *Capital*. He never pictured Jews as inferior to any other, 'higher' or 'more developed' race or people. He never denied his own Jewish origins, several of his close friends were Jews, and he argued in favor of giving Jews full civil rights. At the same time, it is clear [that in some early writing and letters and journalism], Marx spoke disparagingly of the Jews as a group, and of individuals who displayed what he thought were Jewish characteristics" (Seigel 1978: 112–113).

10 The German here is *Die politische Emanzipation ist allerdings ein großer Fortschritt*. We have substituted a more literal translation than the MECW.

11 Bauer treated the "rights of man" as distinct from the "political rights," but Marx correctly rejects that distinction as irrelevant (cf. MECW 3: 161–162).

12 John Stuart Mill, in *On Liberty* (1859), articulated the "Harm Principle" as a limit on the power of the state: the state could only pass laws that restrict liberty when the exercise of that liberty would "harm" others. Mill, by his own admission, was strongly influenced by Wilhelm von Humboldt, whose work would have been known to Marx, as it was to all highly educated Germans of that era.

13 See Wood (1993: esp. 218–219). See also Baynes (2007: 562–565).

14 Kant emphasized laws given by the individual person to himself; Hegel emphasized the necessity of laws imposed by a rational community.

15 Hegel believed that a person's own sense of self was dependent on recognition by others, in particular, by recognition from others who were one's equals, not one's mere "slaves" or instruments. This is the point of the famous "master–slave dialectic" in his *Phenomenology of Spirit* (1977). Of course, it could be true that one's own sense of self depends on recognition by equals, but that is a far cry from establishing that one must identify with the entire community. Why could it not suffice, as it obviously does, that one form a sense of self within the smaller circle of people one recognizes as equals?

16 There are some passing references in the *Grundrisse*, written in 1857–58, where *Gattungswesen* is equated with the idea of humans *originally* being "herd animals," a condition then dissolved by the rise of exchange relations (MECW 28: 420). In *Capital* I, Marx observes that cooperative work "strips off the fetters of [the worker's] individuality, and develops the capabilities of his species" (MECW 35: 334), but no normative or argumentative work is done by this passing observation. Cf. MECW 35: 188 for another discussion that is evocative of the earlier discussion of species-being, without using that concept. Even if Marx leaves his 1844 writings behind, it is not surprising, as we have claimed all along, that some descendants of these ideas should lie in the background of remarks in the mature writings.

17 Recall the discussion of the "fetishism" of commodities in Chapter 4, Section 6.

18 Their interest extends beyond the treatment of "alienation," especially for understanding Marx's break with the philosophical tradition that precedes him in German philosophy: see esp. the discussion in Dallman (2021), Chapters II–IV, VII. *Contra* writers like Marcuse (1932), if Dallman is correct (as we believe he is), then the *Manuscripts* should not change our understanding of Marx's published corpus.

19 Jon Elster calls alienation "the lack of a sense of meaning," but then adds that this "does not imply the sense of a lack of meaning," i.e., it does not imply an *awareness* of lacking meaning (1986: 41). But, consistent with his methodological individualism—"the view that all institutions, behavioral patterns, and social processes can in principle be explained in terms of individuals only: their actions, properties, and relations. It is a form of reductionism" (1986: 22)— Elster says that only the phenomenology or experience of lacking meaning "could provide a motivation for action" (1986: 41). This assumes, falsely, that the motivation has to be conscious. It could be that the *fact* of being alienated creates dispositions to act in certain ways, but the attendant dispositions are not conscious ones—i.e., the agent never has the experience of lacking meaning.

20 Some of these forms of alienation would also obtain under earlier relations of production, but Marx's focus is on the alienation of workers under capitalism.

21 This is the part of Marx's account that most clearly echoes Hegel's idea of self-actualization through producing things, i.e., self-objectification.

22 See Engels, *The Condition of the Working-Class in England* (MECW 4: esp. 457, 537–538).

23 Elster claims that "Marx's models of self-realization are the artist, the scientist, or the preindustrial artisan, not the industrial worker. Although he always insisted that there was no turning back from industrial production, he did not really explain how there could be room for creative work in the modern factory" (1986: 46). Yet, as the discussion of alienation in the text makes clear, Marx harbored no illusions about the debilitating and dehumanizing nature of factory work (a view he never abandoned). And, as we saw in Chapter 4, Marx believed, obviously correctly, that those who were not "wage slaves" would not choose factory work, but other kinds of productive activity.

24 See the discussion of "freedom from necessity" in Chapter 3, Section 4C.

25 For a somewhat different reading than what we offer here, see Chitty (1993).

26 Recall the discussion in Chapter 5, Section 3C.

27 Late in the 1844 *Manuscripts*, Marx criticizes Hegel's "double error." First, Hegel treats the "whole *history of the alienation-process* and the whole *process of the retraction of* the alienation" as "nothing but the *history of the production* of abstract (i.e., absolute) thought—of logical, speculative thought" (MECW 3: 331). Second, Hegel obscures the "human *character* of nature and of the nature created by history— man's products" by treating them simply as "*products of abstract mind and as such, therefore, phases of mind—thought entities*" (MECW 3: 332). This is just to say, as we saw in Chapter 2, that Hegel mistakenly thinks ideas and their evolution are the essence of history, when in fact they are largely epiphenomena.

28 Kandiyali (2020) tries to respond to this worry, in part by weakening what is required for labor to be "unalienated." Our view is that productive abundance is a requirement for communism.

29 For defense of a very different view, see O'Connor (2018).

30 Recall Marx's famous observation about John Milton: "Milton produced *Paradise Lost* for the same reason as a silkworm produces silk. It was an expression of *his own* nature. Later on he sold the product for £5" (MECW 34: 136).

31 The *Grundrisse* is replete with discussions of alienation, much like Marx's earlier *1844 Manuscripts*. Unlike the *Manuscripts*, where the concept of "species-being" is central, in the *Grundrisse* this concept almost entirely disappears (there are two passing uses of the term) and it instead emphasizes the relationship between living labor and objectified labor (these terms are used hundreds of times). Living labor represents the active, human aspect of work, while objectified labor includes commodities, machinery, and other means of production. In the *Grundrisse*, Marx outlines how objectified labor dominates living labor by setting the conditions and pace of work, leading to a form of alienation where human activity becomes subordinate to inanimate objects and systems. This specific form of domination and alienation is further elaborated in *Capital*. Thus, the *Grundrisse* and *Capital*, while retaining some notion of alienation, move away from Marx's earlier, controversial philosophical anthropology and towards a focus on the very clear, practical harms done by the capitalist system. See Carver (2008) for an illuminating discussion.

Further Reading

Brixel (2024) is a recent reading of Marx's idea of alienated labor, connecting it to what we have been emphasizing as the need for "spontaneous" activity, but differing from our reading in other ways.

Brudney (1998), Chapter 3, presents a helpful account of the philosophy of Bruno Bauer.

Kandiyali (2020) is a recent philosophical effort to understand what is wrong with "alienation."

Leopold (2007) offers a sympathetic and historically sensitive account of "On the Jewish Question" and the *1844 Manuscripts* in Chapters 3 and 4, respectively.

Raekstad (2022) is a thoughtful philosophical reconstruction of the normative theory of the early Marx, which also contains a useful Appendix discussing competing views of Marx's normative commitments.

7

Legacy and Influence

When Marx died in 1883, no one could have imagined how dramatic his influence and legacy would become. He had finally come through the most dire years of his exile in London, which had been marked by desperate poverty and relative intellectual obscurity. Still, he was primarily known only among a relatively small group of international socialists and intellectuals. *Capital* had gained some recognition, but it was not a mainstream text by any means; and, while he was recognized as a leader in the International Workingmen's Association, the organization itself had splintered and had little remaining influence. However, shortly after his death, socialist parties inspired by his work gained in prominence, and in the century that followed revolutions were carried out across the world in his name. Even those inspired by him, however, interpreted and extended his ideas in myriad and often conflicting ways. Here we trace out this complex history, both outside and inside the academy.

1. Engels

Friedrich Engels had more influence on Marxism than anyone other than Marx himself, and, for a time, arguably even more. There are several ways that Engels contributed directly to the creation and promotion of Marx's work. First, Engels served early on as Marx's collaborator. In the 1840s, a young Marx had been impressed by Engels's *The Condition of the Working-Class in England* (1845), and the pair soon

DOI: 10.4324/9781315658902-7

began working together on three substantial projects—The Holy Family (1845), The German Ideology (1846), and The Communist Manifesto (1848).

Second, Engels served as Marx's financial benefactor. After the failed revolutions of 1848 and Marx's subsequent exile to London, Engels moved to Manchester and worked in his father's mill throughout most of the 1850s and 1860s, which enabled him to help fund a financially desperate Marx as he worked out his economic theories in London.

Third, Engels served as an early promotor and interpreter of Marx's works. Engels published a detailed review of Marx's A Contribution to the Critique of Political Economy (1859) and numerous reviews of the first volume of Capital (1867), both under his own name and anonymously. After Marx's death in 1883, as his influence grew, Engels wrote influential new prefaces both to reissues of their jointly authored Communist Manifesto and to numerous reissues of Marx's other works.

Fourth, Engels served as Marx's literary executor, which proved to be a massive undertaking. From thousands of pages of often disjointed and very nearly illegible notes, Engels began an effort to edit Marx's unfinished volumes of Capital into publishable form. Two years after Marx's death, he published the second volume (1885); nine years later he published the third (1894); and he worked towards publishing what was to be the fourth (later published as Theories of Surplus Value), but was unable to do so before his own death in 1895.

In addition to aiding and promoting Marx's work, Engels made independent contributions to Marxist theory later in his career— most influentially, the account of dialectical materialism that he developed in Anti-Dühring (1877) and Dialectics of Nature (1883). An enthusiastic scientific autodidact, Engels sought to show how the key elements of the Hegelian dialectic were in accord with or explanatorily useful for understanding (he was not entirely clear on which) the remarkable scientific advances of the era. Whereas Marx had focused primarily on the dialectical transformation of society compelled by class conflict, Engels claimed to show that:

> In nature … the same dialectical laws of motion force their way through as those which in history govern the apparent

fortuitousness of events; the same laws which similarly form the thread running through the history of the development of human thought and gradually rise to consciousness in thinking man.

(MECW 25: 11)

Engels's ambition in these works was to articulate a synthesis of materialism and dialectics that would provide the emerging Marxist movement with a complete "communist world outlook" (MECW 25: 8). His writings from this period are alternately insightful, obscure, and slightly amateurish, and their critical legacy has been pernicious, helping to give rise to a dogmatic "scientific" Marxism whose ambitions went well beyond those of Marx himself. Whatever their shortcomings as Marx interpretation, they exerted an immediate and profound influence on the theorists of the nascent Marxist movement who considered Engels to have provided the "philosophical foundation of Marxism" and to have articulated its "final shape" (Plekhanov 1969: 23).

In addition to his theoretical contributions, Engels played the role of elder statesman, advising the growing Marxist movements throughout Europe, particularly the Social Democratic Party (SPD) in Germany. The SPD was founded in 1875 (as a coalition of two socialist parties themselves founded a decade earlier). The German government enacted anti-socialist laws that officially banned the party from 1878 to 1890; but, once these were lifted, it quickly became the largest political party in the country. For the SPD, this electoral success raised the question to what extent it should continue to conceive of itself as a revolutionary party seeking to overthrow the state from without, rather than a reforming party seeking to gradually change it from within. Engels's position combined the views into a two-step process. First, the party needed to continue to grow its numbers and influence from within as it was doing until it became the dominant political power. Armed revolt before that point would be doomed to fail and threaten the standing of the party. Second, having achieved sufficient numbers and power, the party would be in a position to succeed in the armed conflict with the capitalist classes Engels expected would inevitably come. Thus, in his 1895 Introduction to a reissue of Marx's *Class Struggles in France*, written the year of Engels's death, he states:

[The party would soon] grow into the decisive power in the land, before which all other powers will have to bow ... To keep this growth going without interruption until it of itself gets beyond the control of the prevailing governmental system, not to fritter away this daily increasing shock force in vanguard skirmishes, but to keep it intact until the decisive day, that is our main task ... the normal development would be impeded, the shock force would, perhaps, not be available at the critical moment.

(MECW 27: 522)

The nuance of Engels's position, however, was lost on many of the reformists, who took him to be rejecting revolutionary Marxism altogether, much to his consternation.[1]

2. The Second International and Its Theoreticians

The SPD was itself a member of the Second International. The Second International, also known as the Socialist International, was an organization of socialist and labor parties that existed from 1889 to 1916. It was formed as a successor to the First International, also known as the International Workingmen's Association. The Second International was created to promote cooperation and coordination among socialist parties around the world, with the goal of achieving a socialist revolution. It held a total of fifteen congresses during its existence, in various cities around Europe and North America, in which delegates from member parties would discuss and vote on resolutions and plan joint action.

Karl Kautsky (1854–1938), a prominent socialist theorist and a leading member of the Second International, occupied a central role among Marxist intellectuals for over thirty years as the editor of Die Neue Zeit (The New Times), the party's theoretical monthly founded in 1883, becoming the leading theoretician of Marxism soon after Engels's death in 1895. He exerted considerable influence on the next generation of notable figures, such as Rosa Luxemburg, Vladimir Lenin, and Leon Trotsky. Kautsky was regarded as the key proponent of "orthodox Marxism," which consisted of three main principles. First, he was committed to the strongest reading of historical materialism, holding that the forces of production determine the economic, political, and cultural character of society, without any dynamic interaction between the other levels of society (what is sometimes called "Vulgar Marxism"). Second, Kautsky was a strong advocate of the class struggle, and argued that the workers needed to organize politically and economically to overthrow the capitalist system. Finally, he was critical of the idea of socialism through parliamentary reform, which he saw as a form of opportunism that would ultimately lead to the co-optation of the socialist movement by the capitalist class. Instead, he argued for a revolutionary approach that relied on mass action and the development of a strong socialist party.

Eduard Bernstein (1850–1932) was a German socialist theorist and politician widely regarded to be the co-heir, along with Kautsky, to the position of leading Marxist theorist after Engels's death. He was a member of the Social Democratic Party of Germany, and from 1881 editor of the party's official paper *Sozialdemokrat*, and eventually the leading proponent of what became known as Marxist revisionism within the Second International. Bernstein saw himself as reformulating the theoretical underpinnings of the SPD to align with its already established practice, which he viewed as largely reformist; and he sought to harmonize the theory with this reformism by invoking Engels's 1895 Introduction to *The Class Struggles in France*.

Bernstein's revisionism essentially negated the key claims of Kautsky's orthodox Marxism. First, he argued that historical materialism is false. In his book *Evolutionary Socialism* (1899), Bernstein claimed that the predictions of Marx and Engels about the collapse of capitalism were not accurate, and that the capitalist system was capable of adapting and evolving in ways that would prevent its collapse.[2] Second, he argued that socialism could be achieved through a gradual process of reforms within the existing capitalist system, rather than through a revolutionary overthrow of the capitalism. He believed that the working class could make political and economic gains through the use of parliamentary democracy, trade unions, and other forms of collective action. He also argued that the socialist movement should focus on winning political power within the existing system, rather than on revolutionary overthrow. Finally, Bernstein argued that the party, not the proletariat, was the key agent of change. He believed that socialism could be achieved without the need for a dictatorship of the proletariat, and that the role of the state in a socialist society should be to facilitate social and economic reforms rather than to control the means of production. Bernstein's ideas were highly controversial and led to a split within the socialist movement, with many accusing him of betraying its core principles.

The Second International was formed to coordinate the activities of socialist parties across national borders, to promote international solidarity among the working class, and to work towards the overthrow of capitalism. The outbreak of World War I (which pitted Germany and the Austro-Hungarian Empire against much of the rest of Europe) presented a significant challenge for the Second International, as its member parties were faced with the decision of how to respond to the war. Some socialist parties, particularly those in countries aligned with the Entente Powers—such as France, Russia, and Britain—chose to support their respective governments and the war effort. These parties believed that the war was necessary to defend their countries from the aggression of the Central Powers and to preserve the gains made by the working class. However, other socialist parties—particularly those in the Central Powers, such as Germany and Austria-Hungary—opposed the war and called for an international workers' revolution to overthrow capitalism and end the war. The split between these factions led to bitter debates and disagreements within the Second International, and ultimately contributed to its dissolution in 1916.

3. Lenin and the Nominally Marxist 20th-Century Revolutions

Vladimir Lenin (1870–1924) was a political theorist, Russian revolutionary leader, and the first head of the Soviet Union. He was born in Simbirsk, and was raised in a well-educated, middle-class family. He was a gifted student, and graduated from the University of Kazan in 1891 with a degree in law. Lenin became interested in Marxist ideology and revolutionary politics while studying at university, and became a committed Marxist after his brother's execution for plotting to assassinate Tsar Alexander III in 1887. In 1895, he was introduced to Georgi Plekhanov, a leading Marxist thinker and founder of the Russian Social Democratic Labour Party, or Workers' Party

(RSDLP), who became his mentor. Lenin became increasingly prominent within Russian Marxist circles (whose members were largely in exile) as well as in the Second International, where he made a name for himself as a fierce critic of reformist socialists, and he would eventually break with the organization over its perceived lack of revolutionary commitment.

In the two decades before the 1917 Russian Revolution, Lenin established himself as the leader of the Bolsheviks, who, together with the Mensheviks, constituted the primary factions within the RSDLP. The Bolsheviks and Mensheviks had two key theoretical disputes. The first was over the role of the party in the revolution. The Mensheviks believed that the party should be a broad-based, democratic organization that would include a range of political tendencies and organizations. They argued that a diverse and open party would be better suited to the task of building a popular movement capable of achieving social change. In contrast, the Bolsheviks believed that the party should be a small, tightly organized group of professional revolutionaries who would lead the working class in the struggle for power. They argued that only a disciplined, centralized "vanguard party" could achieve the revolutionary goals of overthrowing capitalism and establishing a socialist state.

The second dispute was over the nature of the revolutionary process itself. The Mensheviks, hewing closely to the classical theory of historical materialism, argued that Russia was still a largely feudal and backward country, and that the working class would need to ally with other progressive forces to achieve a democratic revolution that would first establish a capitalist system, which would then lay the foundation for further social and economic development, eventually creating the conditions necessary for a socialist revolution. (As readers will realize by now, we believe the Mensheviks were correct.) The Bolsheviks, in contrast, argued that Russia could successfully transition from feudalism to communism if a communist political revolution in Russia could quickly act as the catalyst for communist revolutions in the advanced capitalist countries of Western Europe, which would result in communist governments that would in turn help Russia in its economic transition to communism. The Bolshevik view involved wishful thinking, which subsequent historical events made clear.

These theoretical positions were soon put to the test in the real world. In February 1917, the Tsarist autocracy was overthrown in a revolution largely driven by widespread dissatisfaction with the Tsar's handling of World War I and the deteriorating economic conditions in Russia.[3] The Provisional Government was formed by a group of liberal and moderate socialist politicians who aimed to create a democratic government in Russia. However, it failed to address the country's deteriorating conditions, leading to further unrest. Lenin returned to Russia from a seventeen-year exile and led a Bolshevik seizure of power in October 1917, establishing the world's first nominally communist government. This revolution was followed by a period of brutal civil war in which opponents of the Bolshevik regime (funded in large part by capitalist powers like the United Kingdom, France, and the United States) waged war against the new regime; the war lasted from 1918 to 1922 and resulted in millions of deaths and untold suffering. (It also cut short the "war-time capitalism" that Lenin had instituted initially, recognizing that Russia was still a predominantly agricultural society.)

The Bolsheviks ultimately emerged victorious, consolidating their power and establishing the Soviet Union in 1922. However, the hoped-for communist uprisings in the industrialized West never materialized, leaving Lenin's government economically unstable and diplomatically isolated. Lenin died just two year later; and, in his final writings and speeches, he expressed concern about the rise of a bureaucratic elite within the party, and warned of the dangers of excessive centralization and authoritarianism.

After Lenin's death, the Russian regime became even more untethered from anything resembling Marx's own ideas. Joseph Stalin (1878–1953) became the General Secretary of the Communist Party and consolidated power through a series of purges and repressions. Acknowledging the failure of communist revolutions in the industrialized West, Stalin's central strategy was based on the notion of building "socialism in one country." He argued that the Soviet Union needed to focus on rapid industrialization and modernization in order to catch up with the industrialized nations of the West, which he believed could be achieved through intense central planning. The policy had some measure of success, as the Soviet Union became a major global power with a strong industrial base, but with significant costs: forced collectivization of farms that caused widescale famine, shortages of consumer goods, and generally low living standards for Soviet citizens. Moreover, Stalin's regime was a cruel parody of Marx's liberatory aspirations. The Russian regime sought to exercise complete control over all aspects of society, including political, social, and cultural life. The government used a variety of methods to maintain this control, including censorship, propaganda, secret police, and terror. Stalin's regime sought to eliminate all opposition and dissent, and any individuals or groups that were seen as a threat to the regime were subject to mass persecution, imprisonment, and execution. Stalin, who began his Bolshevik career as a gangster who robbed banks for the cause, ultimately proved to be not very different once he had total power.[4]

The Russian Revolution had a significant impact on world history, inspiring communist revolutions in other parts of the world and shaping the geopolitical landscape for much of the 20th century. Some of the most significant nominally Marxist revolutions include the Chinese Revolution led by Mao Zedong, the Cuban Revolution led by Fidel Castro, and the Vietnamese Revolution led by Ho Chi Minh. These revolutionaries self-identified as Marxist insofar as they saw their movements as mass mobilizations driven by a desire to overthrow colonial or neocolonial capitalist powers and replace them with regimes that would address economic inequalities through nationalization of industries, land reform, and the establishment of a planned economy. However, each of these revolutions would have been unrecognizable to Marx, since they were self-avowed peasant uprisings in deeply agrarian societies, often led by revolutionaries who were dubious of the revolutionary intentions and abilities of the industrial working class. This was contrary to historical materialism's claim that genuine communist revolutions could only occur in the most advanced industrial nations. Nor could these revolutions count on support from other industrialized nations to help them skip the capitalist-industrializing phase, as Lenin had earlier hoped would be the case in Russia.

These nascent regimes could certainly not count on Western support; and, by the time the Soviet Union was capable of doing so, it tended to treat these regimes as dependencies to be exploited for material goods or geopolitical advantage, rather than as partners whose advancement through the stages of historical materialism was to be hastened. As a result, none of these regimes bore a resemblance to Marx's own sketches of the post-revolutionary order. Even those less prone to the anti-liberatory totalitarian impulses that characterized the Soviet regime were too poor to ensure their citizens the material basis for a flourishing life: in this regard, they fully vindicated Marx's observation in *The German Ideology* that, for a successful communist revolution, an advanced

> development of productive forces … is an absolutely necessary practical premise, because without it privation, want is merely made general, and with want the struggle for necessities would begin again, and all the old filthy business would necessarily be restored.
>
> (MECW: 5: 49)

4. The Birth of Western Marxism: Lukács and Gramsci

Western Marxism is the umbrella term used to describe the various Marxist intellectual ideas that began to gain prominence in Western Europe after the First World War (1914–1918). Responding to the failures of revolutionary movements in the West, and increasingly disillusioned with the authoritarian turn of Soviet Russia under Stalin, Western Marxists moved away from the economic focus that characterized Marxism up to that point. They instead directed their attention toward the ideological mechanisms by which the ruling class continued to secure the acquiescence of the masses, exploring an often underappreciated dimension of social control, though often at the risk of becoming sociological idealists, like the Left Young Hegelians, whom Marx loathed (see Chapter 5, Section 1). In general, Western Marxism marked a shift of emphasis from purely economic and overtly political concerns toward a broader exploration of cultural and psychological phenomena. Western Marxists, moreover, variously incorporated ideas from other traditions (psychoanalysis, phenomenology, existentialism, and so on) into their theorizing, as well as returning sympathetically to ideas of Hegel, including Hegelian ideas Marx seemed to have left behind after 1845.

Georg Lukács (1885–1971) is widely regarded as the founding figure of Western Marxism. Known initially as a literary critic influenced by Neo-Kantianism, German Idealism, and the German sociology of his day (particularly Georg Simmel[5] and Max Weber[6]), Lukács embraced Marxism after World War I, and in 1923 published Western Marxism's seminal work, History and Class Consciousness. At the core of this work is the question of why the proletariat in the advanced Western countries has failed to revolt against the capitalist system. (He did not consider the possibility that capitalism was not sufficiently developed for communism to make sense.) On the one hand, he argues, there are "acute crises in capitalism ... [and] as a result of the crises even the ordinary social environment can be seen and felt to be problematical," even as "capitalism has been so greatly weakened that it would no longer be able to maintain its position by force if the proletariat were to oppose it consciously and resolutely" (Lukács 1972 [1923]: 262). On the other hand, however,

> even in the very midst of the death throes of capitalism[7] broad sections of the proletarian masses still feel that the state, the laws and the economy of the bourgeoisie are the only possible environment for them to exist in ... it remains the "natural" basis of society.
>
> (Lukács 1972: 262)

According to Lukács, "only ideology stands in the way" (1972: 262) of the proletariat revolting, and the task of his work is to aid the proletariat in achieving "ideological maturity ... a true understanding of its class situation and a true class consciousness" upon which "the fate of the revolution ... and with it the fate of mankind" depends (1972: 76, 70). Lukács's more detailed diagnosis and prescription of this situation proceed through three key ideas—totality, reification, and the proletariat as the subject/object of history.

The concept of "totality" is the foundational category in Lukács's work. As we discussed in Chapter 1, both Hegel and Marx were committed to versions of holism—the idea that, although particular things may appear to be simple, they are typically part of a larger complex, and that the condition of adequately understanding any particular thing requires understanding its position in this whole (or, totality). Embracing this idea, Lukács claims that Marx's "dialectical method" of analyzing social facts holistically, rather than any of his particular claims, constitutes the real core of Marxism:

> It is not the primacy of economic motives in historical explanation that constitutes the decisive difference between Marxism and bourgeois thought, but the point of view of totality … Proletarian science is revolutionary not just by virtue of its revolutionary ideas which it opposes to bourgeois society, but above all because of its method.
>
> (Lukács 1972: 27)

Lukács goes so far as to claim that a Marxist need not be troubled even "if research disproved once and for all every one of Marx's individual theses" because "Marxism … does not imply the uncritical acceptance of the results of Marx's investigations. It is not the 'belief' in this or that thesis, nor the exegesis of a 'sacred' book. On the contrary, orthodoxy refers exclusively to method" (1972: 1). Lukács claims that this method requires analyzing the ways that the individual facts stand in relation to one another at a particular moment, as well as analyzing these facts as moments in a process of historical development.[8] Moreover, and again following Hegel and Marx, Lukács is committed to a view that the historical development of this totality is both teleological and progressive.

Lukács introduces the concept of "reification" (*Verdinglichung*) as the key explanation of why the social interrelations and dynamics that constitute the totality are so difficult to perceive. As we discussed in Chapter 5, Lukács adopts Lenin's non-pejorative use of the term "ideology" to refer to a social and political worldview; but, whereas Lenin explained the presence of ideological thought (both good and bad) as the result of elite messaging, Lukács instead focuses primarily on the way in which such thought develops spontaneously in people's minds based on the way things appear to them as they go about their daily lives in the capitalist system.[9]

Lukács begins with Marx's account of "commodity fetishism" (see Chapter 4, Section 6), which claims that in their economic activities (buying and selling goods) the social relations of people (who makes what, under which conditions, while working for whom) appear merely as relations between things (this object is worth such-and-such compared to that one). Lukács then extends this idea, arguing that, as the market has increasingly come to dominate all aspects of social life under capitalism, commodity fetishism begins to shape every aspect of experience, "stamp[ing] its imprint upon the whole consciousness of man" (1972: 100). People come to see not only objects but also other people, and eventually even themselves, as merely instrumentally valuable things of calculable worth: "his qualities and abilities are no longer an organic part of his personality, they are things which he can 'own' or 'dispose of' like the various objects of the external world" (Lukács 1972: 100).

Less persuasively, Lukács argues that the various "dualisms" that preoccupied the German Idealist tradition (between subject and object, human and nature, etc.) are a result of the misperception of subjects as objects that constitutes reification. More persuasively, he claims that, to the extent that we come to see the world (including ourselves) as objects of exchange, the more the capitalist system will seem natural and inevitable. Within this system, Lukács concludes, human agency is reduced to "the adjustment of one's way of life, mode of work and hence of consciousness, to the general socio-economic premises of the capitalist economy" (1972: 98–99).

Lukács's final step is to argue that the proletariat will be the class that finally overcomes the reification that leads people to misperceive the social relationships and dynamics that constitute the totality. Lukács believes the proletariat's unique position within the capitalist system, as both the creators of value (in the sense of the labor theory of value) and the exploited class, gives them a privileged standpoint. They are, in his term, the "subject-object" of history. They are the *subject* of history insofar as they are both the ones that carry out the key tasks necessary to perpetuate the capitalist system and the ones who will overthrow it. They are the *object* of history insofar as they are the ones most affected by the capitalist system, bearing the brunt of capitalist exploitation. Given the centrality that this standpoint plays in his account, Lukács is frustratingly unclear exactly how members of the proletariat are able in virtue of their position to overcome the reification that initially grips them and everyone else: does their standpoint enable them to perceive the totality directly? Or does the frustration of their circumstances compel them to infer its relevant features? Compounding the difficulty, Lukács, like Lenin, maintained that the party played an indispensable role in the formation of class consciousness and in steering the proletariat towards revolutionary action.

Whatever the exact nature of the proletariat's supposed epistemic advantage, Lukács emphasizes that the knowledge of the totality (of themselves, of their relationships, and of the historical dynamic) it provides is to be understood as a process that is tied to its practical transformation of social reality: in carrying out the revolution, the proletariat simultaneously comes to understand itself, the social world, and the historical role it itself plays.

The trajectory of Lukács's thought in History and Class Consciousness owes more to Hegel's idealism than to Marx's materialism. Although he agrees with Marx that the proletariat will serve as the key agent of historical change, Lukács's proletariat bears more resemblance to Hegel's Geist than to Marx's proletariat in terms of its historical mission: a self-understanding that finally resolves philosophical dualisms, rather than a classless society free from economic domination. Lukács attempts to emphasize the importance of "praxis" (practical action as opposed to mere theorizing), and he expressly aims to develop an account in which action and ideation are coextensive in the good cases; yet throughout this work consciousness often appears to be an autonomous power producing the key transformative effects. It is in this fashion that, sounding very much like the Left Young Hegelians Marx rejected, Lukács concludes that the "reform of consciousness is the revolutionary process itself" (1972: 259).

The sociological idealist drift throughout this work is something for which Lukács later criticized himself:

> What I failed to realise, however, was that in the absence of a basis in real praxis, in labour as its original form and model, the over-extension of the concept of praxis would lead to its opposite: a relapse into idealistic contemplation.
>
> (Lukács 1972: xviii)

Lukács attributes to History and Class Consciousness the view that the proletariat as subject-object of history is "created by self-knowledge" in an "act of cognition ... freed of its alienated nature." Consequently, he comes to reject the proletariat as he had earlier conceived of it—as a purely metaphysical invention rather than an actual agent of historical transformation: "the proletariat seen as the identical subject-object of the real history of mankind is no materialist consummation that overcomes the constructions of idealism. It is rather an attempt to out-Hegel Hegel" (1972: xxiii). However, despite Lukács's personal repudiation of the idealist themes of this work, these themes would greatly influence Western Marxism.[10]

Antonio Gramsci (1891–1937), a contemporary of Lukács, would similarly influence Western Marxism. However, while Lukács's impact was felt almost immediately, Gramsci's work remained relatively obscure for several decades, only gaining widespread recognition and influence from the 1970s onward. He was born in the rural and primarily peasant region of Sardinia, Italy, and faced numerous adversities, including poverty and severe physical ailments from which he would suffer his entire life. A talented student, he studied linguistics at the University of Turin. However, he never completed his degree, due in part to financial difficulties and in part to his growing political activities. His time in Turin coincided with the rise of the industrial working class in Italy, whose struggles greatly influenced his political leanings. Gramsci helped establish the Italian Communist Party in 1921 and became its leader in 1924. His position brought him into contact with the Bolsheviks in Russia, with whom he generally aligned, though he advocated for a more flexible approach to revolution adapted to each country's unique conditions. This position also made him a central target of the fascists who had come to power in Italy. His outspoken opposition led to his arrest and imprisonment by Benito Mussolini's regime in 1926, a sentence that lasted until his health-related death in 1937. While in prison, Gramsci wrote prolifically, producing his most acclaimed work— what became known as the *Prison Notebooks*.[11]

Gramsci's account of ideology is the core of this later work. In his view, the ruling class maintains control not solely through coercion or the explicit exercise of power, but also, crucially, through cultural "hegemony." Drawing from the ideas of Marx and Lenin, Gramsci highlights the significance of the ruling class's control over key institutions involved in shaping and propagating ruling-class ideologies (such as religious, educational, and media institutions), while distinguishing himself by providing a more comprehensive examination of the specific methods employed by the ruling class in this endeavor. Moreover, Gramsci's unique perspective emphasizes that ideology involves not only the implantation of ideas but also the cultivation of attitudes and orientations: "[ideologies] organise human masses, and create a terrain on which men move, acquire consciousness of their position, struggle etc." (Gramsci 1971: 377). He contends that religion exemplifies ideology in this sense, as it engenders "a unity of faith between a conception of the world and a corresponding norm of conduct" (1971: 326). Gramsci's focus on attitudes and orientations extends the concept of ideology beyond Marx's account. Ideological beliefs are not merely a set of beliefs one holds, but a part of one's way of life. This, Gramsci contends, helps to elucidate why ideological belief is so often resistant to rational critique.[12]

For Gramsci, as with Lenin and Lukács, the problem does not lie with ideology in general but with bourgeois ideology, and the aim is to promote a proletariat ideology that can effectively oppose it. In contrast to Lenin's perspective that culture was subordinate to political ends, Gramsci positioned it at the forefront, viewing the establishment of cultural hegemony as a foundational step to gaining power. According to Gramsci, and contrary to Marx, a class cannot achieve dominance in industrialized countries solely by promoting its specific economic interests; nor can it establish control strictly through the use of force or coercion. Instead, to challenge the idea that bourgeois values were the normal or inherent standards for society, it was necessary for the working class to establish its own cultural identity. He distinguished between "traditional intellectuals" (who deludedly see themselves as autonomous from the dominant social group while in fact upholding the status quo) and "organic intellectuals" who are closely associated with particular social classes, emerging from within these groups to articulate their specific interests.[13] Organic intellectuals give voice to the sentiments and experiences that the masses, especially the "subalterns" (i.e., marginalized groups) find difficult to articulate for themselves, thus articulating alternative ideologies than can begin to challenge the hegemony. Gramsci underscores the importance of a national-popular collective project and the formation of a "historic bloc" (1971: 168)—an alliance among various subaltern groups aiming to enhance their agency and engage them in political action capable of effectively countering the prevailing hegemony.

Gramsci, adopting terms from military science, characterizes the formation of a counter-hegemony as a "war of position" in contrast to a "war of manoeuvre" (Gramsci 1971: 238–239). The former, a prolonged ideological struggle, allows the working class—guided by their organic intellectuals organized into a working-class party—to supplant the prevailing bourgeois ideology with their own, presenting an alternative worldview challenging the status quo. This is particularly necessary in developed capitalist societies where the ruling class's cultural and ideological control is deeply rooted and spread across a wide social stratum. In contrast, Russia—where the Tsar held state power but lacked genuine cultural hegemony—did not require this process. The absence of robust ideological domination allowed the Bolsheviks to execute a "war of manoeuvre"—a sudden and direct overthrowing of the ruling class and seizure of political power.[14] However, Gramsci maintained that this approach could only be feasible in developed capitalist societies once the "war of position" has succeeded: "A social group can, and indeed must, already exercise [intellectual and moral] 'leadership' before winning governmental power (this indeed is one of the principal conditions for the winning of such power)" (1971: 57). Consequently, in these societies, successful challenges to existing capitalist power structures require the interplay of both the foundational work of the "war of position" and the decisive action of the "war of manoeuvre."

As with Lukács, Gramsci's work contributed to a change in the focus of Western Marxism from the primarily economic or "material" perspective of Marx's historical materialism to an examination of culture and ideology.[15] His concept of cultural hegemony recognized culture as an element that could maintain power structures, quite apart from the level of development of technology. Gramsci's understanding of intellectuals, particularly his distinction between "traditional" and "organic" intellectuals, emphasized their role in shaping and transforming ideologies. His ideas on the "wars of position" and "wars of manoeuvre" highlighted the role of cultural and ideological struggle in societal change. This shifted focus in Western Marxism towards the examination of culture and ideology broadened its critique beyond purely economic structures. Consequently, Gramsci's theories have influenced how contemporary Western Marxism approaches social analysis and political strategy.

5. Western Marxism: The Frankfurt School

The Frankfurt School was a group of interdisciplinary theorists associated with the Institute for Social Research established in 1923 in Frankfurt, Germany. Its most prominent members were the philosophers Theodor Adorno (1903–1969), Max Horkheimer (1895–1973), and Herbert Marcuse (1898–1979). The philosopher and literary theorist Walter Benjamin (1892–1940), though not officially affiliated with the school, was an associate and influence on many of its members. The Frankfurt School attracted several other theorists drawn from various disciplines (sociology, psychology, and economics), reflecting the group's commitment to interdisciplinary work, and its members drew on a range of thinkers in addition to Marx (Hegel, Freud, Nietzsche, Weber, among others). The Nazi regime's rise to power in 1933 forced the institute to close in Germany and its core members fled to the United States, where the it became affiliated with Columbia University in New York. Adorno and Horkheimer returned to Frankfurt in 1953 to reestablish the institute, fostering a second generation of theorists, most prominently Jürgen Habermas (b. 1929), who strayed even further from Marxist roots.[16] Marcuse remained in the United States, where he became a prominent figure in the New Left movement during the 1960s.

The Frankfurt School practiced a form of social critique it called "critical theory," outlined in Horkheimer's 1937 essay "Traditional and Critical Theory."[17] He characterizes traditional theory as a type of inquiry that often reinforces the status quo because it tends to treat societal structures as static and natural.[18] Critical theory, in contrast, is a method of inquiry oriented towards revealing the latent contradictions inherent in societal systems, thereby paving the way for potential transformation. Horkheimer says that this form of inquiry is fundamentally self-reflective, consistently scrutinizing its own principles and societal impacts—an attribute standing in stark contrast to the alleged neutrality of traditional theory. Further, he maintains that critical theory should be interdisciplinary, as it requires an amalgamation of insights from diverse fields to execute a comprehensive critique of societal structures. Most importantly, Horkheimer maintains that critical theory is committed to emancipation and betterment of human conditions, deviating from the aloof, purely descriptive stance typically associated with traditional theory. Integral to this approach is the method of "immanent critique"—a form of critique that seeks to expose contradictions or inconsistencies from within a system or framework of thought itself, rather than appealing to external criteria or standards.[19] In this view, critique is not a matter of imposing external standards but of highlighting the theory's internal contractions, and hence irrationality. This, of course, represented a return to Left Young Hegelianism of a kind Marx had repudiated.

Horkheimer and Adorno's critique of "instrumental reason," most notably developed in their 1947 *Dialectic of Enlightenment*, can be seen as one of the most prominent applications of their critical approach. Instrumental rationality, as they define it, is a form of rationality that sees everything, including human beings, as resources to be efficiently managed. They suggest this form of rationality was initially a tool honed early in the Enlightenment era to master nature, but inevitably transformed into a mechanism of domination more broadly, organizing social structures into systems of control. The Enlightenment's demythologizing of the world initially served to liberate humans from religious dogma, yet soon paved the way for a new form of domination. Once the world was thoroughly objectified, everything, including humans, was reduced to calculable objects lacking inherent worth, and there was nothing to appeal to but an outmoded moral superstation to resist the domination and exploitation of nature and humans alike. "Enlightenment," they conclude, "understood in the widest sense as the advance of thought, has always aimed at liberating human beings from fear and installing them as masters. Yet the wholly enlightened earth is radiant with triumphant calamity" (Horkheimer & Adorno 2002: 1). This trajectory, of course, found particularly horrifying expression in the fascist regimes in Europe. It could be seen too, they argued, in capitalist societies where efficiency and profitability are paramount; and so human beings are increasingly reduced to consumers to be manipulated, and human relationships reduced to marketplace transactions.

This instrumental thinking impoverishes our understanding of the world and our relationships within it, curbing critical thought and thus the possibility of genuine freedom. Here, again, Horkheimer and Adorno treat philosophical ideas as having causal impact—devastating causal impact!—on the course of historical events, which from Marx's perspective would be an extreme case of sociological idealism (see Chapter 5, Section 1).

A second prominent application of the Frankfurt School's critical approach is found in the critique of the "culture industry," which Adorno and Horkheimer begin to elaborate in "The Culture Industry: Enlightenment as Mass Deception" (a chapter of *Dialectic of Enlightenment*) and which Adorno develops in numerous subsequent essays.[20] Throughout these writings, Adorno argues that mass culture operates as an industry whose primary focus is profitability and standardization rather than artistry. These cultural products are systematically produced and distributed based on market principles—manufactured using standardized formulas, designed for mass appeal, and marketed for maximum profitability. Adorno details examples from the film, television, and music industries, where items are produced following formulaic templates that prioritize entertainment and immediate gratification over the critical engagement and creative innovation of which real art is capable.

The culture industry stimulates a culture of pseudo-needs, manipulating individuals into first desiring and then endlessly seeking out the cultural items it produces, despite the fact these ultimately bring little fulfillment, yet always somehow fostering the expectation that the next goods purchased may finally satisfy the craving. This endless repetition thereby maintains patterns of consumerism that helps to keep the capitalist system functioning. Worse still, Adorno argues that the culture industry's commodification and homogenization of culture legitimizes and reinforces existing power structures by promoting a consensus culture that discourages critical thinking and fosters passive acceptance of the status quo:

> The culture industry no longer has anything in common with freedom. It proclaims: you shall conform … conform to that which exists anyway, and to that which everyone thinks anyway as a reflex of its power and omnipresence. The power of the

culture industry's ideology is such that conformity has replaced consciousness.

(Adorno 2001: 104)

Adorno draws a bleak picture of a society whose members are increasingly oriented around the consumption of cultural products, a society in which conformity displaces space for critical engagement.[21]

Marcuse's most distinctive contribution to the Frankfurt School is his fusion of Marxist and Freudian ideas in his analysis of social and political phenomena, particularly his integration of Freud's concepts of repression and desire into a broader Marxist critique of capitalist society. In his 1955 Eros and Civilization, Marcuse emphasizes the socio-political implications of Freud's psychoanalytic theory of human nature. He proposes that advanced industrial societies sustain a condition he terms "surplus-repression" applying constraints on people's desires over and above what is necessary for basic societal order (Marcuse 1974 [1955]: 35).[22] He suggests the feasibility of a non-repressive society— that is, a societal structure wherein human desires are not excessively stifled, and creativity and fulfillment are not subordinated to labor and productivity. He hypothesizes that such a society could potentially be realized through "non-repressive sublimation" (Marcuse 1974: 208), a process where primal human desires are redirected and expressed in ways that are socially beneficial without being excessively repressed. He also critiques what he calls the "performance principle" (1974: 35), the ceaseless quest for achievement and productivity, asserting that it results in an unnecessary degree of repression.

In 1964's One-Dimensional Man, the book which made Marcuse a public figure in America, Europe, and elsewhere, he rearticulates several familiar Frankfurt School themes, in particular, the idea that advanced industrial societies foster what he dubs "one-dimensionality"—a state in which individuals, conditioned by a steady diet of mass media and consumer culture, become passively accepting of the status quo and lose their capacity for critical resistance. Similarly, he critiques the capitalist system's creation of "false needs" (Marcuse 2007 [1964]: 7)—that is, needs created and sustained by consumerist culture that bind individuals to continual consumption of new products and entertainments, and foreclose critical engagement with the world.

Despite drawing on similar intellectual sources as Adorno and Horkheimer, Marcuse's writing was typically more accessible and conveyed a comparatively more optimistic vision for societal transformation, qualities that appealed to the 1960s' student movement and positioned him as a key figure of the "New Left," and in many ways the public face of the Frankfurt School.[23]

Like Lukács and Gramsci, the Frankfurt School foregrounded the role of culture within Marxist theory. However, while Marx indeed saw the ideological superstructure as helping maintain existing relations of production (see Chapter 2, Section 1) the Frankfurt School extended this idea. Having made the mistake of presuming the material conditions were already in place for a communist revolution in the West, they looked for reasons to explain why it failed to materialize; and to answer this they looked to the ideological realm. Thus, they came to believe that the ideological superstructure possessed a causal influence that greatly surpassed Marx's original conception. The school posited that culture, transmitted through various media and institutions, has the power to mold individual consciousness, values, and behaviors in ways that cement the status quo and prevent revolutionary change, regardless of the level of material development. This viewpoint suggests that culture operates quite autonomously from the underlying economic base.

In contrast to Lukács and Gramsci, most Frankfurt School theorists, partly excepting Marcuse, grew increasingly doubtful about the possibility of overcoming the prevailing cultural hegemony. Their belief was that the omnipresent culture industry and the societal norms it fosters pose significant challenges to achieving critical consciousness and instigating systemic reform. Thus, the Frankfurt School's theoretical approach diverges from Marx's perspective both in challenging the primacy of economic development as the primary impetus for historical change and in evincing a marked skepticism about the possibility of such change occurring at all.

6. Althusser

Louis Althusser (1918–1990) was born in Algeria to French parents. He was first a student at the *École Normale Supérieure* in Paris, where he studied under the prominent philosopher of science Gaston

Bachelard, before later becoming a professor there. Althusser joined the French army during World War II, but was captured by German forces and spent the remainder of the war in a prisoner of war camp. After the war, he joined the French Communist Party, although he was often critical of it and eventually fell out of favor with its leaders. Althusser rose to prominence in the 1960s in a series of influential and controversial works on Marx, most notably two volumes published in 1965—*For Marx* and *Reading Capital*. Althusser suffered for decades from severe mental health issues, and in 1980, during a bout of mental illness, he killed his wife. Following this, Althusser was institutionalized and did not publish any significant works for the remainder of his life.

Althusser challenged the humanist interpretations of Marx that had become prominent in Western Marxism. These interpretations drew heavily from the perceived emphasis on liberating humans from the alienation imposed by capitalism in Marx's early writings before 1845, which were seen as continuous with or complementing his later work. Althusser, however, challenged their continuity and complementarity. He claimed that there were two markedly distinct phases in Marx's thought, with his early writings heavily influenced by the idea of Hegel and the humanistic philosophy of Feuerbach, resulting in a strong focus on issues like human alienation and self-realization.[24]

Yet, a decisive shift or "epistemological break" in Marx's intellectual development occurred around the period of *The German Ideology* and *Theses on Feuerbach*. Following this break, Althusser argues, Marx's work transformed into a rigorous scientific exploration of societal structures, leaving behind the dubious speculative accounts of human nature and moralizing of his early work. (We agree with Althusser on the broad outlines of this change, although not for his reasons.[25]) Althusser's notion of "scientific" refers to a methodological, analytical inquiry into social structures rather than to empirical observation. Marx analyzed society into its constituent parts (such as the economy, class relations, and political power) and scrutinized their interrelationships, focusing on how alterations in one component, like the mode of production, could instigate changes across the entire societal structure. Althusser thus sees in the later Marx a progenitor of the structuralism he himself promoted.[26]

Although he praises the structural approach of Marx's later writings, Althusser's own structural Marxism in fact departs significantly from Marx's historical materialism. In contrast to Marx's view that the development of productive power (technology) is the primary causal influence on historical change, Althusser instead proposes a model where the economy and superstructural elements are components of a complex structure. They remain distinct but also continuously influence one another. Although the economy often has causal primacy, other elements of the superstructure retain relative autonomy and possess a "specific effectivity" of their own, even demonstrating independent historical progression to some extent. Here Althusser looks favorably to Engels's 1890 letter to Joseph Bloch, where he states that economic production is determinative, "but only in the *last instance* [*in letzter Instanz*] ... more than this neither Marx nor I have ever asserted" (Althusser 2005: 111–112).[27] Engels here, in his effort to recast historical materialism in a more commonsense light, introduced a great degree of vagueness regarding the determinacy of economic factors in historical events.[28]

Althusser, however, views it as a positive departure from what he sees as an overly "reductive" understanding of historical materialism. Althusser argues that the elements of the structure are overdetermined,[29] by which he means that, rather than a singular cause–effect relation, there is a network of multiple interconnected factors influencing societal events. Althusser argues for the relative autonomy of the superstructural elements like law, culture, and politics, suggesting they have a significant role in shaping historical developments. Notably, the dominance of any one element, such as the economy, is not fixed but can vary depending on historical conditions. Althusser emphasizes that the analysis of these structures should focus on the structures themselves, rather than the individuals (their beliefs, desires, etc.) that operate within their confines. Instead of viewing individuals as originators of societal processes, he sees them as byproducts and conduits of social structures, roles which they assume through ideology.

As we discussed in Chapter 5, according to Althusser, ideology operates as a force that molds individuals into types of subjects that align with the requirements of the existing economic structure, ensuring they continue to serve its purposes. The ruling class, holding sway over the "repressive state apparatuses" such as the government, military, and police, is thus positioned to control the subordinate classes, either through the implied threat or actual application of violence. Equally significant, the ruling class exerts influence over "ideological state apparatuses" like educational institutions, the media, and civil organizations, which they leverage to uphold social unity and perpetuate the current socio-economic relations (Althusser 2014: 256).

As with Gramsci, Althusser treats ideology as a constellation of beliefs, attitudes, and perspectives that bolsters the domination of the ruling class. Althusser goes further, however, portraying ideological indoctrination as an influence so comprehensive and effective that it essentially creates the individual: "ideology 'acts' or 'functions' in such a way that it 'recruits' subjects among the individuals … or 'transforms' the individuals into subjects" (2014: 190).[30] In this process, society offers the nascent subject a defined assortment of socially useful roles. The subject, in turn, embraces and fulfills these roles, culminating in an "interpellation" process that concurrently constructs and subjugates the individual.

Each of the aspects of Althusser's account outlined above faces serious objections. First, his portrayal of Marx as a staunch anti-humanist is an overstatement.[31] Marx did move away from the influence of Hegel and the Young Hegelians, and from his interest in "alienation" and "species-being," and abandoned entirely the attempt we see in the 1844 Manuscripts to develop a moral "theory" that would explain and justify his claims about the "good life" for human beings. Yet his later works continue to reflect what we might call a "humanistic" concern—namely, with the damage that capitalism does to human well-being and the possibility of freedom, damage that communism would undo. Marx also maintains his belief in human agency, arguing that people can collectively reshape their destiny and challenge oppressive socio-economic structures, at least under certain material preconditions; his call for global unity among workers was premised precisely on that idea. His later work places significant emphasis on human potential and self-realization, envisioning a society where individuals, free from "wage slavery," can express their talents and abilities in "spontaneous" productive activity (recall the discussion of "freedom from necessity" in Chapter 3, Section 4C).

Second, Althusser's "structural Marxism"—while purportedly aiming to offer a more intricate depiction of social structures than Marx's own rendering of historical materialism in the 1859 Preface—rejects what is distinctive in Marx's position, and ends up saying hardly anything at all of substance.[32] Althusser asserts that all elements of society influence each other in varying ways and at different times, without providing specific and consistent criteria for measuring the influence of these different societal elements. Lastly, Althusser's concept of "interpellation," which distinguishes his theory of ideology, is suggestive but woefully underexplained. With Althusser, one can see how individuals are seemingly drawn into existing societal roles and norms through a process of recognition and response; however, this falls short of the complete constitution of the subject that Althusser's stark anti-humanism seems to be after.

7. Analytical Marxism

Analytical Marxism is a school of thought that emerged in the late 1970s, characterized by its commitment to clarity and rigor and which described itself as "no bullshit" Marxism in response to the obscurities of Althusser's work in particular. Key figures in this school include G.A. Cohen, Jon Elster, and John Roemer. This approach treats Marxism not as a comprehensive worldview to be defended *in toto*, but as a set of hypotheses to be tested and refined. This group of theorists focus on key concepts in Marxism, drawing on the resources made available by contemporary social science and analytic philosophy, with the goal of rendering Marxism more coherent, precise, and amenable to empirical testing. Here we highlight three topics that have received sustained focus in the tradition: historical materialism, exploitation, and the normative desirability of socialism over capitalism.

G.A. Cohen's examination of historical materialism in his 1978 *Karl Marx's Theory of History: A Defence* was the landmark work in analytical Marxism, offering a defense of what we called "Orthodox Functionalism" in Chapter 2. Cohen argued that, on Marx's account, the development of productive forces (technology and human skills) determine (or explain) the relations of production of society, which in turn determines (or explains) the superstructure (the various ideological domains). Cohen uses functional explanation, commonly employed in biological sciences, to justify his thesis. He argues that certain social structures exist because they serve the function of facilitating the development of productive forces.

It is here that Elster criticized Cohen's interpretation of historical materialism. Elster contended that Cohen's account lacked a clear causal mechanism that explains how changes in the productive forces lead to changes in the social and political superstructure; and he argued that, unless a mechanism can be identified, the functional explanation in question depends on scientifically discredited teleological reasoning (see Chapter 2, Section 4). Cohen's initial response was to acknowledge that the theory's plausibility required that a causal mechanism must exist, but it did not require that we presently know what that mechanism is (just as Darwin's functional rendering of the theory of evolution was plausible before the discovery of genetics identified its causal mechanism). Peter Railton's solution, which we defended in Chapter 2, identified class struggle as the mechanism in question. Cohen himself, however, eventually turned away from his defense of historical materialism.

Exploitation was another key topic of analytical Marxism. While obviously drawing inspiration from Marx, analytical Marxists departed from his account in two significant ways: (1) they sought to articulate an account of exploitation that does not depend on the discredited labor theory of value; and (2) they emphasized the question "What is wrong with exploitation?", whereas Marx insisted his account was purely descriptive. On John Roemer's approach, for example, an individual or group is technically exploited when three conditions hold: (1) the individual or group would be better off if they could withdraw from society with their per capita share of resources; (2) this withdrawal would make certain others worse off; and (3) these same others would themselves be worse off if they were to withdraw from society. Roemer adds, however, that this technical exploitation is "a bad thing only when it is the consequence of an unjust unequal distribution in the means of production" (1988: 130). So, for example, Roemer considers workers (and the unemployed poor) to be technically exploited because they would be better off taking their per capita share of the economy and opting out; and he considers this exploitation to be unjust because capitalists have long monopolized the productive resources, which has left the workers, through no fault of their own, no option other than being exploited.

A central criticism from Marxists and non-Marxists alike is that Roemer's account fails to consider what many see as a key feature of exploitation—namely, those in dominant positions taking advantage of those who are vulnerable, regardless of how those involved came to be in their relative positions.[33] Common to Roemer and these critics alike, however, is an emphasis on explaining what is "morally wrong" with exploitation, an ahistorical and practically irrelevant question from the point of view of the mature Marx.

Finally, there was a marked shift towards normative theorizing more generally in analytical Marxism, enumerating the various ways that socialism was to be preferred over capitalism on moral grounds. In his later work, Cohen (starting most clearly with *If You're an Egalitarian* in 2000), argued that communism was not inevitable because of the dissolution of the 19th-century proletariat class and the constraints imposed by the climate on the growth of productive power.[34] Cohen argued, instead, that we needed a transformation in moral consciousness, and thus turned toward articulating and defending socialist values. In *Why Not Socialism?*, for example, Cohen proposes a luck-egalitarian "socialist equality of opportunity" principle. This demands not just the removal of barriers due to factors like race and gender (as "bourgeois" equality of opportunity requires) or just the removal of barriers due to economic disadvantages experienced early in life (as "left-liberal" equality of opportunity requires), but corrects for "all unchosen disadvantages ... for which the agent cannot herself reasonably be held responsible," including differing natural abilities (Cohen 2009: 12–18). Cohen, recognizing that even his socialist egalitarianism could permit inequalities that could strain the socialist ideal as he understands it, supplements it with "the requirement of community"—which is "that people care about, and, where necessary and possible, care for, one another, and, too, care that they care about one another" (2009: 34–35).

It is this ethos that similarly motivated Cohen's *Rescuing Justice and Equality* (2008), which is a sustained critique of Rawls's *Theory of Justice*. Cohen here takes issue with Rawls's difference principle, which allows for some inequalities if they are to the advantage of

the least well-off. Cohen finds this principle at odds with an egalitarian ethos, as it permits inequalities for the sake of incentives.
However, having defended the normative desirability of socialism,
Cohen offers only a faintly optimistic assessment of the feasibility of
ever bringing it about: he claims that "we now know that we do not
now know how to do that," adding the distinctly un-Marxian claim
that, "left to itself, the Capitalist dynamic is self-sustaining," before
noting that he nevertheless does not "think the right conclusion is
to give up" (Cohen 2009: 81–82). Of course, from Marx's point of
view, the idea that promoting an "egalitarian ethos" could actually
be effective in the absence of a change in the material circumstances
in which people live would have seemed like just another Left Young
Hegelian fantasy.[35]

8. Feminist Extensions of Marx

"Feminist Marxism" emerged in response to perceived gaps in traditional Marxist theory, particularly its insufficient focus on gender
oppression: classical Marxism, with its emphasis on class struggle
and economic exploitation under capitalism, overlooks the systemic
oppression of women and the role of the patriarchy (Hartmann
1979). As it has evolved, feminist Marxism has stimulated new conversations in Marxist discourse about the ways capitalist structures
might perpetuate gender-based inequalities, including the valuation
of domestic and reproductive labor, the role of women in the workforce, and the intersection of capitalism with gender and race.

Social reproduction theory, a key development within feminist
Marxism, examines the undervaluation and invisibility of reproductive labor in capitalist societies (Federici 2020). It highlights the
critical yet unpaid tasks of child-rearing, caregiving, and household
maintenance, which, despite their centrality to the labor force's sustenance, go unrecognized in the capitalist framework. Debates in
this area often explore whether such reproductive labor constitutes
exploitation similar to that found in wage labor, and discuss ways
capitalist systems could be reimagined to properly acknowledge and
remunerate this work. For example, in many countries, the lack of
comprehensive childcare policies reflects the systemic undervaluation of reproductive labor, contributing to gender inequalities in the

workforce. Another area of concern is the global care chain, where women from poorer countries often fill care roles in wealthier ones, highlighting the international dimension of reproductive labor's exploitation.

Advocates for this theory argue that acknowledging reproductive labor challenges the fundamental structures of capitalism and necessitates a radical reevaluation of value and labor's definitions (Bhattacharya (2017). Emphasizing that these activities are crucial for workforce reproduction and the overall functioning of the capitalist economy, some advocate for systemic reforms to appropriately value and compensate reproductive labor, thereby confronting economic models that exclusively value market-based labor. Others, however, suggest that focusing intensely on the revaluation of reproductive labor could inadvertently overshadow the need for systemic changes across all labor forms to address the broader inequities and exploitations inherent in capitalism. Social reproduction theory thus reveals the gendered labor division as a key site of capitalist exploitation, underscoring the imperative to incorporate reproductive labor considerations into wider anti-capitalist efforts.

Two major figures in broadly Marxist feminism have been the philosopher Nancy Fraser and the philosopher and political activist Angela Davis. Fraser's (2014) work is characterized by her critique of what she identifies as capitalism's shortcomings and her advocacy for a model of justice that includes redistribution, recognition, and representation. Like much Western Marxism, Fraser revives elements of Hegel in her treatment of Marxist themes. She is especially interested in how capitalist societies perpetuate economic inequality and cultural injustices through misrecognition. "Recognition" here refers to the acknowledgment of and respect for the diverse identities and contributions of individuals. Fraser, in a very un-Marxian vein, argues that injustices related to recognition are as detrimental as those concerning economic distribution. Her analysis of the "crisis of care" (2016) also points to contradictions within capitalism that devalue essential care work, typically performed by women, leading to societal and economic instability.

Angela Davis, who was a student of Herbert Marcuse and has long been active in communist politics, has focused in her theoretical writings on the intersectionality of race, class, and gender oppression (1983),[36] along with a critique of the prison-industrial complex (2011). She views the latter as a mechanism of capitalist and racial exploitation, linking it to broader economic and social structures. Davis calls for a radical reimagining of the current criminal justice system, suggesting alternatives that emphasize rehabilitation and restorative justice, and addressing the root causes of crime. Her work has played a pivotal role in debates on the feasibility and implications of prison abolition.

As the preceding overview would suggest, there are ongoing debates within feminist Marxism between those inspired by Marx, but finding his approach inadequate in addressing gender and racial injustices (e.g., Eisenstein 1979), and those who believe that Marx's work contains the foundations for a feminist-Marxist analysis (e.g., Vogel 2013, Wills 2018).

9. Marx after the "Great Recession" of 2008

The global crisis of capitalism around 2008 generated renewed popular interest in Marx, which also helped stimulate attention to academic work purportedly related to Marx. Most of the attention, alas, accrued to superficial and unserious work, with a couple of exceptions. The French economist Thomas Piketty published *Capital in the Twenty-First Century* in 2013, its title an obvious echo of Marx's three volumes. Piketty, however, was no Marxist; and his book does not offer accounts of exploitation, the theory of value, or make prognoses about capitalism's demise. According to Piketty, the rate of return on capital (e.g., dividends, interest, etc.) outstrips and will continue to outstrip economic growth, leading to greater economic inequality; only state intervention (through, e.g., wealth taxes) can avert this development. Piketty's is a vision for greater social democracy, of the Western European kind, rather than a revolutionary transformation of society.

Those taking themselves to be more committed to the traditional Marxian project have returned to *Capital*, sometimes trying to salvage its mistaken labor theory of value, at times through tortured hermeneutics. Heinrich (2012) has been the most valiant and illuminating of these efforts, although unsuccessful for reasons discussed in footnotes in Chapter 4.

10. Conclusion

As the preceding account suggests, Marxism after Marx has had several very un-Marxian features—most strikingly, treating culture and ideas as independent causal forces in history, and treating ahistorical moral critique of capitalism as a central part of the Marxian project. In both Western Marxism and Analytical Marxism, the discovery of the 1844 *Manuscripts* (see Chapter 6) was greeted with enthusiasm and an outpouring of philosophical writing—although Marx himself lost interest in working on the 1844 topics, seeing, obviously correctly, that they were irrelevant to revolutionary transformation. The hermeneutics of *Capital* over the last quarter-century has been more faithful to Marx, but often less sensitive to developments in economics since Marx and less adept at sorting the wheat from the chaff, something Analytical Marxism tried to do with a vengeance.

After the excesses of Hegelian idealism in early 19th-century Germany, there was a "back to Kant" movement by mid-century. We hope this volume will contribute to a "back to Marx" turn—one that eschews the Young Hegelian tendencies of Western Marxism and the unduly gullible embrace of Marx's economics. In his theory of history, his theory of ideology, and his economics minus the labor theory of value there remains one of the most potent and insightful challenges to modernity, one even more relevant today as capitalism (finally) conquers the entire globe.

Notes

1 Shortly before his death, Engels wrote an angry letter berating an editor who had co-produced and published a version of his 1895 Introduction to Marx's *Class Struggles in France* that had highlighted its reformist elements: "I was amazed to see today in the Vorwärts an excerpt from my 'Introduction' that had been printed without my knowledge and tricked out in such a way as to present me as a peace-loving proponent of legality *quand même* [come what may]. Which is all the more reason why I should like it to appear in its entirety in the *Neue Zeit* in order that this disgraceful impression may be erased. I shall leave Liebknecht in no doubt as to what I think about it and the same applies to those who, irrespective of who they may be, gave him this opportunity of perverting my views" (MECW 50: 486).

2 We addressed versions of this worry in Chapter 4, Section 7, although mostly from the perspective of contemporary neoclassical economics. Bernstein was, in fact, correct about the timeline that Marx had envisioned for the unravelling

of capitalism. See https://www.marxists.org/reference/archive/bernstein/works/1899/evsoc/index.htm.

3 Tsar Nicholas II, who reigned from 1894 to 1917, is often characterized by historians as a particularly ineffective and out-of-touch leader. His lack of administrative acumen and resistance to meaningful reforms exacerbated Russia's existing social and political issues, leading the nation towards revolutionary upheaval. His poor decisions during World War I, coupled with his inability to address the domestic crises of famine and poverty, further eroded public confidence. The culmination of his inadequacies was the 1917 Russian Revolution, after which Nicholas and his family were executed, marking the end of the Romanov dynasty after three centuries of rule. See Service (2017) for a thorough account of his failings.

4 See Khlevniuk (2017) for an excellent biography of Stalin.

5 Georg Simmel (1858–1918) was a German sociologist who explored various aspects of modern social and cultural theory. He is particularly known for his analyses of social interactions and the philosophical implications of monetary exchange and urban life. See Simmel (2009).

6 Max Weber (1864–1920) was a major German sociologist, most widely known for *The Protestant Ethic and the Spirit of Capitalism* (2003 [1905]), which analyzes the relationships between religion, bureaucracy, and capitalism, particularly examining the interplay between Protestant beliefs and the development of Western economic systems. His view was decidedly anti-Marxist, assigning a decisive role to the Protestant religion, rather than technological innovation, in the development of capitalism.

7 Marx, of course, would have denied that these were the death throes of capitalism; the fact that, a century later, capitalism continues to expand its global reach makes clear how mistaken Lukács was.

8 Given its centrality in Lukács's account, however, much remains obscure as to the exact nature of this totality and of the method of its analysis. He says that the totality is not itself an empirical fact, yet it is "the real, ultimate ground of their [the various empirical facts] reality and their factual existence and hence also of their knowability even as individual facts" (1972: 152), and that "totality is, therefore, the category that governs reality" (1972: 10). But he does not explain how exactly this totality "grounds" or "governs" the individual facts. Nor does he explain the nature of our epistemic access to this non-empirical totality. He suggests that this is done "dialectically" and credits Marx for having taken this "method" over from Hegel and having "brilliantly transformed [it] into the foundations of a wholly new science" (1972: 27), but says little about exactly how he takes this method to work other than to say that it is "the conceptual reproduction of reality" (1972: 8). Lukács acknowledges that "this dialectical conception of totality seems to have put a great distance between itself and reality, it appears to construct reality very 'unscientifically'" (1972: 10). The anti-scientific commitments of the view and the problems this raises for its

intelligibility came into sharper focus during the "positivism dispute" of the 1960s in which Adorno sought to articulate and defend a largely Lukács-ian account of totality against empiricist critics. See O'Connor (2013: 37–44) for an excellent overview. Marx, who took natural science seriously as a model, would clearly not have been on the side of Lukács and Adorno.

9 Lukács does acknowledge the effect of elite messaging, observing, for example, that "large sections of the proletariat remain intellectually under the tutelage of the bourgeoisie; even the severest economic crisis fails to shake them in their attitude" (1972: 304). But it is not his primary focus.

10 In the 1930s, Lukács publicly repudiated the views he expressed in *History and Class Consciousness* and continued to criticize the work in various ways throughout his life. Some of this seems due to a genuine philosophical reevaluation; but certainly much of this was owing to the mounting pressure he faced from the Soviet Communist Party and his desire to ingratiate himself to it. After World War II, Lukács played a role in the Hungarian government, including serving as a minister in Imre Nagy's reformist government in 1956. However, after the suppression of the Hungarian Revolution that same year, he was removed from his position and returned to academic life. In his later years, he focused on aesthetics and the history of philosophy, producing several works that delved into the nature of literature, realism, and artistic expression. These topics had genuinely been lifelong interests of his, as well as areas that now drew less dangerous attention from the authorities.

11 The *Prison Notebooks*, written between 1929 and 1935, encompass roughly 3000 pages of essays, observations, and comments organized thematically. These writings, however, present considerable challenges for interpretation. A few reasons account for this, including the fact that Gramsci did not originally intend these notebooks for publication, leaving them somewhat fragmented and lacking a clear guide for reading order or interpretative approach. Furthermore, since they were composed during his imprisonment, the entries often employ intentional vagueness and allusiveness to bypass censorship.

12 By contrast, as we saw in Chapter 5, there are many psychological mechanisms that render ideology immune to rational critique.

13 Gramsci's views are detailed in his essay "The Intellectuals" (1971: 3–23).

14 Gramsci writes: "In Russia the State was everything, civil society was primordial and gelatinous; in the West, there was a proper relation between State and civil society, and when the State trembled a sturdy structure of civil society was at once revealed. The State was only an outer ditch, behind which there stood a powerful system of fortresses and earthworks" (1971: 238).

15 Gramsci was skeptical throughout his intellectual development of Marxism's focus on economic causes in historical transformation. In his 1917 essay "The Revolution Against *Capital*" (Gramsci 1977: 34–37), he argues that the Russian Revolution, which he took to be a genuine communist revolution occurring in an economically undeveloped country, showed that human agency and not

economic developments motored history. His later comments on the Russian Revolution do not alter this view, but only suggest that what worked in Russia could not succeed in the same manner in Western Europe, where what was needed, as we have seen, was ideological contest.

16 Under Habermas's influence, so-called "critical theory" became much like Anglophone moral and political philosophy after John Rawls's *A Theory of Justice* (1971), trying to offer accounts of the rational foundations of moral and political norms, a kind of ahistorical project foreign to the mature Marx.

17 See Horkheimer (2002: 188–243).

18 "Traditional theory" for Horkheimer is a 1930s'-style positivist conception of science in which scientific methods of explanation and confirmation are uniform across all scientific domains, and science is marked by its somewhat austere empiricism and its commitment to mathematical formalizability. The powerful impact of this essay on the Frankfurt School theorists is quite visible nearly forty years later, in Marcuse's polemic against "positivism"—essentially Horkheimer's "traditional theory" (Marcuse 2007 [1964]: 177 ff.). Almost all serious work in philosophy of science since has repudiated both the unity and the uniformity of methods of scientific inquiry and explanation characteristic of Horkheimer's conception of "traditional theory" and of logical positivism's conception of science (e.g., Kitcher 1993).

19 See O'Connor (2013), Chapter 2, for a detailed discussion of the method of immanent critique, its motivations, virtues, and limitations.

20 Many of these are collected in *The Culture Industry: Selected Essays on Mass Culture* (Adorno: 2001).

21 As some commentators have noted (e.g., Kellner 2002), Adorno's exposure to popular culture was limited, and occurred mostly during World War II while he was living in the United States, when popular culture had clearly been mobilized in support of the war effort. Many of his aesthetic judgments seem more idiosyncratic than insightful: e.g., his hostility toward American jazz, and his laudatory view of Shostakovich's atonal music.

22 Freud (1994) himself suggested this in *Civlization and Its Discontents* from 1930, arguing that human beings had both aggressive instinct that threatened to pull society apart and erotic instincts that drew people to each other. Freud recognized that civilization required significant repression of human instincts, but feared that existing societies demanded an unrealistic and unnecessary amount.

23 One gets a sense of Adorno and Marcuse's differing perspectives by examining their reactions to the 1968 student movements. Adorno, having returned to Frankfurt, not only expressed skepticism towards these movements, fearing they might inadvertently reproduce authoritarian structures, but even called the police on students protesting at his institute. In stark contrast, Marcuse, having remained in California, took an active role in supporting the student movements. He embarked on campus speaking tours, becoming a role model and vocal advocate for the revolutionary potential of the protests, which he believed

could challenge the capitalist status quo and established order. For a detailed discussion of their respective responses to these events, as well as of their moving
correspondence to one another debating the appropriateness of these responses,
see Jeffries (2016).

24 See Althusser (2005), "Introduction," and Chapter 6, "On the Materialist
Dialectic."

25 Dallman (2021) is a philosophically and textually superior account of the break
than Althusser's.

26 Structuralism is a theoretical approach that emerged in the mid-20th century,
especially in France. It asserts that human culture, thought, and behavior are
best understood in terms of their relationship to broader systemic structures.
The theoretical groundwork for structuralism was laid by linguist Ferdinand
de Saussure, who posited that meaning in language is produced not merely by
individual words, but through their differences and relationships within the
linguistic system. Anthropologist Claude Lévi-Strauss expanded this perspective
to cultural phenomena, suggesting that underlying structures, much like the
grammatical rules of a language, shape and give meaning to cultural practices
and beliefs. This idea was further developed and applied to the realms of psychoanalysis and philosophy by Althusser's contemporaries such as Jacques Lacan
and Michel Foucault, in their own ways attempting to illuminate the structures
that underlie human identity and societal institutions.

27 See MECW (49: 33–37) for the letter in its entirety; though note that Althusser
here uses a different translation than that found in the MECW, which renders *in
letzer Instanz* as "in the final analysis."

28 As we discussed in Chapter 2, Section 1, the crux of Marx's materialism is the
claim that the level of development of technology is explanatorily prior: no
other causal forces can make a difference absent the requisite level of productive
power.

29 Detailed in Althusser (2005: Chapter 3), "Contradiction and Overdetermination."

30 This was again a serious departure from Marx, who always emphasized the
presence of "individuality" throughout history. See Chapter 3, Section 1 and
Chapter 6, Section 1A.

31 See Geras (2017: Chapter 5) for particularly measured criticisms of Althusser's
work.

32 See Kolakowski (1971) for an apt, if scathing, assessment of Althusser on this
point.

33 See Goodin (1987), Vrousalis (2013), and Wood (1995).

34 A point on which we agree, although not for Cohen's reasons. See Chapter 4,
Section 7D.

35 For a more extended critique of Cohen, see Leiter (2015b: 35–42).

36 For doubts from a Marxist perspective, see Reed (2023).

Alienation (Entfremdung): The estrangement of people from aspects of their human nature due to living in societies divided into social classes. This describes an objective fact, though alienation may often be felt. Marx believed that the capitalist system, in particular, leads to four types of alienation:

- *Alienation from the product of one's labor:* Workers in a capitalist society do not own the products they produce. Instead, these products belong to the capitalist (the owner of the means of production). This alienation occurs because the worker can only express labor through the production of commodities for the market, rather than for personal use or satisfaction.
- *Alienation in the labor process:* Marx argued that the work process under capitalism is alienating in itself. Workers have no control over the design, process, or pace of their work. The labor process is dictated by the capitalist, aiming to maximize profit, often at the expense of the worker's well-being.
- *Alienation from species-being:* This form of alienation refers to the estrangement of individuals from their "species-being" (*Gattungswesen*), a term Marx uses to describe the inherent nature of humans as free, creative beings capable of shaping the world. In a capitalist society, labor is not a means for personal expression or the fulfillment of communal needs, but rather a means to survive, reducing individuals to their capacity to work.
- *Alienation from others:* Capitalism not only alienates individuals from their work, their own potential, and the products of their

labor but also from other workers. Competition replaces cooperation, and social relations are reduced to market transactions.
This alienation manifests in both the workplace, through competitive labor relations, and in society, through the commodification of social interactions.

Marx believed that overcoming alienation is a key element in the
transition to a communist society, where the means of production
are communally owned, and labor serves both individual and communal needs, allowing for the full realization of human potential.

Analytical Marxism: A school of Marxist thought that emerged in
the late 20th century, aiming to reevaluate traditional Marxist
theory through the lens of analytical philosophy and the empirical methods of social sciences. This approach is characterized by
a rigorous examination of Marxist concepts (such as class struggle, exploitation, and historical materialism) using clear definitions, logical arguments, and empirical evidence. Originating
from scholars like G.A. Cohen, Jon Elster, and John Roemer,
Analytical Marxism seeks to address and refine Marxist theory's perceived ambiguities and contradictions, making it more
accessible and scientifically testable.

Basic needs: Refers to adequate food, clothing, shelter, and leisure
that are necessary for sustaining one's life.

Bolsheviks: One of the primary factions of the Russian Social
Democratic Labor Party, which was led by Vladimir Lenin before
the 1917 Russian Revolution. The Bolsheviks believed that the
party should be a small, tightly organized group of professional
revolutionaries who would lead the working class in the struggle for power.

Bourgeois ideology: This refers to the set of beliefs, values, and
norms that justify and maintain the capitalist system, primarily
serving the interests of the bourgeoisie, the class that owns the
means of production. This ideology promotes individualism,
private property, competition, and the free market as natural
and unchangeable aspects of human society. Marxists argue that
bourgeois ideology functions to obscure the realities of class
struggle, exploitation, and the social relations of production,

thereby naturalizing the inequalities and injustices inherent in capitalism. It operates through various institutions, including the media, education, and religion, to perpetuate the dominance of the bourgeoisie by shaping public consciousness in ways that align with capitalist interests.

Bourgeoisie: The class that owns the main forces of production under capitalism.

Capital: Capital is defined as wealth used to generate more wealth, primarily through the exploitation of labor. This concept goes beyond mere money or physical assets to include the investment in means of production like factories, materials, and land, which are owned by the capitalist class (bourgeoisie). The capitalist employs workers (proletariat), who must sell their labor power because they do not own the means of production. Workers produce value that exceeds their wages, and this surplus value is captured by capitalists as profit, highlighting a fundamental mechanism of wealth accumulation and exploitation under capitalism.

Capitalism: The economic system in which Marx expects the history of class conflict to reach its peak before finally ushering in the age of communism. It is characterized by capitalists (who own the major forces of production) employing wage laborers to produce commodities for exchange on the market for profit. Marx recognizes and celebrates the incredible power of capitalism but thinks the system is fundamentally unstable.

Causal theory of historical materialism: This states that members of a class flourish and become dominant because they make effective use of the forces of production. If this class fails to make use of more advanced forces of production, then a different class that does will triumph over the previously dominant class.

Chattel slaves: These are individuals who are treated as personal property, owned outright by another person. Unlike other forms of servitude, chattel slavery allows slaves to be bought, sold, and traded as commodities. This form of slavery was fundamental to the economies of ancient civilizations and colonial empires, notably in the transatlantic slave trade.

Class conflict: Economic systems sort individuals into groups whose members are similarly situated with respect to realizing their material interests. Groups acting in pursuit of their own self-interest inevitably clash with one another. Class conflict arises from these clashes, as the interests of different classes within an economic system. In the present capitalist society, this struggle is most centrally between the proletariat, who must sell their labor to survive, and the bourgeoisie, who own the means of production and profit from labor exploitation. Class conflict drives historical change and social revolution by challenging existing power structures and economic arrangements.

Class consciousness: An understanding of one's place within the class structure. Class consciousness enables one to challenge the ruling class when one is in the right position vis-à-vis the prevailing economic structure.

Cognitive bias: A bias that causes a theorist to respond too uncritically to the evidence before them.

Cognitive judgment: Judgment that can be true or false. Some theorists contend that Marx was making a cognitive judgment about exploitation and seeking to describe some moral truth about it.

Command economy: An economy that involves centralized power dictating what will be produced, in what quantities, and often who will be enlisted in its production.

Commodity: A good or service produced for exchange on the market. It has a dual nature: it possesses use-value (it satisfies some human need or desire) and exchange-value (it can be traded for other commodities). Commodities are central to capitalist economies, where the production of goods is driven not by the need to fulfill human needs directly but by the potential to generate profit through their exchange. This focus on exchange value over use value is a key factor in the dynamics of exploitation and alienation in capitalist societies.

Communism: Communism is a classless, stateless society where the means of production are owned collectively, aiming to eliminate the exploitation and inequalities of capitalism. It envisions a world where goods and services are distributed according to need rather than profit, promoting communal living and shared wealth. Marx saw communism as the ultimate goal of social development, achieved through the proletariat's overthrow of capitalist structures and the establishment of a socialist state as a transitional phase.

Constant capital: the investment in physical assets like machinery, buildings, and raw materials used in the production process. Unlike variable capital, which is spent on labor power and can produce surplus value, constant capital does not create new value by itself. Its value is transferred to the final product in the course of production, maintaining its worth without generating an excess.

Contradiction (Widerspruch): A contradiction exists for Marx when the growth of productive power is stymied by the existing relations of production and the existing ideology. A contradiction exists when the dominant ideology serves to legitimate and sustain relations of production that are a hindrance to the further development of the productive forces.

Contribution principle: Economic principles under the dictatorship of the proletariat that are still shaped by the capitalist views of the previous era. Under the contribution principle, people would expect to be paid for work they have done, no more and no less.

Critical theory: Practiced by theorists of the Frankfurt School, this form of social critique is a method of inquiry oriented towards revealing latent contradictions inherent in societal systems, thereby paving the way for potential transformation.

Cultural hegemony: A concept developed by Antonio Gramsci which describes the dominance of a societal ruling class's worldview, values, norms, and ideologies over others. This dominance is maintained not just through coercive means but also through the consensual acceptance of the ruling class's ideals by the subordinate classes. Hegemony is achieved by controlling cultural institutions like education, the media, and religion, shaping public consciousness in ways that naturalize and legitimize the status quo. Gramsci argued that for a social group to challenge power, it must first question and alter the prevailing cultural hegemony.

Culture industry: This idea, developed by theorists of the Frankfurt School such as Theodor Adorno and Max Horkheimer, criticizes the mass production of cultural goods in capitalist societies. They argue that popular culture is manufactured by the culture industry to manipulate mass society into passivity and conformity, undermining critical thinking and individuality.

This process commodifies culture, making it another product aimed at profit rather than fostering genuine creativity or critical engagement. The culture industry serves to reinforce capitalist ideologies and maintain social hierarchies by promoting a standardized culture that supports the status quo.

Cunning: An attribute of Hegel's philosophy of history which posits that history is a process of Spirit coming to know itself. This process is cunning insofar as the actual structure of the process is unknown to historical actors, who act for motives and reasons unrelated to the dialectical and teleological structure of the process.

Dialectical: A process in which contradictions in an earlier stage (of thought, of economic production) lead to a transformation in which the later stage (of thought, of economic production) sublates the earlier form.

Dictatorship of the proletariat: This is the transitional period following the overthrow of capitalism, where the working class (proletariat) holds political power and suppresses the resistance of the former ruling classes (bourgeoisie). This phase aims to dismantle the capitalist state apparatus and reorganize society's productive forces and relations to build socialism, leading towards a classless, stateless society (communism). Marx and Engels posited this as a necessary step to eradicate class distinctions and create an equitable distribution of wealth and power.

Economic structure: The totality of the relations of production.

Eliminative materialism: A view of materialism that claims that any entities that are not reducible to material ones are to be eliminated from our picture of what the world is like.

Epistemic capacity: An individual's capacity to recognize what is happening in their social and economic environment and how it affects their interests.

Exchange-value: This is the measure of a commodity's worth in relation to other commodities in the market, determined by the amount of labor required for its production. It allows different goods and services to be traded based on a common standard, facilitating the complex web of exchanges in a capitalist economy. Unlike use-value, which reflects a commodity's practical utility, exchange-value embodies the social relations of trade and capital accumulation.

Exploitation: The value-creating work done beyond that needed for the worker's sustenance that is now owned by the capitalist. According to Marx, workers are "exploited" since they produce more value than they are actually paid for. Exploitation has a negative valence for Marx, but it is a technical notion rather than one that connotes injustice.

False consciousness: Accepting as true beliefs that are both false and whose falsity is contrary to one's own interests.

False needs: Term used by Frankfurt School theorist Herbert Marcuse to describe the capitalist system creating and sustaining a consumerist culture that binds individuals to continual consumption of new products and entertainments and forecloses critical engagement with the world.

Fetishism: To fetishize an entity means to invest it with inherent powers or attributes that it does not really have. These powers and attributes are entirely derivative from, or dependent upon, human beings.

Feudalism: System of economic production characterized by a feudal lord who controls the land and tools that serfs use to work the land.

Forces of production: These refer to the physical and technological resources—such as tools, machinery, raw materials, and labor—used to produce goods and services within a society. They represent the material basis for economic activity, and determine the potential for wealth creation and material abundance. The development and utilization of the forces of production are central to understanding the dynamics of economic growth and societal change.

Frankfurt School: This refers to a group of German theorists who founded the Institute for Social Research in Frankfurt in 1923. Influential figures include Theodor Adorno, Max Horkheimer, Herbert Marcuse, and Walter Benjamin. They critically analyzed the cultural and political conditions of modern capitalist societies, blending Marxian theory with psychoanalytic insights and cultural critique. The school is known for its analyses of the culture industry, authoritarianism, and the ideological conditions that underpin the persistence of capitalism.

Freedom: The fundamental aim of communism according to Marx. Freedom enables people to engage in productive activity because they want to do so, and not simply out of necessity.

Functionalism: A theory that claims that the level of development of the forces of production explains functionally the other features of society. A functional explanation explains the existence of something by appeal to the function it performs. Functional explanations are peculiar because the thing to be explained predates the thing that explains it.

Globalization: The process whereby capitalism presses beyond national borders to secure raw materials, cheaper labor, and new markets for its goods. This process greatly extends the life cycle of capitalism.

Hegemony: A concept used by the Italian Marxist thinker Antonio Gramsci to describe the cultural control through which the other classes come to endorse their own economic and political domination by the ruling classes.

Heuristics: Automatic and simplifying mental shortcuts that focus our attention on certain features of a situation while ignoring others.

Historical materialism: This is a methodological approach to understanding society, history, and social change through the lens of material conditions and economic activities. It posits that the mode of production—how goods are produced and how work is organized—shapes societal structures, including social relations, political institutions, and cultural beliefs. Marx argued that history progresses through stages of economic development, each defined by a specific mode of production and the class conflict it generates. This perspective sees social change as driven by the struggle between classes for control of the means of production, leading to the eventual overthrow of one economic system by another.

Holism: An idea that both Marx and Hegel were committed to. It is the idea that although particular things may appear to be simple, they are typically part of a larger complex, and the condition of adequately understanding any particular thing requires understanding its position in this whole.

Human emancipation: In Marxist thought, this refers to the comprehensive liberation of individuals from the social, political, and economic constraints imposed by class societies, especially capitalism. Marx envisioned human emancipation as the end of all forms of exploitation and alienation, achieved through the collective action of the proletariat to overthrow capitalist structures. This concept encompasses not just economic liberation but also the freedom from ideological and political domination, aiming for a society where individuals can fully develop and express their capacities and needs without being constrained by class interests.

Ideological critique: Aims at unmasking false beliefs that harm the interests of those who hold them, while also explaining the genesis of these beliefs in a way that simultaneously explains their prevalence and intractability.

Ideological superstructure: Dominant or influential religious, philosophical, moral, and economic ideas in a society.

Ideology: An ideology, for Marx, is a cluster of inferentially related *beliefs* (and *causally* related *attitudes*) that have three characteristics: (1) at least some of the ideology's central beliefs are false; (2) the ideology is the product of ideologists (economic, religious, and philosophical "theorists") who systematically make claims underdetermined (or even contradicted) by evidence (typically due to shared biases that undermine their theorizing); and (3) the ideology supports the interests of the ruling class and harms the interest of the vast majority, most often by misrepresenting how the existing state of affairs affect their interests.

Immanent critique: A method central to the Frankfurt School, this involves analyzing a society or system from within, using its own values and logic to expose contradictions and shortcomings. This approach does not rely on external moral standards, but identifies the internal discrepancies between what a society claims to stand for and the reality of its practices. The Frankfurt School applied immanent critique to capitalist societies, revealing how ideals of freedom and equality are undermined by the actual dynamics of exploitation and domination. This method aims to illuminate the potential for transformation and emancipation inherent within the existing social order.

Instrumental reason: A form of rationality that sees everything, including human beings, as resources to be efficiently managed. This form of rationality was initially a tool honed early in the Enlightenment era to master nature, but inevitably transformed into a mechanism of domination more broadly.

Interpellation: According to Louis Althusser, this is the process by which individuals are constituted as subjects through the workings of ideology and ideological state apparatuses, such as schools, churches, and the media. Althusser argues that ideology "calls" individuals into social roles, shaping their identities and beliefs in ways that support existing power structures and social relations. This concept highlights how power and control are maintained not just through coercion but through the more subtle mechanism of shaping consciousness and self-identity, ensuring individuals comply with and reproduce the dominant ideology of their society.

Just world theory: Proposed by psychologist Melvin Lerner, this theory posits that people have a fundamental need to believe in a just world where individuals get what they deserve. This belief motivates them to rationalize injustices and suffering, often blaming victims for their own misfortunes to maintain the perception of a fair and orderly world. Lerner's theory illuminates the psychological underpinnings of social attitudes and behaviors, particularly how individuals justify inequality and resist social change that challenges their belief in a just world.

Labor power: An ability to work with the physical and cognitive capacities one has. Under capitalism, the worker owns his labor power, which he can sell in the marketplace. Human labor power has the unusual attribute that it can create value, which is the secret of profit generation under capitalism.

Labor theory of value: This is a principle in classical economics, notably refined by Marx, asserting that the value of a commodity is determined by the total amount of socially necessary labor required for its production. This theory underpins Marx's critique of capitalism, highlighting how the exploitation of labor (paying workers less than the value of their output) is the source of capitalist profit. It contrasts with market-driven theories of value, emphasizing that labor, rather than subjective consumer preferences or market dynamics, is the essential determinant of economic value. This framework is crucial for understanding Marx's analysis of exploitation, surplus value, and the dynamics of capitalist economies.

Luck egalitarianism: One approach to socialist theorizing that demands not just the removal of barriers due to economic disadvantages or barriers due to race and gender, but the removal of all unchosen disadvantages.

Majoritarian electoral democracy: Power that is distributed evenly amongst citizens who represent their interests directly through democratic processes.

Majoritarian pluralism: This theory holds that the state is an impartial coordinator of a power that is distributed evenly across a range of organizations and interest groups representing the citizenry.

Mensheviks: The second primary faction of the Russian Social Democratic Labor Party, along with the Bolsheviks. The Mensheviks, in contrast to the Bolsheviks, thought the party should be a broad-based, democratic organization that would include a range of political tendencies and organizations.

Marginal utility: This is an economic concept that describes the additional satisfaction or benefit gained from consuming one more unit of a good or service. It is foundational to the theory of consumer choice in neoclassical economics, illustrating how the value of a good to a consumer decreases as the quantity consumed increases. This principle helps explain consumer behavior, market demand curves, and the determination of prices in a market economy, contrasting with labor-based theories of value by emphasizing subjective individual preferences and the diminishing additional satisfaction derived from consuming more of any good.

Market price: The price of a commodity which, in contrast to the natural price, varies with supply and demand. Adam Smith noted that the market price will tend to gravitate towards the natural price.

Mode of production: This refers to the overall economic system and social organization through which production is carried out within a society. It encompasses both the forces of production (the physical and technological resources used in production) and the relations of production (the social relationships and roles individuals have in the production process). The mode of production determines how goods and services are produced, who owns and controls the means of production, and how wealth is distributed within society. Different modes of production, such as capitalism, socialism, and feudalism, are characterized by distinct arrangements of productive forces and social relations.

Modern state: Marx claimed that the modern state under capitalism simply follows the orders of the capitalist ruling class concerning economics affairs, and lacks any other apparent purpose than representing the bourgeoisie.

Motivated bias: A bias that occurs when theorists evaluate evidence and argument in a way that enables them to reach a desired conclusion.

Natural price: The natural price of a commodity prevails in a perfectly competitive market. According to Adam Smith, in a primitive economy, the natural price is determined by the labor that went into producing the commodity.

Neoclassical economics: This explains the value of commodities not in terms of their utility, but instead in terms of their marginal utility. Neoclassical economics treats instrumental reason as the only kind of thinking that could count as rational.

Non-cognitive judgments: Judgements that express attitudes or feelings that are neither true nor false.

Non-repressive sublimation: A process developed by Frankfurt School theorist Herbert Marcuse where primal human desires are redirected and expressed in ways that are socially beneficial without being excessively repressed.

Objectivist view: A view according to which what is good for someone does not depend at all on their subjective desires or attitudes, even the desires or attitudes they might have under different, "ideal" conditions.

Oligarchy: A system of government characterized by a handful of powerful elites who hold disproportionate economic and political power. Marx's theory of elite domination predicted that capitalist societies would be characterized by oligarchic control, wherein politics serves the interests of the capitalist class.

One-dimensionality: A term used by Frankfurt School theorist Herbert Marcuse to describe a state in which individuals, conditioned by a steady diet of mass media and consumer culture, become passively accepting of the status quo and lose their capacity for critical resistance.

Order-of-information bias: A bias that describes a tendency to support and sustain status quo beliefs. These beliefs bias the judgments we go on to make about the social and political world in a way that confirms our initial expectations.

Organic composition of capital: This is a concept in Marxist economic theory that refers to the ratio of constant capital (investment in physical assets like machinery, equipment, and raw materials) to variable capital (investment in labor power). This ratio reflects the technological and organizational structure of production, indicating the degree of capital intensiveness or the extent to which production relies on machinery versus human labor. Marx argued that, as capitalism develops, there is a tendency for the organic composition of capital to rise due to technological advancements and the capitalist's pursuit of greater efficiency and profit, which in turn influences the rate of profit and the dynamics of capitalist economies, including the potential for crises.

Organic intellectuals: Intellectuals who, according to Antonio Gramsci, are closely associated with particular social classes that emerge from these groups to articulate their specific interests. Organic intellectuals give voice to the sentiments and experiences that the masses find difficult to articulate for themselves.

Orthodox Marxism: Popularized by the socialist theorist Karl Kautsky. Other theorists of orthodox Marxism include Rosa Luxemburg, Vladimir Lenin, and Leon Trotsky. It consisted of three features: a strong reading of historical materialism; emphasis on the class struggle; and being critical of socialism through parliamentary reform.

Performance principle: A critique developed by Frankfurt School theorist Herbert Marcuse where the ceaseless quest for achievement and productivity results in an unnecessary degree of repression.

Plurality of values: Also referred to as the "incommensurability" of values, this posits that different kinds of things and activities should be valued and have their value assessed in different ways, depending on the kind of thing or activity they are.

Political emancipation: This is primarily concerned with extending the realm of civic and political rights to all citizens regardless of other facts about their status or identity. Marx welcomes political emancipation, but thinks this sort of emancipation remains compatible with continued widespread oppression and degradation.

Political superstructure: This refers to the state, legal, and political institutions that arise from and serve to protect a society's economic base (the mode of production). This concept emphasizes that the superstructure is shaped by the economic base and, in turn, reinforces it, reflecting the interests of the ruling class. The superstructure not only includes government and laws, but also encompasses cultural and ideological institutions (such as education, religion, and the media) that help maintain the dominance of the ruling class by promoting and legitimizing the existing social and economic order.

Private property: In the context of Marxist critique, this refers to the ownership of the means of production (factories, land, capital, etc.) by individuals or corporations for the purpose of generating profit. Marx distinguished private property from personal possessions, focusing on its role in capitalist economies where it enables the exploitation of labor and the accumulation of capital by a small ruling class. This system of property rights is seen as the foundation of social inequalities and class divisions as it allows the bourgeoisie to control the wealth and resources of society, while the proletariat is alienated from the fruits of their labor. Marx advocated for the abolition of private property in means of production as a step towards achieving a classless society.

Production price: This refers to the price of a commodity given the costs of production (raw materials, technology, and labor), and assuming some rate of profit for the capitalist.

Progressive: A characteristic whereby later forms represent improvements over earlier forms. Marx and Hegel's conception of history is progressive since, for them, later historical epochs represent improvements in the development of the productive forces.

Proletariat ideology: While Marx treated ideology as a pejorative concept, some Marxists after him promoted the development of a proletariat ideology that could supplant the bourgeois ideology as foundational to the working classes establishing their own cultural identity and gaining power.

Proletariat: The social class that sells their labor power for wages. According to Marx, the proletariat—comprised of the urban industrial working class that emerged from the industrial revolution—is a unique class that will eventually bring about a revolution that will finally end the cycle of class conflict.

Rate of exploitation: This measures the extent to which capitalists extract surplus value from workers, calculated as the ratio of surplus value to variable capital (wages).

Rate of profit: This refers to the ratio of surplus value (the value produced by labor beyond what is required for workers' wages) to the total capital invested, including both constant capital (investment in means of production) and variable capital (wages paid to labor). It represents the exploitation of labor by capital, where profit arises from the extraction of surplus value from workers. Marx argued that the tendency of the rate of profit to fall over time due to factors such as technological advancements and the rising organic composition of capital is a fundamental contradiction within capitalism, leading to economic crises.

Rational actor: This is the principal agent of neoclassical economics who calculates the most efficient way to satisfy his desires. This actor is presumed to face serious obstacles to engaging in collective activities, since he may always be tempted by the possibility of free riding on the efforts of others.

Reductive materialism: Reductive materialism is a philosophical theory that asserts that all phenomena, including mental states and consciousness, can be ultimately explained by physical processes. It holds that everything can be reduced to or explained by the interactions of physical matter and energy, without the need for non-physical or supernatural explanations.

Reification (Verdinglichung): A term popularized by Georg Lukács, reification is the process of attributing human qualities, relationships, and behaviors to human-made objects, perceiving them as independent entities that govern human existence. It also involves viewing human beings as object-like entities subject to the laws of the material world, rather than expressing their humanity. Under capitalism, individuals and their relationships are commodified, treated as interchangeable commodities with calculable value, reinforcing the perception of capitalism as a natural and inevitable system.

Relations of production: These refer to the social relationships and arrangements that individuals enter into as they engage in the process of production within a given economic system. These relations involve ownership and control of the means of production, the division of labor, and the distribution of the products and services. Understanding relations of production is crucial for analyzing class structures, power dynamics, and social inequality within societies.

Repressive state apparatuses: A term used by the French Marxist philosopher Louis Althusser to describe state institutions such as the government, the military, police, and so on. According to Althusser, the ruling classes control the repressive state apparatuses and use them to secure social cohesion and sustain prevailing socio-economic relations.

Ruling class: This is the economically dominant class in a particular epoch. The ruling class monopolizes state power and employs it to secure its interests.

Serfs: An economic class under feudalism that controls only their ability to work. A serf has no other option to meet his basic needs than working for the feudal lord.

Sociological idealism: A term introduced by Charles Mills to describe the sort of idealism Marx was primarily critiquing in the *German Ideology*. The idealist, in this sense, treats ideas as independent of the social and economic contexts that in fact gave rise to them, while also granting ideas explanatory pride of place in their accounts of social transformation.

Species-being (*Gattungswesen*): This refers to the inherent characteristics and potential of human beings as social and creative creatures. It encompasses humanity's capacity for purposeful activity, creative production, and establishment of cooperative social relations. The concept highlights the importance of realizing these potentials for individual fulfillment and societal progress.

Spirit (Geist): A term used by Hegel to refer to the self-conscious and self-determining subject who posits the objects and institutions of the world in its quest for self-realization.

Spontaneous activity: The opportunity to engage in productive labor independent of the need to survive.

Structuralism: A theoretical approach that emerged in the mid-20th century, especially in France. It asserts that human culture, thought, and behavior are best understood in terms of their relationship to broader systemic structures.

Subaltern: Antonio Gramsci's term for a marginalized group. Gramsci highlights the importance of various subaltern groups forming a "historic bloc," an alliance to enhance their agency and enable them to counter the prevailing hegemony.

Subject–object of history: According to Lukács, the proletariat is the subject-object of history. They are the subject of history insofar as they are both the ones that carry out the key tasks necessary to perpetuate the capitalist system and the ones who will overthrow it. They are the object of history insofar as they are the ones most affected by the capitalist system, bearing the brunt of its exploitation.

Sublation (Aufhebung): A term often used in Hegelian philosophy, sublation refers to a dialectical process of transcendence and preservation. It involves both negating and preserving aspects of a concept or phenomenon within a higher-level synthesis. In this process, contradictions or oppositions are resolved by integrating them into a higher unity, preserving what is valuable while overcoming limitations. Sublation represents a dynamic movement of development where contradictions are resolved, leading to a deeper and more comprehensive understanding or form of existence.

Surplus-repression: A theory developed by the Frankfurt School theorist Herbert Marcuse. Surplus-repression occurs when advanced industrial societies apply constraints on people's desires over and above what is necessary for basic societal order.

Surplus value: This arises from the generation of value beyond the point that labor has already created enough exchange-value for its own sustenance. It refers to the additional value created by the worker and embodied in the commodity that is the source of the capitalist's profit.

Teleological: This refers to when a process has a necessary endpoint. History, for Marx, is teleological since its necessary endpoint is communist relations of production, a situation where the main forces of production are collectively owned and used for collective benefit.

The Second International: Also known as the "Socialist International," this was an organization of socialist and labor parties that existed from 1889 to 1916. It was created to promote cooperation and coordination among socialist parties around the world, with the goal of achieving a socialist revolution.

Totality: Totality, as understood by Lukács, refers to the interconnectedness and unity of all social phenomena within a given historical context. It emphasizes that social reality is not a collection of isolated elements but a complex and interdependent whole. For Lukács, understanding totality is essential for grasping the underlying structures and dynamics of society, including how various aspects (such as economics, politics, culture, and ideology) intersect and influence each other. This holistic approach enables a deeper analysis of social phenomena and their historical development.

Traditional intellectuals: These are intellectuals who, according to Antonio Gramsci, deludedly see themselves as autonomous from the dominant social group, while in fact upholding the status quo.

Transformation problem: The transformation problem refers to a challenge in Marxist economics concerning the conversion of labor values into prices of production within a capitalist economy. Specifically, it addresses the difficulty of reconciling the labor theory of value, which posits that the value of a commodity is determined by the socially necessary labor time required for its production with the observed prices of goods and services in a market economy. Resolving the transformation problem involves explaining how the abstract labor values of commodities are translated into their market prices, accounting for factors such as differences in productivity, input costs, and profit rates across industries.

Underconsumption: The process that describes how capitalists, in the drive to cut the costs of variable capital, also eliminate the potential consumers for their commodities.

Use-value: This refers to the inherent utility or practical usefulness of a commodity in satisfying human needs or desires. It represents the tangible qualities of a commodity that make it valuable for consumption or use. Use-value contrasts with exchange-value, which refers to the value a commodity has in terms of its ability to be exchanged for other commodities in the market.

Variable capital: The amount a capitalist spends on labor power.

Vulgar Marxism: A view that holds that the forces of production determine the economic, political, and cultural character of society without any dynamic interaction between the other levels of society.

Wage slaves: The class that sells their labor power in return for a wage and, under certain circumstances, can sell their labor for better wages, thus having an advantage over serfs and chattel slaves—at least as long as there are buyers for their labor power,

War of maneuver (manoeuvre): Antonio Gramsci adopts terminology from military science to characterize the sudden and direct overthrowing of the ruling class and seizure of political power. This tactic is appropriate in states without robust bourgeois ideological domination.

War of position: Gramsci adopts terminology from military science to characterize the formation of a counter-hegemony in the form of a prolonged ideological struggle that allows workers, guided by their organic intellectuals, to organize into a working-class party that supplants the prevailing bourgeois ideology.

Western Marxism: The umbrella term used to describe the various interpretations and adaptations of Marxist theory that emerged primarily in Western Europe and North America during the 20th century. Unlike orthodox or Soviet Marxism, Western Marxism often focused more on cultural, philosophical, and sociological analyses rather than solely on economic and political matters. Figures associated with Western Marxism include Georg Lukács, Antonio Gramsci, Theodor Adorno, Herbert Marcuse, and Louis Althusser. These thinkers engaged with diverse intellectual traditions—such as phenomenology, psychoanalysis, and existentialism—to develop critical perspectives on capitalist society, culture, and ideology.

World history: In Hegelian philosophy, this refers to the unfolding of the historical process or the development of human societies over time. Hegel conceived of history as a rational progression toward the realization of human freedom and self-consciousness. He saw history as driven by the dialectical interplay of opposing forces, leading to the advancement of human civilization.

Young Hegelians: The Young Hegelians, also known as the Left Hegelians, were a group of intellectuals in the mid-19th century who were influenced by the ideas of Georg Wilhelm Friedrich Hegel but interpreted them in a more radical and atheistic manner. They criticized the conservative and religious interpretations of Hegelianism prevalent at the time, and sought to apply Hegelian dialectics to social and political issues. Prominent figures among the Young Hegelians include Ludwig Feuerbach, Bruno Bauer, and Max Stirner. Marx was personally acquainted with many of these figures as a doctoral student, and their critiques of religion, morality, and the state were of great importance to him. However he eventually rejected the idealism that he argued characterized their philosophy in favor of his own historical materialism.

Bibliography

Marx and Engels

All references to Marx and Engels, unless otherwise noted, are from the MECW, or Marx/Engels Collected Works, a 50-volume English-language edition of their comprehensive writings. Spanning early articles and letters to foundational treatises, the MECW offers a chronological documentation of their intellectual contributions. Published between 1975 and 2005, this collection emerged from a collaboration between Progress Publishers in Moscow, Lawrence & Wishart in London, and International Publishers in New York, providing an authoritative English translation of their key works. We have sometimes altered the original German translation. In these cases, we have used the Marx/Engels Werke: Marx, Karl and Friedrich Engels (1956–1990), Werke. 50 vols. (Berlin: Dietz Verlag).

Other Primary Philosophical and Economic Texts

Adorno, Theodor. (2005) Critical Models: Interventions and Catchwords. Translated by Henry Pickford. New York: Columbia University Press.

Adorno, Theodor. (2001) The Culture Industry: Selected Essays on Mass Culture. Edited by J.M. Bernstein. New York: Routledge.

Althusser, Louis. (2005) For Marx. Translated by Ben Brewster. New York: Verso.

Althusser, Louis. (2014) On the Reproduction of Capitalism: Ideology and Ideological State Apparatuses. Translated by G.M. Goshgarian. London: Verso.

Althusser, Louis et al. (2016) Reading Capital: The Complete Edition. Translated by Ben Brewster and David Fernbach. New York: Verso.

Feuerbach, Ludwig. (1989 [1841]) The Essence of Christianity. Translated by George Elliot. Amherst, MA: Prometheus Books.

Freud, Sigmund. (1994 [1930]) Civilization and its Discontents. Translated by Joan Riviere. Mineola, NY: Dover Publications.

Gramsci, Antonio. (1971) Selections from the Prison Notebooks of Antonio Gramsci. Edited and translated by Quintin Hoare and Geoffrey Nowell Smith. New York: International Publishers.

Gramsci, Antonio. (1977) Selections from Political Writings (1910–1920). Edited by Quintin Hoare. Translated by John Mathews. London: Lawrence & Wishart.

Hegel, G.W.F. (1977) Phenomenology of Spirit. Translated by Arnold V. Miller. Oxford: Oxford University Press.

Hegel, G.W.F. (1991) Elements of the Philosophy of Right. Translated by H.B. Nisbet. Edited by Allen W. Wood. Cambridge: Cambridge University Press.

Hegel, G.W.F. (2004) The Philosophy of History. Translated by J. Sibree. Mineola, NY: Dover Publications.

Hegel, G.W.F. (2009) Lectures on the History of Philosophy 1825–6: Volume III: Medieval and Modern Philosophy. Translated by Robert F. Brown. Oxford: Oxford University Press.

Horkheimer, Max. (2002) Critical Theory: Selected Essays. Translated by Matthew O'Connell et al. New York: Continuum.

Horkheimer, Max, and Theodor Adorno. (2002 [1947]) Dialectic of Enlightenment: Philosophical Fragments. Edited by Gunzelin Schmid Noerr and Edmund Jephcott. Stanford: Stanford University Press.

Lenin, Vladimir. (1977) Collected Works, Volume 5. Edited by Victor Jerome. Translated by George Hanna. Moscow: Progress Publishers.

Lukács, Georg. (1972 [1923]) History and Class Consciousness: Studies in Marxist Dialectics. Translated by Rodney Livingstone. Cambridge, MA: MIT Press.

Marcuse, Herbert. (1932) "Neue Quellen zur Grundlegung des Historischen Materialismus." Die Gesellschaft 9(3): 136–174.

Marcuse, Herbert. (1969) An Essay on Liberation. Boston: Beacon Press.

Marcuse, Herbert. (1974 [1955]) Eros and Civilization. Boston: Beacon Press.

Marcuse, Herbert. (2007 [1964]) One-Dimensional Man: Studies in the Ideology of Advanced Industrial Society. London: Routledge.

Mill, John Stuart. (2002 [1859]) On Liberty. Mineola, NY: Dover Publications.

Ricardo, David. (2004 [1817]) "On the Principles of Political Economy and Taxation." In Works and Correspondence of David Ricardo, edited by Maurice Dobb and Piero Sraffa. Indianapolis: Liberty Fund.

Simmel, Georg. (2009) Sociology: Inquiries into the Construction of Social Forms. Translated by Anthony J. Blasi, Anton K. Jacobs, and Mathew Kanjirathinkal. Leiden: Brill.

Smith, Adam. (1976 [1776]) An Inquiry into the Nature and Causes of the Wealth of Nations. Edited by Edwin Cannan. Chicago: University of Chicago Press.

Secondary and Other Literature

Acemoglu, Daron, and James A. Robinson. (2015) "The Rise and Decline of General Laws of Capitalism." *Journal of Economic Perspectives* 29(1): 3–28.

Acemoglu, Daron, and Pascual Restrepo. (2019) "Automation and New Tasks: How Technology Displaces and Reinstates Labor." *Journal of Economic Perspectives* 29(1): 3–30.

Acemoglu, Daron, and Simon Johnson. (2023) *Power and Progress: Our Thousand-Year Struggle over Technology and Prosperity.* London: Public Affairs.

Alterman, Eric. (2003) *What Liberal Media?* New York: Basic Books.

Asch, Solomon. (1946) "Forming Impressions of Personality." *Journal of Abnormal and Social Psychology* 41(3): 1230–1240.

Aston, T.H., and C.H.E. Philpin. (1985) *The Brenner Debate: Agrarian Class Structure and Economic Development in Pre-Industrial Europe.* Cambridge: Cambridge University Press.

Azmanova, Albena. (2020) *Capitalism on Edge.* New York: Columbia University Press.

Bacon, Francis. (2000) *The New Organon.* Edited by Lisa Jardine and Michael Silverthorn. Translated by Michael Silverthorn. Cambridge: Cambridge University Press.

Bagdikian, Ben. (1997) *The Media Monopoly.* Boston: Beacon Press.

Bakunin, Michael [Mikhail]. (2012) *Statism and Anarchy.* Translated and edited by Marshall S. Shatz. Cambridge: Cambridge University Press.

Bartels, Larry M. (2016) "Elections in America." *Annals of the American Academy of Political and Social Science* 667(1): 36–49.

Baynes, Kenneth. (2007) "Freedom as Autonomy." In *The Oxford Handbook of Continental Philosophy*, edited by Brian Leiter and Michael Rosen, 551–587. New York: Oxford University Press.

Bègue, Laurent, and Marina Bastounis. (2003) "Two Spheres of Belief in Justice: Extensive Support for the Bi-Dimensional Model of Belief in a Just World." *Journal of Personality* 71(3): 435–463.

Beiser, Frederick C., editor. (1993) *The Cambridge Companion to Hegel.* New York: Cambridge University Press.

Benanav, Aaron. (2022) *Automation and the Future of Work.* London: Verso.

Bergholt, Drago et al. (2022) "The Decline of the Labor Share: New Empirical Evidence." *American Economic Journal: Macroeconomics* 14(3): 163–198.

Bhattacharya, Tithi, editor. (2017). *Social Reproduction Theory: Remapping Class, Recentering Oppression.* London: Pluto.

Blaug, Mark. (1985) *Economic Theory in Retrospect.* Cambridge: Cambridge University Press.

Block, Fred. (1977) "The Ruling Class Does Not Rule: Notes on the Marxist Theory of the State." *Marxist Revolution* 33 (May–June): 6–28.

Bornstein, Robert. (1989) "Exposure and Affect: Overview and Meta-Analysis of Research." *Psychological Bulletin* 106(2): 265–289.

Brenner, Robert. (1976) "Agrarian Class Structure and Economic Development in Pre-Industrial Europe." *Past & Present* 70(1): 30–75.

Brenner, Robert. (1977) "The Origins of Capitalist Development: A Critique of Neo-Smithian Marxism." *New Left Review* 104(1): 25–92.

Brink, David O. (1989) *Moral Realism and the Foundations of Ethics*. Cambridge: Cambridge University Press.

Brixel, Pascal. (2024) "The Unity of Marx's Concept of Alienated Labor." *Philosophical Review* 133(1): 33–71.

Brudney, Daniel. (1998) *Marx's Attempt to Leave Philosophy*. Cambridge, MA: Harvard University Press.

Buchanan, Allen E. (1982) *Marx and Justice: The Radical Critique of Liberalism*. Lanham, MD: Rowman & Littlefield.

Buchanan, Allen E. (forthcoming) *Ideology and Revolution: How the Struggle Against Domination Drives the Evolution of Morality and Institutions*. Cambridge: Cambridge University Press.

Campbell, Danielle, Stuart C. Carr, and Malcolm MacLachlan. (2001) "Attributing 'Third World Poverty' in Australia and Malawi: A Case of Donor Bias." *Journal of Applied Social Psychology* 31(2): 409–430.

Carver, Terrell. (2008) "Marx's Conception of Alienation in the Grundrisse." In *Karl Marx's Grundrisse: Foundations of the Critique of Political Economy 150 Years Later*, edited by Marcello Musto, 48–66. New York: Routledge.

Chitty, Andrew. (1993) "The Early Marx on Needs." *Radical Philosophy* 64: 22–31.

Choma, Russ. (2014, January 9) "Millionaires' Club: For First Time, Most Lawmakers Are Worth $1 Million-Plus." *OpenSecrets News*. https://www.opensecrets.org/news/2014/01/millionaires-club-for-first-time-most-lawmakers-are-worth-1-million-plus/

Chomsky, Noam. (1989) *Necessary Illusions: Thought Control in Democratic Societies*. Boston: South End Press.

Christiano, Thomas. (2012) "Money in Politics." In *The Oxford Handbook of Political Philosophy*, edited by David Estlund, 241–258. New York: Oxford University Press.

Cohen, G.A. (1978) *Karl Marx's Theory of History: A Defense*. Princeton: Princeton University Press.

Cohen, G.A. (1979) "The Labor Theory of Value and the Concept of Exploitation." *Philosophy & Public Affairs* 8(4): 338–360.

Cohen, G.A. (1983) [Review of *Karl Marx*, by A.W. Wood (1981)]. *Mind* 92: 441–446.

Cohen, G.A. (2000) *If You're an Egalitarian, How Come You're So Rich?* Cambridge: Harvard University Press.

Cohen, G.A. (2008) *Rescuing Justice and Equality*. Cambridge, MA: Harvard University Press.

Cohen, G.A. (2009) *Why Not Socialism?* Princeton: Princeton University Press.

Cohen, Joshua. (1982) "Review of *Karl Marx's Theory of History: A Defense*, by G.A. Cohen." *Journal of Philosophy* 79(5): 253–273.

Correia, Isabel, and Jorge Vala. (2003) "When Will a Victim Be Secondarily Victimized? The Effect of Observer's Belief in a Just World, Victim's Innocence and Persistence of Suffering." *Social Justice Research* 16: 379–400.

Curtis, Gregory. (2008) *The Cave Painters: Probing the Mysteries of the World's First Artists*. New York: Knopf Doubleday.

Dallman, Lawrence. (2021) *Marx's Naturalism: A Study in Philosophical Methodology* (Doctoral dissertation, University of Chicago).

Dallman, Lawrence, and Brian Leiter. (2019) "Marx and Marxism." In *The Routledge Handbook of Relativism*, edited by Martin Kusch, 88–96. London: Routledge.

Davis, Angela Y. (1983) *Women, Race & Class*. New York: Vintage.

Davis, Angela Y. (2011) *Are Prisons Obsolete?* New York: Seven Stories Press.

De Judicibus, Margaret, and Marita McCabe. (2001) "Blaming the Target of Sexual Harassment: Impact of Gender Role, Sexist Attitudes, and Work Role." *Sex Roles* 44: 401–417.

Dobb, Maurice. (1946) *Studies in the Development of Capitalism*. London: Routledge.

Draper, Hal. (1986) *Karl Marx's Theory of Revolution III*. New York: New York University Press.

Edwards, Jaime. (2018) *The Marxian Theory of Ideology: A Reconstruction and Defense* (Doctoral dissertation, University of Chicago).

Eidelman, Scott, and Christian Crandall. (2009) "A Psychological Advantage for the Status Quo." In *Social and Psychological Bases of Ideology and System Justification*, edited by John T. Jost et al., 85–106. New York: Oxford University Press.

Eidelman, Scott, and Christian Crandall. (2012) "Bias in Favor of the Status Quo." *Social and Personality Psychology Compass* 6(3): 270–281.

Eisenstein, Zillah R. (1979) *Capitalist Patriarchy and the Case for Socialist Feminism*. New York: Monthly Review Press.

Ellard, John, and Douglas Bates. (1990) "Evidence for the Role of the Justice Motive in Status Generalization Processes." *Social Justice Research* 4: 115–134.

Elster, Jon. (1985) *Making Sense of Marx*. Vol. 4. Cambridge: Cambridge University Press.

Elster, Jon. (1986) *An Introduction to Karl Marx*. Cambridge: Cambridge University Press.

Evans, Trevor. (1997) "Marxian Theories of Credit, Money and Capital." *International Journal of Political Economy* 27(1): 7–42.

Federici, Silvia. (2020) *Revolution at Point Zero: Housework, Reproduction, and Feminist Struggle*. Binghamton, NY: PM Press.

Finkelman, Paul. (2019) *Defending Slavery: Proslavery Thought in the Old South: A Brief History with Documents*. Boston: Bedford/St. Martin's Press.

Fleischacker, Samuel. (2021) *Adam Smith*. London: Routledge.

Foley, Duncan K. (1982) "The Value of Money, the Value of Labor Power and the Marxian Transformation Problem." *Review of Radical Political Economics* 14(2): 37–47.

Forster, Michael N. (1993) "Hegel's Dialectical Method." In *The Cambridge Companion to Hegel*, edited by Fredrick C. Beiser, 130–170. New York: Cambridge University Press.

Forster, Michael N. (2015) "Ideology." In *The Oxford Handbook of German Philosophy in the Nineteenth Century*, edited by Michael N. Forster and Kristin Gjesdal, 829–852. New York: Oxford University Press.

Fraser, Nancy. (2014) *Justice Interruptus: Critical Reflections on the "Postsocialist" Condition*. New York: Routledge.

Fraser, Nancy. (2016) "Contradictions of Capital and Care." *New Left Review* 100: 99–117.

Friedman, Milton. (1970, September 13) A Friedman Doctrine—The Social Responsibility of Business Is to Increase Profits. *New York Times*, 17.

Frey, Carl Benedikt, and Michael A. Osborne. (2017) "The Future of Employment: How Susceptible Are Jobs to Computerisation?" *Technological Forecasting and Social Change* 114: 254–280.

Geras, Norman. (1989) "The Controversy about Marx and Justice." In *Marxist Theory*, edited by Alex Callinicos. Oxford: Oxford University Press.

Geras, Norman. (2017) *Literature of Revolution: Essays on Marxism*. New York: Verso.

Gilens, Martin. (2012) *Affluence and Influence: Economic Inequality and Political Power in America*. Princeton: Princeton University Press and Russell Sage Foundation.

Gilens, Martin, and Benjamin I. Page. (2014) "Testing Theories of American Politics: Elites, Interest Groups, and Average Citizens." *Perspectives on Politics* 12(3): 564–581. https://doi.org/10.1017/S1537592714001595

Gilovich, Thomas. (1991) *How We Know What Isn't So: The Fallibility of Human Reason in Everyday Life*. New York: Free Press.

Goodin, Robert. (1987) "Exploiting a Situation and Exploiting a Person." In *Modern Theories of Exploitation*, edited by Andrew Reeve, 166–200. London: Sage.

Grossman, Gene, and Ezra Oberfield. (2022) "The Elusive Explanation for the Declining Labor Share." *Annual Review of Economics* 14: 93–124.

Hafer, Carolyn, and Laurent Bègue. (2005) "Experimental Research on Just-World Theory: Problems, Developments, and Future Challenges." *Psychological Bulletin* 131(1): 128–167.

Hamilton, David, and Terrence Rose. (1980) "Illusory Correlation and the Maintenance of Stereotypic Beliefs." *Journal of Personality and Social Psychology* 39(5): 832–845.

Hardimon, Michael O. (1994) *Hegel's Social Philosophy: The Project of Reconciliation*. Cambridge: Cambridge University Press.

Harris, Marvin. (1989) *Cows, Pigs, Wars, and Witches*. New York: Vintage.

Hartmann, H.I. (1979) "The Unhappy Marriage of Marxism and Feminism: Towards a More Progressive Union." *Capital & Class* 3(2): 1–33.

Heinrich, Michael. (2012) *An Introduction to the Three Volumes of Marx's Capital*. Translated by Alex Locascio. New York: Monthly Review Press.

Heller, Agnes. (1976) *The Theory of Need in Marx*. London: Allison and Bundy.

Herman, Edwards S., and Noam Chomsky. (1988) *Manufacturing Consent: The Political Economy of the Mass Media*. New York: Pantheon.

Hitchcock, Christopher. (2011) "Counterfactual Availability and Causal Judgment." In *Understanding Counterfactuals, Understanding Causation: Issues in Philosophy and Psychology*, edited by Christoph Hoerl et al., 171–185. Oxford: Oxford University Press.

Hobsbawm, Eric. (1989) *The Age of Empire: 1875–1914*. New York: Vintage.

Hobsbawm, Eric. (1996a) *The Age of Revolution: 1789–1848*. New York, Vintage.

Hobsbawm, Eric. (1996b) *The Age of Capital: 1848–1875*. New York: Vintage.

Hohendahl, Peter Uwe. (2016) *Building a National Literature: The Case of Germany, 1830–1870*. Translated by Renate Baron Franciscono. Ithaca, NY: Cornell University Press.

Jeffries, Stuart. (2016) *Grand Hotel Abyss: The Lives of the Frankfurt School*. New York: Verso.

Jones, Edward E. et al. (1968) "Pattern of Performance and Ability Attribution: An Unexpected Primacy Effect." *Journal of Personality and Social Psychology* 10(4): 317–340.

Jost, John. (2020) *A Theory of System Justification*. Cambridge, MA: Harvard University Press.

Jost, John, and Mahzarin Banaji. (1994) "The Role of Stereotyping in System-Justification and the Production of False Consciousness." *British Journal of Social Psychology* 33(1): 1–27.

Johnston, David Cay. (2001, April 8) "Talk of Lost Farms Reflects Muddle of Estate Tax Debate." *New York Times*. https://www.nytimes.com/2001/04/08/us/talk-of-lost-farms-reflects-muddle-of-estate-tax-debate.html

Kahneman, Daniel. (1982) "The Simulation Heuristic." In *Judgment under Uncertainty: Heuristics and Biases*, edited by Daniel Kahneman, Paul Slovic, and Amos Tversky, 201–210. Cambridge, Cambridge University Press.

Kandiyali, Jan. (2020) "The Importance of Others: Marx on Unalienated Production." *Ethics* 130(4): 555–587.

Kellner, Douglas. (2002) "T. W. Adorno and the Dialectics of Mass Culture." In *Adorno: A Critical Reader*, edited by Nigel C. Gibson and Andrew Rubin, 86–109. Oxford: Wiley-Blackwell.

Khlevniuk, Oleg. (2017) *Stalin: New Biography of a Dictator*. Translated by Nora Seligman Favorov. New Haven: Yale University Press.

Kitcher, Philip. (1993) *The Advancement of Science: Science without Legend, Objectivity Without Illusions*. New York: Oxford University Press.

Kolakowski, Leszek. (1971) "Althusser's Marx." *Socialist Register* 8: 111–128.

Krugman, Paul. (2003, September 14) "The Tax-Cut Con." *New York Times*. https://www.nytimes.com/2003/09/14/magazine/the-tax-cut-con.html

Kunda, Ziva. (1990) "The Case for Motivated Reasoning." *Psychological Bulletin* 108(3): 480–498.

Kuran, Timur, and Cass R. Sunstein. (1999) "Availability Cascades and Risk Regulation." *Stanford Law Review* 51: 683–768.

Larraín, Jorge. (1979) *The Concept of Ideology*. London: Hutchinson.

Lazarus, Jeffrey, Amy McKay, and Lindsey Herbel. (2016) "Who Walks through the Revolving Door? Examining the Lobbying Activity of Former Members of Congress." *Interest Groups & Advocacy* 5: 82–100.

Leist, Anton. (2008) "The Long Goodbye: On the Development of Critical Theory." *Analyse & Kritik* 30 (2): 331–354.

Leiter, Brian. (2015a) "Marx, Law, Ideology, Legal Positivism." *Virginia Law Review* 101(4): 1179–1196.

Leiter, Brian. (2015b) "Why Marxism Still Does Not Need Normative Theory." *Analyse und Kritik* 37(1): 23–50.

Leiter, Brian. (2024) "How are Ideologies False? A Reconstruction of the Marxian Concept." *Social Philosophy & Policy* 41(1).

Leiter, Brian, and Michael Rosen, editors. (2007) *The Oxford Handbook of Continental Philosophy*. Oxford: Oxford University Press.

Leopold, David. (2007) *The Young Karl Marx: German Philosophy, Modern Politics, and Human Flourishing*. Cambridge: Cambridge University Press.

Lerner, Melvin. (1980) *The Belief in a Just World: A Fundamental Delusion*. New York: Springer.

Liedman, Sven-Eric. (2018) *A World to Win: The Life and Thought of Karl Marx*. London: Verso.

Lippmann, Walter. (1922) *Public Opinion*. New York: Harcourt, Brace and Company.

Mansel, Philip. (2003) *Paris between Empires, 1814–1852*. London: Phoenix.

Maß, Sandra. (2019) "Teaching Capitalism: The Popularization of Economic Knowledge in Britain and Germany (1800–1850)." In *Moralizing Capitalism*, edited by Stefan Berger and Alexandra Przyrembel, 29–59. London: Palgrave Macmillan.

Mayer, Jane. (2016) *Dark Money: The Hidden History of the Billionaires behind the Rise of the Radical Right*. New York: Doubleday.

McChesney, Robert. (1997) *Corporate Media and the Threat to Democracy*. New York: Seven Stories Press.

Miliband, Ralph. (1977) *Marxism and Politics*. Oxford: Oxford University Press.

Miliband, Ralph. (1983) "State Power and Class Interests." *New Left Review* 138(1): 57–68.

Miller, Richard W. (1984) *Analyzing Marx: Morality, Power, and History*. Princeton: Princeton University Press.

Mills, Charles W. (1992) "'Ideology' in Marx and Engels' Revisited and Revised." *Philosophical Forum* 23(4): 301–328.

Montada, Leo. (1998) "Belief in a Just World: A Hybrid of Justice Motive and Self-Interest?" In *Responses to Victimizations and Belief in a Just World*, edited by Leo Montado and Melvin J. Lerner, 217–246. New York: Plenum Press.

Morris, Ian. (2015) *Foragers, Farmers, and Fossil Fuels: How Human Values Evolve*. Edited by Stephen Macedo. Princeton: Princeton University Press.

Napier, Jaime et al. (2006) "System Justification in Responding to the Poor and Displaced in the Aftermath of Hurricane Katrina." *Analyses of Social Issues and Public Policy* 6(1): 57–73.

Neville, Helen et al. (2000) "Construction and Initial Validation of the Color-Blind Racial Attitudes Scale (CoBRAS)." *Journal of Counseling Psychology* 47(1): 59–70.

Nisbett, Richard, and Lee Ross. (1980) *Human Inference: Strategies and Shortcomings of Social Judgment*. Englewood Cliffs, NJ: Prentice-Hall.

O'Connor, Brian. (2013) *Adorno*. New York: Routledge.

O'Connor, Brian. (2018) *Idleness: A Philosophical Essay*. Princeton: Princeton University Press.

Pancer, Mark. (1988) "Salience of Appeal and Avoidance of Helping Situations." *Canadian Journal of Behavioral Science* 20(2): 133–139.

Parfit, Derek. (2011) *On What Matters:Volume 1*. Oxford: Oxford University Press.

Perkins, Dwight. (2017) *Agricultural Developments in China 1368–1968*. New York: Routledge.

Piketty, Thomas. (2014) *Capital in the Twenty-First Century*. Translated by Arthur Goldhammer. Cambridge, MA: Belknap Press of Harvard University Press. Originally published in French, 2013.

Plekhanov, George. (1969) *Fundamental Problems of Marxism*. Translated by Julius Katzer. New York: International Publishers.

Poulantzas, Nicos. (1978) *Political Power and Social Classes*. London: Verso.

Raekstad, Paul. (2022) *Karl Marx's Realist Critique of Capitalism*. London: Palgrave Macmillan.

Railton, Peter. (1986) "Explanatory Asymmetry in Historical Materialism." *Ethics* 97(1): 233–239.

Rawls, John. (2009 [1971]) *A Theory of Justice*. Cambridge, MA: Harvard University Press.

Reed Jr., Adolph. (2023, February 20) "Race and Class: The Beginnings of an Argument." *The Nation*. https://www.thenation.com/article/society/race-class-intersectionality-atlanta

Roberts, William Clare. (2016) *Marx's Inferno: The Political Theory of Capital*. Princeton: Princeton University Press.

Roemer, John E. (1981) *Analytical Foundations of Marxian Economic Theory*. Cambridge: Cambridge University Press.

Roemer, John E. (1985) "Should Marxists Be Interested in Exploitation?" *Philosophy & Public Affairs* 14(1): 30–65.

Roemer, John E. (1988) *Free to Lose:An Introduction to Marxist Economic Philosophy*. Cambridge, MA: Harvard University Press.

Roemer, John E. (1990) "Marxian Value Analysis." In *Marxian Economics*, edited by John Eatwell et al., 257–265. New York: W.W. Norton & Co.

Roose, Kevin. (2019, January 25) "The Hidden Automation Agenda of the Davos Elite." *New York Times*. https://www.nytimes.com/2019/01/25/technology/automation-davos-world-economic-forum.html

Rosen, Michael. (1996) *On Voluntary Servitude: False Consciousness and the Theory of Ideology*. Cambridge, MA: Harvard University Press.

Ross, Lee. (1977) "The Intuitive Psychologist and His Shortcomings: Distortions in the Attribution Process." *Advances in Experimental Social Psychology* 10: 174–221.

Ross, Lee, David Greene, and Pamela House. (1977) "The False Consensus Effect: An Egocentric Bias in Social Perception and Attribution Processes." *Journal of Experimental Social Psychology* 13(3): 279–301.

Saito, Kohei. (2016) "Marx's Ecological Notebooks." *Monthly Review* 67(9): 25–42.

Sanbonmatsu, David, Sharon Akimoto, and Bryan Gibson. (1994) "Stereotype-Based Blocking in Social Explanation." *Personality and Social Psychology Bulletin* 20(1): 71–81.

Schakel, Wouter. (2021) "Unequal Policy Responsiveness in the Netherlands." *Socio-Economic Review* 19(1): 37–57.

Seigel, Jerrold. (1978) *Marx's Fate: The Shape of a Life.* Princeton: Princeton University Press.

Service, Robert. (2017) *The Last of the Tsars: Nicholas II and the Russian Revolution.* London: Macmillan.

Smith, Kevin B. (1985) "Seeing Justice in Poverty: The Belief in a Just World and Ideas about Inequalities." *Sociological Spectrum* 5(1–2): 17–29.

Sowell, Thomas. (2006) *On Classical Economics.* New Haven: Yale University Press.

Sperber, Jonathan. (2014) *Karl Marx: A Nineteenth-Century Life.* New York: Liveright/Norton.

Srnicek, Nick and Alex Williams. (2015) *Inventing the Future: Postcapitalism and a World without Work.* London: Verso.

Strauss, David Friedrich. (2010) *The Life of Jesus, Critically Examined.* Translated by George Elliot. Cambridge: Cambridge University Press.

Sweezy, Paul. (1970) *The Theory of Capitalist Development: Principles of Marxian Political Economy.* New York: Monthly Review Press.

Sweezy, Paul. (1976) "A Critique of Maurice Dobb, *Studies in the Development of Capitalism.*" In *The Transition from Feudalism to Capitalism,* edited by Rodney Hilton. Saint Lucia: Verso.

Thompson, E.P. (1968) *The Making of the English Working Class.* Harmondsworth: Penguin.

Tversky, Amos, and Daniel Kahneman. (1973) "Availability: A Heuristic for Judging Frequency and Probability." *Cognitive Psychology* 5(2): 207–232.

Tversky, Amos, and Daniel Kahneman. (1974) "Judgment under Uncertainty: Heuristics and Biases." *Science* 185: 1124–1130.

Vogel, Lise. (2013) *Marxism and the Oppression of Women: Toward a Unitary Theory.* Leiden: Brill.

Vrousalis, Nicholas. (2013) "Exploitation, Vulnerability, and Social Domination." *Philosophy and Public Affairs* 41(2): 131–157.

Weber, Max. (2003 [1905]) *The Protestant Ethic and the Spirit of Capitalism.* Translated by Talcott Parsons. Mineola, NY: Dover Publications.

Wills, Vanessa. (2018) "What Could It Mean to Say, 'Capitalism Causes Sexism and Racism'?" *Philosophical Topics* 46(2): 229–246.

Winters, Jeffrey. (2011) *Oligarchy.* Cambridge: Cambridge University Press.

Wood, Allen W. (1981) *Karl Marx.* London: Routledge.

Wood, Allen W. (1993) "Hegel's Ethics." In *The Cambridge Companion to Hegel,* edited by Frederick C. Beiser, 211–233. Cambridge: Cambridge University Press.

Wood, Allen W. (1995) "Exploitation." *Social Philosophy and Policy* 12: 136–158.

Wolff, Robert Paul. (1984) *Understanding Marx: A Reconstruction and Critique of Capital.* Princeton: Princeton University Press.

Wolff, Robert Paul. (1990) "Methodological Individualism and Marx: Some Remarks on Jon Elster, Game Theory, and Other Things." *Canadian Journal of Philosophy* 20(4): 469–486.

Wright, Larry. (1976) *Teleological Explanations: An Etiological Analysis of Goals and Functions*. Berkeley: University of California Press.

Xenophanes. (1992) *Xenophanes Fragments*. Translated by James H. Lesher. Toronto: University of Toronto Press.

Zaller, John. (1992) *The Nature and Origins of Mass Opinion*. Cambridge: Cambridge University Press.

Index

For Product Safety Concerns and Information please contact our EU
representative GPSR@taylorandfrancis.com Taylor & Francis Verlag GmbH,
Kaufingerstraße 24, 80331 München, Germany

Printed and bound by CPI Group (UK) Ltd, Croydon, CR0 4YY
08/06/2025
01897005-0006